Conte

More Predictive Analytics: Microsoft Excel

Conrad Carlberg

800 E. 96th Street

Indianapolis, Indiana   46240

More Predictive Analytics: Microsoft Excel

ISBN-13: 978-0-7897-5614-5
ISBN-10: 0-7897-5614-5

Library of Congress Control Number: 2015941441

Printed in the United States of America

First Printing: August 2015

Trademarks

Warning and Disclaimer

Special Sales

For information about buying this title in bulk quantities, or for special sales opportunities (which may include electronic versions; custom cover designs; and content particular to your business, training goals, marketing focus, or branding interests), please contact our corporate sales department at corpsales@pearsoned.com or (800) 382-3419.

For government sales inquiries, please contact governmentsales@pearsoned.com.

For questions about sales outside the U.S., please contact international@pearsoned.com.

Editor-in-Chief
Greg Wiegand

Acquisitions Editor
Joan Murray

Development Editor
Charlotte Kughen

Managing Editor
Sandra Schroeder

Project Editor
Seth Kerney

Copy Editor
Cheri Clark

Indexer
Ken Johnson

Proofreader
Megan Wade

Technical Editor
Michael Turner

Editorial Assistant
Cindy Teeters

Cover Designer
Mark Shirar

Compositor
Jake McFarland

Contents

About the Author

Conrad Carlberg (www.conradcarlberg.com) is a nationally recognized expert on quantitative analysis and on data analysis and management applications such as Microsoft Excel, SAS, and Oracle. He holds a Ph.D. in statistics from the University of Colorado and is a many-time recipient of Microsoft's Excel MVP designation.

Carlberg is a Southern California native. After college he moved to Colorado, where he worked for a succession of startups and attended graduate school. He spent two years in the Middle East, teaching computer science and dodging surly camels. After finishing graduate school, Carlberg worked at US West (a Baby Bell) in product management and at Motorola.

In 1995 he started a small consulting business, which provides design and analysis services to companies that want to guide their business decisions by means of quantitative analysis—approaches that today we group under the term "analytics." He enjoys writing about those techniques and, in particular, how to carry them out using the world's most popular numeric analysis application, Microsoft Excel.

Dedication

In loving memory of Peter M. Messer, 1942-2015.

We Want to Hear from You!

As the reader of this book, *you* are our most important critic and commentator. We value your opinion and want to know what we're doing right, what we could do better, what areas you'd like to see us publish in, and any other words of wisdom you're willing to pass our way.

We welcome your comments. You can email or write to let us know what you did or didn't like about this book—as well as what we can do to make our books better.

Please note that we cannot help you with technical problems related to the topic of this book.

When you write, please be sure to include this book's title and author as well as your name and email address. We will carefully review your comments and share them with the author and editors who worked on the book.

Email: feedback@quepublishing.com

Mail: Que Publishing
            ATTN: Reader Feedback
            800 East 96th Street
            Indianapolis, IN 46240 USA

Reader Services

Visit our website and register this book at quepublishing.com/register for convenient access to any updates, downloads, or errata that might be available for this book.

In 2011, I wrote *Predictive Analytics: Microsoft Excel.* The book went into techniques that are heavily used in the field of predictive analytics but that we don't necessarily think of as "predictive."

Those techniques included logistic regression, a technique that's often used in place of least squares regression when the outcome variable is measured with categories; principal components analysis, which groups not records but variables into mutually independent components of related variables; and factor rotation, a technique that helps make the interpretation of principal components more straightforward.

These topics are important ones in predictive analytics, and I personally find them intrinsically interesting and fun to write about. But they soft-pedal the predictive part. You can use logistic regression to predict—on the basis of such variables as state of residence, amount loaned, and annual income—who is likely to repay a loan and who isn't. But that's not the main purpose of logistic regression.

You can use principal components and factor analysis to reduce a database that contains hundreds of related variables down to a manageable few, without significant loss of information. Doing so often makes a forecast feasible, when—using hundreds of variables—it would not have been sensible even to attempt one.

So these techniques get you ready to make predictions, but none of them actually looks at the history of a diagnosis-related component in a given hospital and tells you how many patients to expect next quarter. None looks at a principal component that quantifies customers' interest in particular types of products and predicts what they'll spend on given products next year. Any of those techniques might help you develop useful information about which sorts of patients are likely to develop symptoms, without giving you a clue about when that will happen.

In that earlier book on predictive analytics, I did discuss the use of regression, moving averages, and smoothing to predict upcoming results. I also discussed the use of Box-Jenkins techniques to identify different sorts of time series patterns: autoregressive and moving average. But there just wasn't enough room in the book to cover the handling of time series that occur frequently and that are among the most interesting: series that are trending up or down, and series that have distinct seasonal components.

So I decided to focus this book on the predictive end of things. That still leaves some choices because even from 30,000 feet you can see three distinct approaches to quantitative forecasting: least squares regression, smoothing, and autoregressive integrated moving averages (or *ARIMA*).

It made sense to me that this book's topic ought to be the second of those three, smoothing. I didn't want to spend my time and yours on simple regression, whether multiple or not. Projecting an outcome variable forward in time based on its relationship to a predictor variable has limited applicability. This is particularly true when you begin to consider all the reasons that it can be a bad idea.

Spurious correlation is one such reason. That effect takes place when two variables that are not causally related are nevertheless correlated because each rises (or falls) as time passes. Suppose the per capita incidence of a disease has risen each year during the past decade and the per capita incidence of vaccination has risen similarly. Standard least squares regression might convince you that the correlation is too strong to be due to anything other than causation. Your analysis might argue that the vaccinations are causing the disease that they are meant to prevent.

Regression itself isn't to blame for this kind of misunderstanding, but it is susceptible to the confusion of spurious correlation. It seems to me that the opportunities for legitimate and informative use of the regression technique, at least for predictive purposes, simply don't fill a book.

That's not to say that multiple regression doesn't have a place in predictive analytics. It does, particularly when it comes to time series that are both trended and seasonal. I discuss the use of multiple regression in support of seasonal smoothing in Chapter 5, "Working with Seasonal Time Series."

ARIMA is another matter. I've been using it successfully since the mid-1980s in various business situations, from product sales to inventory control, and I intend to continue doing so. But it's not at all transparent, at least when it comes to the more complex models. ARIMA analysis can become heavily loop-dependent, and that makes it difficult to visualize specifically what's going on in the black box. The loop dependency also makes it difficult to discuss in the context of Excel worksheets.

Certainly Excel can accommodate iterative analysis by means of Visual Basic for Applications (VBA), add-ins coded in C, and similar tools. But it's difficult to learn anything other than coding from looking at code. Excel is a nearly ideal environment for learning how numerics that are in place at time 15 affect those in place at time 16. The Excel worksheet, properly designed, can illuminate those relationships better than anything except, perhaps, for an Excel chart.

Furthermore, there's some evidence—buttressed by sentiment—that for certain common business applications ARIMA is overkill, that it's unnecessarily complex and burdensome as compared to the somewhat simpler smoothing approaches. As I noted earlier, I'm not about to give up ARIMA just because some authors think it's too much of a good thing. I particularly like having a largely objective tool in the form of ARIMA's correlograms to help me select a model. But I'd just as soon wait for the jury to weigh in some more before I take the time to write another book about ARIMA analysis, or ask you to read it.

I do ask you to read this one. Smoothing approaches have come under some criticism since the mid-1980s. They've been called ad hoc, not grounded in careful statistical theory, and there's some truth to that. The mathematical and statistical groundwork that underlies, for example, multivariate statistical analysis outweighs the theory behind smoothing many times over.

Another drawback is the variety of methods touted by writers and practitioners of prediction via smoothing. For example, smoothing requires that forecasts be *initialized*. You can take many different routes to arrive at those initial values, and your choice can have a significant impact on your forecasts—particularly early in the time series. There's little in the way of theory to guide you here, and the result is that many sources use different methods, often without explanation, to initialize their forecasts. A stronger theoretical superstructure would help steer a path through the rubble.

And yet forecasts from smoothing have turned out to be accurate far more than you might expect of a technique that's so transparent and intuitively appealing. Excel even has a tool in its Data Analysis add-in that performs a (very rudimentary) version of simple smoothing. So this book pays only brief attention to the basics of smoothing. I assume that you know something about what it is, and I review the very basics primarily to make sure that we're using the same vocabulary. (If you don't yet have simple exponential smoothing in your bag of tricks, you might want to check out that *Predictive Analytics: Microsoft Excel* book I mentioned earlier.)

The topics of diagnosing time series (for example, to decide whether a time series is in fact trended), dealing with trend, dealing with seasonality, using additive or multiplicative models, and extending damped trend forecasts constitute most of this book.

You won't find any VBA here, for good or ill. (One exception: There's an Excel workbook named ACF.xls, which contains code to calculate and chart autocorrelation functions for you.) Everything I have to say about the smoothing part of predictive analytics can take place on the worksheet and can be illustrated in Excel charts. You can download all the Excel workbooks, and there's one for each chapter, from the publisher's website. That's so you don't have to enter data to explore the examples in this book.

After you've downloaded them, I suggest that you open the workbook for Chapter 1, "Smoothing and Its Alternatives," and then have a look at Chapter 1 itself, which has more to say about how regression and smoothing differ and how they help one another out.

Smoothing and Its Alternatives

1

Back around 1997 (my gosh, has it been that long?), I walked into the office of the chief operating officer of a mid-sized hospital for a meeting. He was an empiricist. He believed in what data, carefully gathered and intelligently analyzed, could tell him about the hospital's operations, its value to the community, its compliance with the spirit and the letter of the regulatory environment, and its fiscal health.

I had been consulting at that hospital for around six months—long enough, if only just barely, to have developed some measure of credibility with the client. The man I was meeting with had concerns about how the hospital was going about its demand-based staffing. A hospital has to maintain minimum nurse-to-patient ratios in its various units, sometimes based on patient acuity, which is a measure of the frequency, intensity, and duration of nursing care a patient requires. It can be disastrous to a hospital's standard of care if too few nurses are on site for a given hospital census; it can be disastrous to a hospital's fiscal health to routinely have many more nurses than are needed on the various units.

So I had arranged a meeting with this executive to suggest that we take a look at one of several ways to forecast patient census, perhaps tuned to patient acuity. I hadn't even finished my elevator pitch when I saw that he was starting to shake his head and it wasn't the "Yes, go on" kind of shake. It was the "Might as well drop it" kind of shake.

I knew this guy well enough to realize that I wasn't going to get anywhere with my suggestion, but I also knew that he'd clue me to the source of the problem. "I don't think it works. We've looked at forecasting already and it gets us nowhere."

I moved on to something else entirely. Later that day I learned that the consultant I had replaced was under the impression that statistical process control was a satisfactory forecasting technique, and had thereby poisoned the well.

The COO was wicked smart and he had both a CPA and an MBA from good schools. As I mentioned earlier, he respected data. But I was going to have to invest a lot of time and personal resources to show him that forecasting does so work. You have to understand how different measures call for different approaches. A technique that works beautifully in one context can easily turn out to be a real dog in another.

Regression in Forecasting

Which brings me to the role of regression analysis in forecasting, where it's neither dog nor best in show.

One popular way to forecast is to calculate the relationship between an outcome of interest and some measure of time. For example, can you forecast Microsoft's annual revenue if you know which year you're interested in? The material in Figure 1.1 addresses that question.

Figure 1.1
Excel has good support for ordinary least squares regression.

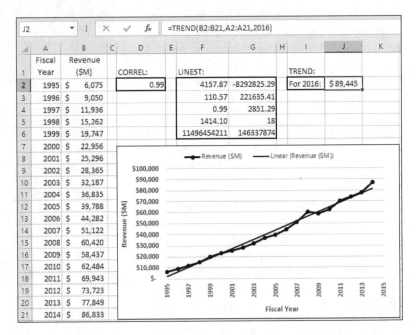

With even a marginally reasonable baseline of data such as the one shown in the range A2:B21 in Figure 1.1, it's possible to make a regression-based forecast for an upcoming year and have some confidence in it. Of course, in this example you're working with a very strong relationship:

- The correlation between Year and Revenue is 0.99. It's hard to get stronger than that without resorting to some trivial relationship such as the correlation between height in inches and height in centimeters.

- One result of the strong correlation is that the standard error of estimate is relatively small. You can find that statistic in the LINEST() results, in cell G4. Bracketing the observed revenue for a given year by plus and minus two standard errors gives you an interval of around $11,000M. That huge number of dollars is relatively small in the context of observations in the $80,000M range in 2013 and 2014.

- A small error of estimate shows up in the way the individual observations stick close to the regression line (which Excel terms a *trendline*). In Figure 1.1, the regression line is the straight diagonal line that the legend labels "Linear (Revenue ($M))." The stronger the relationship, the smaller the standard error of estimate and the closer the observations hew to the regression line.

Such a strong relationship can give you good confidence that the actual 2016 revenue will be fairly close to $89,445M, as forecast by Excel's TREND() function, even with a baseline of only 20 observations. The chart, with its linear trendline almost indistinguishable from the actual revenues, would tell you that it's probably unnecessary to look any further than simple linear regression for a forecasting technique with this data.

Curvilinear Relationships

Things are seldom as neat as Microsoft's annual revenues. Figure 1.2 shows the monthly U.S. unemployment rate for 2005 through 2013, as reported by the Bureau of Labor Statistics. It also suggests how useful ordinary linear regression can be when reality doesn't follow a straight line.

Figure 1.2 applies linear regression to Unemployment Rate—the predicted variable—and Period—a predictor variable with equally spaced values. The analysis calculates intercepts and slopes that describe the straight regression lines in Figures 1.1 and 1.2. (The intercept identifies where the regression line intercepts the chart's vertical axis, and the slope defines the steepness of the regression line.)

Regression calculates the intercept and slope such that the sum of the squared distances, or *deviations*, between the actual observations and the regression line are minimized—hence the term *least squares*. Clearly, when the charted observations (the reported unemployment rates) follow a curved path, they simply cannot track closely to a straight regression line.

Many phenomena that we're interested in describe a cycle, such as the rates charted in Figure 1.2. Or they respond to seasonal variation, the way that home sales peak in spring and summer months and bottom out during the winter. Or they follow a trend, a unidirectional trend as in Figure 1.1, or an up-and-down trend such as outdoor hourly temperatures. (The difference between a trend and a cycle is that up-and-down trends recur regularly; you never know when a cycle is going to turn up or down.)

Figure 1.2
This time series is surely a cycle rather than a trend or seasonal effect.

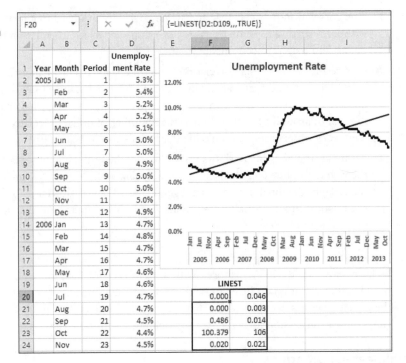

	A	B	C	D
	Year	Month	Period	Unemployment Rate
1	Year	Month	Period	ment Rate
2	2005	Jan	1	5.3%
3		Feb	2	5.4%
4		Mar	3	5.2%
5		Apr	4	5.2%
6		May	5	5.1%
7		Jun	6	5.0%
8		Jul	7	5.0%
9		Aug	8	4.9%
10		Sep	9	5.0%
11		Oct	10	5.0%
12		Nov	11	5.0%
13		Dec	12	4.9%
14	2006	Jan	13	4.7%
15		Feb	14	4.8%
16		Mar	15	4.7%
17		Apr	16	4.7%
18		May	17	4.6%
19		Jun	18	4.6%
20		Jul	19	4.7%
21		Aug	20	4.7%
22		Sep	21	4.5%
23		Oct	22	4.4%
24		Nov	23	4.5%

F20 $\{=LINEST(D2:D109,,,TRUE)\}$

LINEST

0.000	0.046
0.000	0.003
0.486	0.014
100.379	106
0.020	0.021

Piecewise Regression

Standard linear regression does not lend itself well to nonlinear measures such as those that describe economic outcomes, whether those outcomes are seasonal, trended in alternating directions, or cyclic. Some analysts like to apply what's called *piecewise regression* in that sort of case. Figure 1.3 has an example.

Using piecewise regression, the analyst admits that a single straight regression line will not properly describe the relationship between the predicted and the predictor variable or variables. But several regression lines just might do so.

In Figure 1.3 we deal with the difficulty shown in Figure 1.2, the large deviations between the observations and the single straight regression line, by running three separate regression analyses. The three instances of Excel's LINEST function are run against the first 39 records, and then the second 19, and then the third 50. Both the second and the third resulting equations are more accurate predictors of unemployment rate than is the single regression equation in Figure 1.2.

There are a several ways to construct a piecewise regression analysis. One is to actually run multiple regression analyses, as shown in Figure 1.3. A different method is to run just one regression, but to include additional predictor variables that identify which of (in this case) three groups each observation belongs to.

Figure 1.3
Piecewise regression breaks up a single linear regression line into several regression lines.

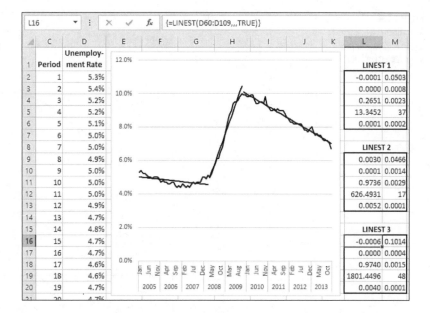

That approach is getting very close to the analysis of covariance, which among other tasks tests the interactions between the new variables and the covariate. Those tests help determine whether differences in the groups' regression lines can be considered random. In that event, it's not implausible that the groups share a common regression line, and we can resort to a single regression. But in a case such as the unemployment rates in Figure 1.3, it's clear that the regression lines are so discrepant that we cannot act as though they represent random departures from one shared regression line.

> **NOTE** The approach that involves creating new predictor variables that represent group membership is a useful technique when it comes to quantifying seasonality in an analysis of a time series that relies predominantly on smoothing. Later chapters on initializing smoothing analyses and on accounting for seasonal differences return to this approach and examine it in some detail.

Polynomial Regression

Still, piecewise regression often turns out to be a needless complication in forecasting. There's a different approach, still in the regression family, which can do a better job without having to piece together several regression equations. See Figure 1.4.

What you see in Figure 1.4, besides the original plot of the data, is a *polynomial regression line*. The term "polynomial" refers to the fact that there are "many names" or "many values" in the predictor variable, just as "binomial" means that a variable has two names, such as True and False, zero and nonzero, or Male and Female. (With two or more predictor variables, as here, the term *multiple regression* also applies.)

Figure 1.4
A polynomial regression equation allows for non-linear regression lines.

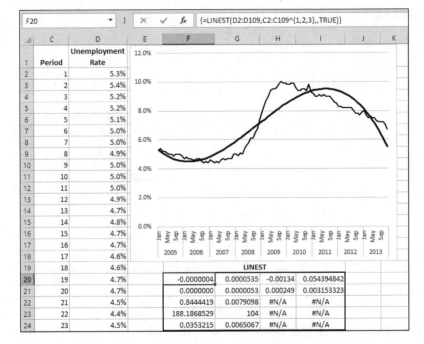

| F20 | ▼ : × ✓ fx | {=LINEST(D2:D109,C2:C109^{1,2,3},,TRUE)} |

C	D	LINEST			
Period	Unemployment Rate				
1	5.3%				
2	5.4%				
3	5.2%				
4	5.2%				
5	5.1%				
6	5.0%				
7	5.0%				
8	4.9%				
9	5.0%				
10	5.0%				
11	5.0%				
12	4.9%				
13	4.7%				
14	4.8%				
15	4.7%				
16	4.7%				
17	4.6%				
18	4.6%		LINEST		
19	4.7%	-0.0000004	0.0000535	-0.00134	0.054394842
20	4.7%	0.0000000	0.0000053	0.000249	0.003153323
21	4.5%	0.8444419	0.0079098	#N/A	#N/A
22	4.4%	188.1868529	104	#N/A	#N/A
23	4.5%	0.0353215	0.0065067	#N/A	#N/A

In this case, the values are the original values of the time period itself, the original values squared, and the original values cubed. When you use only the original values and those values squared, the term is "quadratic equation"; when you add the cubed values, it's "cubic equation."

Here's a method that can save you the time of explicitly entering the squares and cubes of the original predictor values directly on the worksheet, where you can use LINEST()'s or TREND()'s arguments to point at them. Assuming the layout used in Figure 1.4, with the number of the month in column C and the unemployment rate in column D, you can skip putting the squares and cubes on the worksheet and, instead, simply array-enter this formula in F20:G24:

```
=LINEST(D2:D109,C2:C109^{1,2,3},,TRUE)
```

Notice the curly braces around 1,2,3 in the formula. Together they constitute what Excel calls an *array constant*. In effect, this formula instructs Excel to raise the values in C2:C109 to the first, second, and third powers on your behalf, and to use the results as the predictor variables in the regression equation.

Then, the LINEST() function takes over and returns the results, including the intercept and the coefficients of the regression equation. Those results, in combination with the numbers that identify the month when the observation was made, define the regression line. If you chart the results of the equation along with the original unemployment observations, you'll find that you get the trendline shown in Figure 1.4.

You could get the results of the equation, the trendline, in one step by array-entering this TREND() function, again using an array constant, into a range that's 108 rows high and 1 column wide:

```
=TREND(D2:D109,C2:C109^{1,2,3})
```

I've used both the TREND() function and the LINEST() function several times in this chapter, and you'll see them used repeatedly in later chapters. Not because this is a book about using regression to forecast—it isn't—but because regression analysis can be a useful adjunct to this book's main theme, the use of smoothing techniques in forecasting. Therefore it's helpful to bear in mind the difference in the results that the two functions return:

- LINEST() returns the intercept and the coefficients that define the regression equation. At your option, it also returns various statistics that help you evaluate the reliability of the results, such as R^2 and the closely related F-ratio.

- TREND() returns the results of applying the intercept and coefficients to the predictor variables, that is, the values that the regression equation calculates. Those results can be termed forecasts, predicted values, outcomes, or any of various other terms that have more to do with how the data was obtained, and how it's to be used, than with the regression approach itself.

> **NOTE**
>
> Suppose that you have array-entered, using Ctrl+Shift+Enter, an array formula such as the one in F20:I24 in Figure 1.4, and that Excel has accepted it as you intended. If you select any cell in the formula's results and look in the formula box, you'll see the formula you array-entered surrounded by curly braces, like this:
>
> ```
> {=LINEST(D2:D109,C2:C109^{1,2,3})}
> ```
>
> Notice that the complete formula is now surrounded by a pair of curly braces. You didn't type them; Excel supplied them in response to your use of Ctrl+Shift+Enter instead of merely Enter. But the interior curly braces, the ones that demark the array constant—*those* you have to enter yourself.
>
> This probably seems confusing if you're new to Excel's array formulas and array constants, and all I can tell you is that I don't design 'em; I just use 'em. If you want to do the same, type the braces around the array constant and let Excel type the braces around the array formula.

I've thrown a lot at you in this section, including the use of an array constant in an array formula to avoid having to create ranges on the worksheet for the predictor's squared and cubed values. It might help to step back from the minutiae of curly brackets and revisit the purpose of the LINEST() formula in Figure 1.4, in F20:I24:

```
=LINEST(D2:D109,C2:C109^{1,2,3},,TRUE)
```

The arguments to LINEST() are as follows:

1. D2:D109 is the range that contains the variable to be forecast.
2. C2:C109^{1,2,3} implies three columns of values that constitute the predictor variables.

3. The third argument is empty and defaults to TRUE. That tells Excel to calculate the intercept (or *constant*) normally, and not to force it to equal zero. The reasons to calculate the intercept normally are not quite as compelling as they were before the release of Excel 2003, but they're still plenty good.

4. The fourth argument, TRUE, tells Excel to return the full set of LINEST() results, and not just the intercept and coefficients.

In Figure 1.4, notice from the LINEST() results that the cubic regression accounts for more than 84% of the variability in the predicted variable (see cell F22). That compares fairly well with the three different results returned by the piecewise approach shown in Figure 1.3, and of course it's much better than the single linear regression shown in Figure 1.2.

> **NOTE** Cell F22 in Figure 1.4 contains the value 0.844. The third row, first column of the full LINEST() results always provides the R² value. That's the square of the correlation between the predicted variable and the predictor variable or variables. The R² value expresses the proportion (equivalently, of course, the percent) of variability shared by the predicted variable and the predictor variable(s).

Excel offers various ways to get the analysis that's shown and charted in Figure 1.4. One alternative appears in Figure 1.5.

Figure 1.5
Excel's TREND() function returns the regression line.

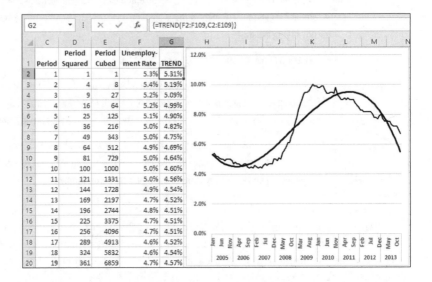

One way to set up a polynomial regression in Excel is to establish the predictor variables directly on the worksheet, instead of using the array constant in a LINEST() or TREND() formula. In Figure 1.5, you can find the predictor variables entered explicitly in columns C through E. Column C, of course, contains the original predictor values: the numbers of the months during which the unemployment rate was measured. Column D contains the values in column C, squared. Column D contains the values in column C, raised to the third power.

Excel's TREND() function is used in column G to forecast the unemployment rate based on its relationship to the elapsing months and to their squared and cubed values in columns C through D. The TREND() function is array-entered into the range G2:G109, using the keyboard sequence Ctrl+Shift+Enter. The formula as array-entered is as follows:

```
=TREND(F2:F109,C2:E109)
```

TREND() and LINEST()

For another way to use Excel's regression tools to calculate a polynomial regression, see Figure 1.6.

Figure 1.6
TREND() is a shortcut to LINEST()'s forecasts.

	A	B	C	D	E	F	G	H	I	J	K
	Year	Month	Period	Period Squared	Period Cubed	Unemployment Rate		LINEST			
2	2005	Jan	1	1	1	5.3%	-0.0000004	0.0000535		-0.00134	0.05439
3		Feb	2	4	8	5.4%	0.0000000	0.0000053		0.00025	0.00315
4		Mar	3	9	27	5.2%	0.8444419	0.0079098		#N/A	#N/A
5		Apr	4	16	64	5.2%	188.1868529	104		#N/A	#N/A
6		May	5	25	125	5.1%	0.0353215	0.0065067		#N/A	#N/A
7		Jun	6	36	216	5.0%					
8		Jul	7	49	343	5.0%	TREND			LINEST Formula	
9		Aug	8	64	512	4.9%	0.05311			0.05311	
10		Sep	9	81	729	5.0%	0.05193			0.05193	
11		Oct	10	100	1000	5.0%	0.05085			0.05085	
12		Nov	11	121	1331	5.0%	0.04988			0.04988	
13		Dec	12	144	1728	4.9%	0.04900			0.04900	
14	2006	Jan	13	169	2197	4.7%	0.04821			0.04821	
15		Feb	14	196	2744	4.8%	0.04752			0.04752	
16		Mar	15	225	3375	4.7%	0.04692			0.04692	
17		Apr	16	256	4096	4.7%	0.04641			0.04641	
18		May	17	289	4913	4.6%	0.04599			0.04599	
19		Jun	18	324	5832	4.6%	0.04565			0.04565	
20		Jul	19	361	6859	4.7%	0.04539			0.04539	

J9 ▾ : × ✓ fx =$K$2+$J$2*C2+$I$2*D2+$H$2*E2

If all you're after is forecast values, you might as well use TREND(). I've learned, though, that if I'm going to the minimal trouble of forecasting values with TREND(), I might as well go to the slight additional trouble of entering LINEST(), because it can point me to problems with my data—and the R^2, the standard error of estimate, and the pieces of an omnibus ANOVA in the final two rows of the LINEST() results might help me understand whether I have something I can rely on.

Figure 1.6 shows how the results of the TREND() function come about from the LINEST() function. The range H2:K6 contains the results of this LINEST() array formula:

```
=LINEST(F2:F109,C2:E109,,TRUE)
```

In Figure 1.6 I have shown the month numbers, squared and cubed, explicitly in columns D and E. (The reason will become apparent shortly.) So both the TREND() and the LINEST() functions refer to columns C through E as the locations of the predictor variables.

I've array-entered this version of the TREND() function in H9:H116:

```
=TREND(F2:F109,C2:E109)
```

That returns the forecast values that you've already seen in Figure 1.5. I repeat them in Figure 1.6 so that you can compare them to the values in the range J9:J116. This formula is in cell J9:

```
=$K$2+$J$2*C2+$I$2*D2+$H$2*E2
```

It sums these terms:

- The regression equation's intercept in cell K2
- The product of the first regression coefficient in J2 and the number of the first month in C2
- The product of the second regression coefficient in I2 and the (squared) number of the first month in D2
- The product of the third regression coefficient in H2 and the (cubed) number of the first month in E2

> **NOTE** If something about the way the coefficients and the predictor variables are paired in the formula seems odd to you, you'll find it discussed near the end of Chapter 2, "Diagnosing Trend and Seasonality."

The addresses of the intercept and the coefficients are fixed by means of dollar signs so that the formula can be copied and pasted, or autofilled, down through row 116, with the values of the predictor variables incrementing accordingly.

If you'll compare the results of the TREND() function in column H with the worked-out formula in column I, you'll note that they are precisely equal. You can use either, and sometimes there's a good reason to use both.

Using the Chart's Trendline

Finally—for now, anyway—there's a quick-and-dirty way to get a look at how a polynomial equation fits your charted data. See Figure 1.8.

The polynomial trendline (shown with dashes) in Figure 1.8's chart requires no calculations on the worksheet, no entering TREND() or LINEST(). You just take these steps:

1. Create a Line or Scatter chart of your observed variables. (If your predictors are anything other than the numbers 1, 2, 3, ..., you should probably use a Scatter chart. I've used Line charts in this chapter because with these month numbers there's no substantive difference between the Line and Scatter charts.)

Figure 1.7
The chart trendline is a
quick way to visualize the
regression equation.

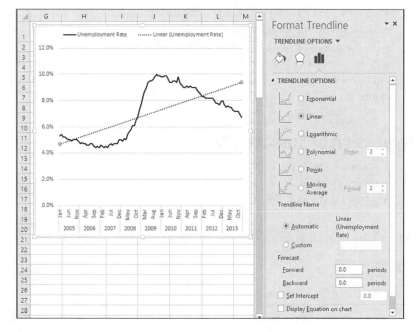

2. Right-click the charted data series and choose Insert Trendline. The pane at the right in Figure 1.7 appears.

3. The default trendline is Linear. With this data set you would surely want to click the Polynomial option button and set the order to 3.

That's all there is to it, although you can make cosmetic adjustments to the trendline's appearance if you want. See Figure 1.8.

Figure 1.8
The chart trendline does
not correspond directly
to any range on the
worksheet.

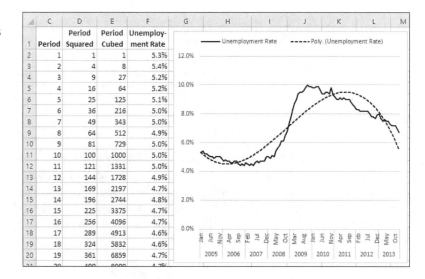

Period	Period Squared	Period Cubed	Unemploy-ment Rate
1	1	1	5.3%
2	4	8	5.4%
3	9	27	5.2%
4	16	64	5.2%
5	25	125	5.1%
6	36	216	5.0%
7	49	343	5.0%
8	64	512	4.9%
9	81	729	5.0%
10	100	1000	5.0%
11	121	1331	5.0%
12	144	1728	4.9%
13	169	2197	4.7%
14	196	2744	4.8%
15	225	3375	4.7%
16	256	4096	4.7%
17	289	4913	4.6%
18	324	5832	4.6%
19	361	6859	4.7%

1

Of course, you have no additional information regarding the reliability of the regression, no quantitative measure of the relationship (you *can* call for the R^2 to be displayed along with the trendline on the chart; the Trendline Options pane includes a check box for that, although you can't see it in Figure 1.7). Nevertheless, it's always advisable to get a visual check on the way your data lay out, and Excel makes it so easy that there's no good reason not to do so.

Regression or Smoothing?

For contrast with the regression examples given in the preceding section, Figure 1.9 provides an example of a smoothing analysis of the unemployment data examined in Figures 1.2 through 1.8.

Figure 1.9
Smoothing can provide much more accurate forecasts than regression.

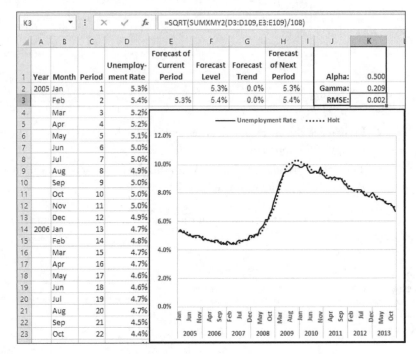

The forecasts are charted via the dotted line, labeled "Holt" in the legend.

I should note right here that the analysis that's suggested by Figure 1.9 is more than a little simplified. It does include a component to forecast the level of the time series as well as a component to forecast its trend. However, before I settled on a strictly level-and-trend model (often termed a Holt model), I would want to undertake various checks that don't belong here in Chapter 1, such as filtering out the trend to look for cyclic or seasonal movement.

NOTE | Throughout this book I use the terms *baseline* and *time series* almost interchangeably. I do tend to use "baseline" when I want to stress, or at least allude to, the desirability of using a lengthy history of observations. The term "time series" is nearly synonymous with "baseline," but in some contexts it also connotes a time series object in the R statistical application, which contains both the data itself and additional attributes.

Comparing Smoothing with Regression with Forecasting Errors

Despite the simplicity of the analysis, the smoothing calculations in Figure 1.9 give us a pretty good set of forecasts. Consider the value in cell K3, which is 0.002. The worksheet labels that value "RMSE," for root mean square error. It is closely related to the standard error of estimate returned by LINEST() and shown in several preceding figures in this chapter.

NOTE | RMSE divides the sum of the squared forecast errors by the number of forecasts; the standard error of estimate divides the sum of the squared forecast errors by their degrees of freedom.

Adjusting for the difference between the number of forecasts and the degrees of freedom, the RMSE for the smoothing forecasts shows smoothing as outperforming the regression of unemployment rate against month by the following amounts:

- Compared to the linear regression shown in Figure 1.2, the standard error of estimate in the regression is 7.23 times greater than the RMSE for the smoothing analysis.

- Compared to the combined piecewise regressions in Figure 1.3, the standard error of estimate for the regressions is 1.04 times greater than the RMSE of the smoothing analysis.

- Compared to the polynomial regression in Figure 1.4, the standard error of estimate for the regression is 3.97 times greater than the RMSE for the smoothing analysis.

So, at least in the case we've been looking at in this chapter, the smoothing approach to forecasting can return much more accurate results than regression. You can confirm that visually by comparing the charts in Figures 1.2 through 1.4 with the chart in Figure 1.9. You can confirm it quantitatively by comparing the size of the standard errors from the regression analyses with the RMSE value in Figure 1.9.

Additional Rationales for Smoothing

That's a strong argument for choosing the smoothing approach, or at least trying it out, if a time series is returning regression forecasts that you aren't finding satisfactory. To that argument, you can add the fact that smoothing itself does not rely on reference distributions in order to quantify probabilities, as do some applications of regression analysis (granted, some optional and auxiliary uses of regression in support of smoothing do precisely that).

> **NOTE** Full disclosure: My own view is that there's nothing wrong, and frequently there's much that's right, with using reference distributions to help understand the probabilities. But if you can discard an assumption without doing damage to the analysis, that's an option that deserves your consideration. Smoothing itself makes no assumptions about normal distributions, homogeneous variances, or independence of observations, although ancillary analyses such as prediction intervals (which are similar to confidence intervals) retain those assumptions.

Furthermore, a regression analysis derives *one* equation to describe the relationship between the predictor variable(s) and the predicted variable. (This is equally true of piecewise regression; the example shown in Figure 1.3 provides three separate equations, but they are derived by three separate regression analyses.)

In contrast, smoothing uses as many equations as there are forecasts. Every new observation that arrives occasions a new forecast, and that new forecast is determined in part by the amount and direction of the error in the immediately previous forecast.

When you recalculate a regression based on the acquisition of a new data point, the new regression equation has an effect on all the forecasts that precede the new data point. Only when you recalculate the constants in a smoothing analysis is the impact of new observations felt at earlier time points, and that recalculation is both infrequent and of little impact after you have a reasonably long time series to work with.

To my mind, though, the most convincing reason to use smoothing in preference to regression for purposes of predictive analytics is that regression requires that you select, measure, and include your predictor variables. That task is often a tug-of-war between including enough predictor variables to get satisfactory forecasts, and keeping the number of predictors small enough to avoid overmodeling and to ensure a stable equation.

But with smoothing you're forecasting the variable of interest from that variable itself. To begin with, that structure helps you avoid the problem of spurious correlation: the attempt to predict one variable from another when the two bear no causal relationship but rather are both correlated with the passage of time.

More compelling is that the complex of variables that bring about change in a variable at, say, Time 98 will also exert their effects at Time 99. By forecasting an unemployment rate at Time 99 based in large measure on its values from Time 1 through Time 98, you subsume into the time series itself all the macroeconomic variables such as the Federal funds rate, whether the business cycle is in a growth or contraction phase, corporate tax rates, and so on. Changes in those causal variables leave their marks in the series of unemployment measurements, and through the smoothing process can alert you to an important change in the nature of the time series.

Pushing the Forecast Horizon

Another difficulty with regression analysis in forecasting situations is the problem of the *forecast horizon*, by which I mean the distance that you want to forecast into the future. The problem extends from forecasting to other, more familiar contexts. For example, consider the probability of purchasing a house given different levels of annual income, shown in Figure 1.10.

Figure 1.10
Simple linear regression can take you into no-man's-land at both ends of the regression line.

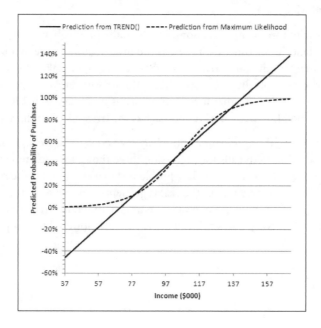

Figure 1.10 shows the (fictitious) relationship between annual income level and the probability of purchasing a house. The linear regression returned by Excel's TREND() function, given this data set, indicates that the probability of making a purchase rises steadily, by constant increments, as the income level rises, again steadily and again by constant increments. The line does not bend up as income increases, nor down as income falls. The probability of purchasing a house exceeds 100% when the income passes roughly $145,000, and falls below 0% when the income is less than $72,000.

If you plotted actually observed probabilities, rather than forecasts, against income, you would see a line much closer to the curved and dashed line in Figure 1.10, which was calculated using a maximum likelihood technique called *logistic regression*. (Despite its name, logistic regression does not use the measures of shared variance that are at the heart of least squares regression; it uses odds, odds ratios, and logarithms.)

With data sets like the one in Figure 1.10, techniques such as logistic regression can model the data much more accurately than can least squares regression. Notice that the dashed line calculated by the maximum likelihood approach conforms to the logic and the reality of the situation much more closely than does TREND()'s straight regression line. The dashed line bends as it approaches 0% and 100%, and in fact it exceeds neither of those limits no matter how much you reduce income on one end or increase it on the other. (I discuss how the smoothing approaches deal with the problem of limits in Chapter 7, "Multiplicative and Damped Trend Models.")

The same is true of forecasting situations, in which the predictor variable is either time itself or some stand-in for time. Certainly, as the investigator, you're in a position to cut off the forecast horizon at the point that a straight regression line takes you beyond the realm of rationality (for example, beyond 100% of anything). But can you confidently tweak a cur-vilinear regression analysis so that it reflects reality as it *approaches* that limit, much as the maximum likelihood line flattens as it approaches the 0% and 100% limits of probability?

The problem is not with regression itself. In my own consulting work, I estimate that the data I'm given to work with calls for regression three times, for each time that I find that a different technique will work better. The problem is that the simpler the regression model, the less it's able to accurately reflect the reality presented by some well-defined situations—such as forecasting. And the more complex the model, the more you risk *over* modeling, a condition that can be every bit as misleading as an underpowered technique.

Diagnosing Trend and Seasonality

2

Much of the work that's done in the smoothing approaches to predictive analytics has nothing to do with the techniques that we generally term *statistical inference*. If you've taken an introductory-to-intermediate-level course in statistics, you've read about those techniques. They include analyses such as confidence intervals, t-tests and the analysis of variance, multiple regression analysis, and so on.

For various reasons, there's not much use for that sort of inferential technique in the smoothing methods. Statistical inference is useful in some smoothing situations, and this chapter discusses them. Sometimes you'd like to see what probability has to say about whether a time series really exhibits trend, or whether the seasonality you see in a charted time series is dependable. Prediction intervals, which in effect are confidence intervals applied to forecasts, don't get as much use as they should. And the ARIMA methods—some of which are identical, or nearly so, to smoothing—make broad use of statistical inference. The interrupted time series models are a good example.

The principal reason that you don't find inferential statistics such as F-tests and Wilks' lambda in smoothing analysis is that they're designed to answer different kinds of questions. You might deploy an F-test when you want to decide whether the differences in the means of three groups are reliable—that is, whether they're likely to recur in a subsequent version of an experiment. Planned orthogonal contrasts might be the way to go if you specify beforehand which group means you want to compare.

Different inferential techniques ask different questions, but they tend to be variations on this basic theme: What is the probability that I would observe a difference between my samples as large as this one if there is no difference between the populations that I drew my samples from?

That is not the sort of question that smoothing analysis asks. When you use smoothing techniques on a time series, you're asking for the value that you can expect to observe at the next time period. There's no empirically observed value or point estimate, such as a group mean, about which you can make a statement of probability under the assumption that a null hypothesis is true. The whole point is to estimate an as yet *unobserved* value.

That said, inferential statistics can be valuable tools in the smoothing process. You tend to resort to them when you want objective guidance in deciding whether you have a trended or a horizontal time series to work with. You tend to use inferential analyses when you want to test whether seasonal peaks and valleys might be more real than apparent. And in a different vein, prediction intervals are useful in putting limits around predicted values.

This chapter discusses the use of inferential statistics in deciding whether a trend is present in your time series, or whether seasonality is present. In either case there are special procedures you'll want to apply to take advantage of the trend or seasonality.

Inside the Autocorrelation

I'm going to recommend that you use something called the *autocorrelation function*, or ACF, for various diagnostic purposes when you're working with time series. There are several reasons for that recommendation. One reason, which is relatively unimportant for present purposes, is that ACFs and partial ACFs are necessary diagnostic tools if you ever find yourself using the Box-Jenkins approach to time series analysis, often termed *ARIMA*.

More important is the closely related purpose of deciding whether your time series is characterized by a trend. A *stationary* series, also termed a *horizontal* series, by definition has no trend. It does not move steadily up or down for a prolonged period. On average, the level of the series is unchanging no matter whether you observe it at time period 1, 100, or any period in between.

Of course, you generally want a source of information that's more objective than eyeballing a chart of the series to decide whether it has a trend. ACFs are a well-established and relatively straightforward method of making that decision. ACFs are also valuable tools for deciding whether residual values—the values that are left over after you have subtracted forecasts from associated actual observations—are themselves autocorrelated. Ideally, the residuals have no autocorrelation. They should represent random error. If there is some systematic component to the relationship between pairs of residual values, that component ought to be taken into account by the forecasting model instead of tossed into the detritus of the actual errors.

So ACFs are useful, among other reasons, for helping you determine whether your raw data series is trended. If it is, you should choose a smoothing model that is designed to take trend into account. They are also useful as a means of checking that residuals are independent of one another. Other reasons that ACFs are so useful exist, but those are the two reasons to discuss ACFs in this chapter. We start with a review of the nature of a correlation.

The Magnitude and the Direction of a Correlation

This section discusses how it comes about that a positive correlation coefficient measures a direct relationship and that a negative correlation coefficient measures an inverse relationship. This section also reviews why a strong relationship has a correlation close to plus or minus 1.0, whereas a weak relationship is close to 0.0. These concepts help to clarify how patterns of ACFs help you identify the presence or absence of trend.

Strictly, an ACF differs from a conventional Pearson correlation coefficient. But the differences, which I discuss later in this chapter in the "Understanding the Meaning of ACFs" section, are minor, and they become vanishingly small as the number of underlying observations increases. It's a lot easier to grasp how the number of time periods between paired observations affects the strength of the relationship when it's discussed in terms of the Pearson correlation than when it's discussed in terms of the ACF. You'll quickly come to see how the line of thought generalizes from the conventional Pearson correlation to the ACF.

The Definitional Formula for Pearson's Correlation

Pearson's correlation coefficient is almost universally abbreviated as r, which stands for *regression*, the statistical phenomenon upon which the notion of correlation is based (as are most other components of the fearsome-sounding General Linear Model). Many mutually equivalent formulas for r exist, but the one that's most pertinent to the current topic is

$$r = \sum_{i=1}^{n} z_{i1} z_{i2} / n$$

where

- r is the correlation coefficient.
- n is the number of pairs of observations that are correlated.
- z_{i1} is the ith observation in the 1st group, converted to a standard or "z" score.
- z_{i2} is the ith observation in the 2nd group, converted to a standard or "z" score.

In words, and assuming that you're forced to use paper and pencil instead of just entering the Excel worksheet function CORREL(), here are the steps:

1. Convert each observation in the first group of scores to a z-score. Do so by subtracting the average of the first group from each observed value, and dividing by the group's standard deviation.

2. Do the same for the second group of scores.

3. Get the product of the z-scores that belong to each member of a pair. If one group consists of 10 girls and the other group consists of their brothers, get the product of the z-scores for each sister and her brother.

4. Total the products and divide by the number of pairs.

The result is the Pearson correlation coefficient. There are several points to note regarding this calculation, but first have a look at Figure 2.1.

Figure 2.1
A simple Pearson correlation between the weights in pounds of brothers and sisters.

	A	B	C	D	E	F	G
				Sisters' z-scores	Brothers' z-scores		Products of z-scores
1	Sisters	Brothers					
2	34	52		-1.48	-0.23		0.35
3	73	63		0.72	0.23		0.16
4	97	98		2.07	1.69		3.48
5	51	84		-0.52	1.10		-0.58
6	44	71		-0.92	0.56		-0.51
7	51	18		-0.52	-1.65		0.87
8	81	75		1.17	0.73		0.85
9	51	30		-0.52	-1.15		0.60
10	61	49		0.04	-0.36		-0.01
11	60	36		-0.02	-0.90		0.02
12							
13	=CORREL(A2:A11,B2:B11)						Average of products
14		0.52					0.52

G14 ▾ : × ✓ *fx*   =AVERAGE(G2:G12)

In Figure 2.1, the raw data—weight in pounds—of sisters and brothers of any young age appears in the range A2:B11. Excel provides the worksheet function CORREL() for just this sort of situation, where you want to know the strength and direction of the relationship between two variables. Cell B14 shows that the correlation between the two is 0.52.

Figure 2.1 also shows the correlation between the sisters' and the brothers' weights worked out using the definitional formula given earlier. That formula gets the average of the products of the z-scores in G2:G11. The z-scores themselves are in D2:D11 and E2:E11 and are calculated with formulas like this one, used in cell D2:

```
=(A2-AVERAGE($A$2:$A$11))/STDEV.P($A$2:$A$11)
```

As discussed earlier in this section, the formula subtracts the average of the scores in A2:A11 from the individual score in A2, and divides the difference by the standard deviation of the scores in A2:A11. This procedure results in a z-score.

Notice what happens when you subtract the average of the scores from an individual score: You wind up with a quantity that's negative or positive depending on where the person's weight falls vis-à-vis the average. The average weight of the 10 sisters is 60.3, and when you subtract that average from the 34-pound weight of the sister in cell A2, you get a negative amount. The amount is smaller, but still negative, when you divide by the standard deviation. Therefore, the sister whose weight is in cell A2 winds up with a negative z-score in cell D2; her weight is below the average weight of the 10 sisters.

As it happens, the same is true of the brother whose weight is given in cell B2. His weight of 52 is below the average weight of the 10 brothers, which is 57.6. Therefore his z-score in cell E2 is negative, as is his sister's in cell D2.

When you multiply the brother's negative z-score in E2 by the sister's negative z-score in D2, you get a positive product, 0.35, in cell G2.

All this is the same when both the sister and the brother in a pair are heavier than their group's average. In row 3 of Figure 2.1, both the brother and the sister are heavier than the average of their respective groups. They both have positive z-scores, and so the product in cell G3 is also positive.

On the other hand, when one member of a pair has a positive z-score and the other member has a negative z-score, the product is negative. See the brother-sister pair in row 5, where the sister's weight is below the sisters' average and the brother's weight is above the brothers' average. That situation (as well as when the sister is heavier and the brother lighter than their respective averages) results in a negative product.

Now, when you take the average of the z-score products, you calculate a positive correlation coefficient if, and only if, the total of the positive products exceeds the absolute value of the negative products. In the absence of really discrepant outliers, you tend to get a positive correlation when the members of the pairs are both either above the average of their group or below the average of their group. If a correlation is positive, high scores go with high scores and low scores with low ones, and you have a *direct relationship*.

Similarly, if the relationship is inverse rather than direct, it's likely that you have more pairs with differently signed z-scores than pairs whose z-scores have the same sign. Suppose that you asked 10 golfers how many years each had been playing the game, and what their handicaps were. You would expect that the more years that had passed since they took up the game, the lower their handicaps. You would expect that years of experience above the average would tend to go with handicaps below the average: an *inverse relationship*.

Furthermore, the product of two relatively large z-scores tends to pull the average product (that is, the correlation coefficient) away from zero and toward either plus or minus 1.0. When a correlation is strong, close to either 1.0 or −1.0, it means that relatively extreme z-scores are linked. If years of experience playing golf is relative to the golfer's handicap, and if the correlation is, say, −0.9, then many years of golf tends to be found in golfers with very low handicaps. And duffers who just took up the game tend to have very high handicaps.

In a very real sense, then, the direction of the correlation depends on whether two linked numbers—brother's weight and sister's weight, or a golfer's experience and handicap—are both on the same side of the average. The strength of the correlation, whether positive or negative, tends to depend on the distance from their respective means of both numbers.

This discussion has been based on the pairing of individual values in two sets of numbers. That pairing could be based on different beings, such as those who share family relationships, or on two conceptually related variables, such as height and weight, that can be measured on the same individual. How do the same concepts play out in the context of serial correlation, when the two related measures come from different time periods in a given time series?

Autocorrelation and Averages

Suppose that you were investigating the relationship—the correlation—between consecutive pairs of values in a time series. That time series might represent the number of gallons of water pumped each day through the sprinklers on a golf course. If the weather conditions are fairly stable and the transpiration rates are carefully measured, you would expect good management to result in consistent levels of pumped water on a daily basis. The amount pumped on June 1 is probably very much like the amount pumped on June 2, on June 3, and so on. But unless the golf course is located in an arid region, you would expect the daily water usage to fall, perhaps considerably, in the winter months when rain and snow are providing moisture that doesn't need to be pumped out of wells.

In a situation such as the one I've just described, you would expect to find many days during the summer months when a relatively large amount of water is pumped every day. Equally, you would expect many winter days when a relatively small amount of water is pumped.

In that case, an amount of water that's greater than the annual average would be pumped on any given summer day. And a similar amount of water would be pumped on the next day. On any given winter day, the amount of water pumped would be smaller than the annual average—and so would the amount of water on the next day.

In other words, and although there will be many exceptions, most two-day spans during the year will both pump more water than average, or less water than average. You'll get a long run of days above the average of the time series, followed by a long run of days below its average. This is termed *autocorrelative drift* for reasons that will shortly become apparent.

Looking at Individual Cases

Let's have a look at a fairly extreme example of autocorrelative drift, because the example's extremity helps make the important points more crisp. Suppose that the number of gallons of water pumped over a 20-day period looks something like the chart in Figure 2.2.

This example is out of the ordinary because the second through tenth observations are each one unit larger than the immediately preceding observation, and the final nine are each one unit smaller than the preceding observation. This degree of regularity isn't found in nature, but the resulting pattern is this: five consecutive observations below the mean of 5.5, then nine above the mean, then another five below the mean.

Figure 2.2 also shows the two series that the original observations are split into, so as to create what's termed a *lag 1* analysis (the second of two observations lags behind the first by 1 period). The Pearson r between the data in the range C2:C19 and the range D2:D19 is 0.93.

Figure 2.2
In this extreme example, each observation is either one unit greater (first half) or lower (second half) than the preceding observation.

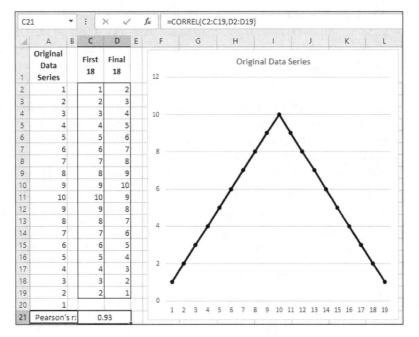

C21 f_x =CORREL(C2:C19,D2:D19)

	A	B	C	D	E	F ... Original Data Series
	Original Data Series		First 18	Final 18		
1						
2	1		1	2		
3	2		2	3		
4	3		3	4		
5	4		4	5		
6	5		5	6		
7	6		6	7		
8	7		7	8		
9	8		8	9		
10	9		9	10		
11	10		10	9		
12	9		9	8		
13	8		8	7		
14	7		7	6		
15	6		6	5		
16	5		5	4		
17	4		4	3		
18	3		3	2		
19	2		2	1		
20	1					
21	Pearson's r:		0.93			

Now convert the observations to z-scores and chart them, as shown in Figure 2.3.

Figure 2.3
The charted data are the z-scores.

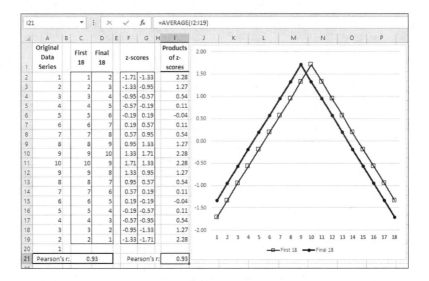

I21 f_x =AVERAGE(I2:I19)

	A	B	C	D	E	F	G	H	I
	Original Data Series		First 18	Final 18		z-scores			Products of z-scores
1									
2	1		1	2		-1.71	-1.33		2.28
3	2		2	3		-1.33	-0.95		1.27
4	3		3	4		-0.95	-0.57		0.54
5	4		4	5		-0.57	-0.19		0.11
6	5		5	6		-0.19	0.19		-0.04
7	6		6	7		0.19	0.57		0.11
8	7		7	8		0.57	0.95		0.54
9	8		8	9		0.95	1.33		1.27
10	9		9	10		1.33	1.71		2.28
11	10		10	9		1.71	1.33		2.28
12	9		9	8		1.33	0.95		1.27
13	8		8	7		0.95	0.57		0.54
14	7		7	6		0.57	0.19		0.11
15	6		6	5		0.19	-0.19		-0.04
16	5		5	4		-0.19	-0.57		0.11
17	4		4	3		-0.57	-0.95		0.54
18	3		3	2		-0.95	-1.33		1.27
19	2		2	1		-1.33	-1.71		2.28
20	1								
21	Pearson's r:		0.93			Pearson's r:			0.93

By now we have divided the original time series of 19 observations into two sets that represent the lag 1 data (C2:C19 and D2:D19 in Figure 2.2). The two resulting data sets have each been converted to z-scores (F2:F19 and G2:G19 in Figure 2.3).

Those two sets of z-scores are charted in Figure 2.3. You would observe exactly the same pattern in the chart if you charted the data in C2:C19 and D2:D19 in Figure 2.2. Converting data to z-scores preserves the original relationships between the data points. But converting to z-scores makes it easier to see where the charted points are with respect to the mean—a complete set of z-scores must have a mean value of 0.0.

Each value in the first 18 observations is exactly one (original) unit smaller than its mate in the final 18 observations. So, nearly all the pairs of points are both on the same side of the mean of zero: –1.71 and –1.33, –1.33 and –0.95, –0.95 and –0.57, and so on through the top of the pyramid, 1.33 and 1.71, and back down to –1.71 and –1.33. In fact, there are only two pairs of z-scores, in F6:G6 and F15:G15, whose members have different signs, and therefore 16 pairs whose members have the same sign.

The result of that situation—positive z-scores paired with positive z-scores and negative with negative—is that the overall correlation for lag 1 is positive. It will also tend to be large (0.93 is a large correlation).

What about lag 5? See Figure 2.4.

Figure 2.4
This figure represents the lag 5 analysis.

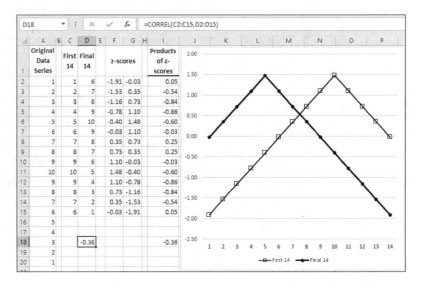

With a lag of five, the pairs of observations are no longer only one original unit apart, as was the case in Figures 2.2 and 2.3. In Figure 2.4 the pairs of observations are five units apart, both in terms of the size of the difference and in terms of the number of time periods. In columns C and D, 1 is paired with 6, 2 is paired with 7, and so on. In situations where autocorrelative drift exists, you often reach a lag that's longer than the length of time during which pairs of observations are on the same side of the mean.

That's the case in Figure 2.4, which pairs observation 1 with observation 6, 2 with 7, and so on. Have a look at the resulting pairs of z-scores in F2:F15 and G2:G15. In Figure 2.3, 16 of 18 pairs had the same sign. In Figure 2.4, only 4 of 14 have the same sign. It should not come as a surprise, therefore, that the correlation between the first 14 values and the final 14 values—the lag 5 pairing—is negative.

Let's step back from the minutiae of the individual lags and have a look at Figure 2.5 for a chart of the first 10 lags in the data series. (This sort of chart, with ACFs associated with different lags, is termed a *correlogram*.)

Figure 2.5
This correlogram is typical of time series that show autocorrelative drift, or are otherwise trended.

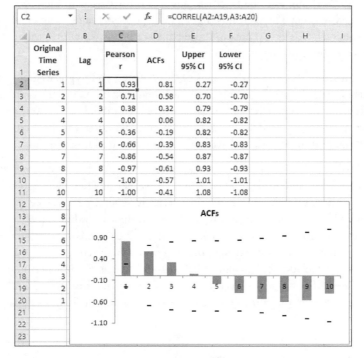

ACFs are not quite the same as Pearson correlation coefficients. They behave similarly, though, and except when the relationship between the two series in the same lag comes very close to 0.0, the signs of the Pearson r's are identical to the ACFs. Furthermore, when you have a data series of any real length, the difference between the Pearson r and the ACF becomes very small.

Later in this chapter, in the "Understanding the Meaning of ACFs" section, I detail the differences in how the ACF and the Pearson r are calculated. I have cast this discussion of the relationship between autocorrelative drift and lags in terms of the traditional Pearson r. That's because it's a lot easier to grasp, initially at least, if you're thinking in terms of traditional correlation coefficients. The points made in earlier sections about where the two members of a pair fall in relation to the mean apply every bit as much to ACFs as to Pearson correlations.

With this in mind, I have provided the Pearson correlations in column C and the ACFs in column D of Figure 2.5. Compare the signs of the two statistics at each lag, and note that the signs are the same, and the absolute values of the correlations and the ACFs aren't far apart.

Note also the pattern of the ACFs in the chart. They start out strong—the lag 1 ACF is well beyond the upper 95% confidence limit sketched by the dashes. Then they decline to zero and might well dip into the negative range, as is the case with the time series that this section has discussed. The reason is that at some point the lag is long enough to capture pairs of points such that first points in those pairs are below (or above) the mean and the second points are above (or below) the mean.

As you'll see in the next few sections of this chapter, you might well encounter a time series that is not clearly trended and is not clearly stationary. You'll want to decide how to treat it, because the way you generate forecasts for trended models is very different from the way you treat stationary models. If charting the raw data doesn't make it clear what sort of time series you're dealing with, a chart of the ACFs very well might do so.

One further point: You'll sometimes see a test for a trended series done by means of calculating the Pearson correlation between the time period (1, 2, 3, and so on) and the observations for those time periods. If the time series is generally increasing (or decreasing) over time in a linear fashion, this can be a reasonable approach. But if the trend is curvilinear, or departs from linearity in some other way, that correlation will be of no use other than as a point of comparison. In particular, the time series analyzed in Figures 2.2 through 2.5 has a Pearson correlation coefficient of 0.0 with the associated time period numbers. But that *doesn't* mean that the series has no relationship with the time periods. All it means is that Pearson's r was not meant to be used with data whose distributions depart so far from the normal.

Testing for Trend in the Observations

You can often tell just by looking at a chart of a time series whether a trend is present or absent. Figure 2.6 shows a clear example of an upward trend.

There's no question that the time series in Figure 2.6 has an upward trend. Smoothing analysis needs to take notice of that and allow for it.

> **NOTE** It's conventional, and even pretty standard, to designate the number that shows the time period an observation belongs to as *t*. I've shown the number as *Period (t)* in column A of Figures 2.6 through 2.8, but some subsequent figures in this book show it simply as *t*.

Figure 2.6
This time series is clearly trended upward.

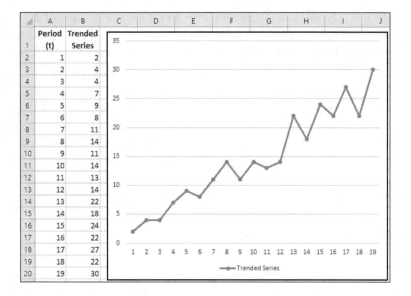

Period (t)	Trended Series
1	2
2	4
3	4
4	7
5	9
6	8
7	11
8	14
9	11
10	14
11	13
12	14
13	22
14	18
15	24
16	22
17	27
18	22
19	30

There are several approaches to dealing with trend, including differencing (the main method used in Box-Jenkins ARIMA models but also useful in smoothing analysis), using a trend smoothing constant, and transformations such as logs and link relatives. In this case it's enough to look at the chart to know that trend is present and that you'll want to apply one of those methods to deal with it.

Now have a look at Figure 2.7.

Figure 2.7
This time series isn't quite so clearly trended.

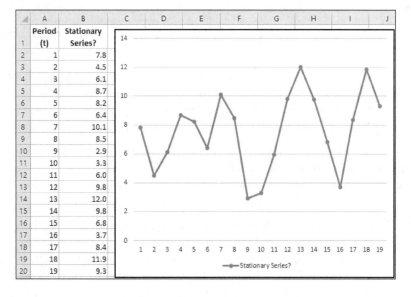

Period (t)	Stationary Series?
1	7.8
2	4.5
3	6.1
4	8.7
5	8.2
6	6.4
7	10.1
8	8.5
9	2.9
10	3.3
11	6.0
12	9.8
13	12.0
14	9.8
15	6.8
16	3.7
17	8.4
18	11.9
19	9.3

What do you think about the time series in Figure 2.7? Its trend, if there is one, is much gentler than in Figure 2.6. If I had to make a call on visual evidence alone, I'd say that it's trended. But I'd be a lot more comfortable with an objective, numeric analysis to back me up.

There are several ways to get that numeric analysis. One quick-and-dirty way is to calculate the simple correlation between the observations and their period numbers. I say "quick-and-dirty" in part because you can get it quickly in Excel. In Figure 2.7, just right-click the charted data series and choose Add Trendline from the shortcut menu. In the Format Data Series panel that appears, accept the default Linear trendline, and fill the Display R-squared Value on Chart check box. You'll get something that looks very much like the chart in Figure 2.8.

Figure 2.8
The dotted trendline suggests the presence of a mild upward trend.

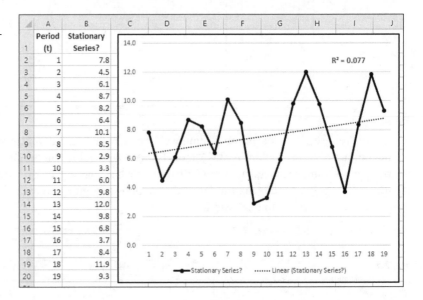

Period (t)	Stationary Series?
1	7.8
2	4.5
3	6.1
4	8.7
5	8.2
6	6.4
7	10.1
8	8.5
9	2.9
10	3.3
11	6.0
12	9.8
13	12.0
14	9.8
15	6.8
16	3.7
17	8.4
18	11.9
19	9.3

Another reason I say "quick-and-dirty" is that the quantitative information you get is limited to the R^2 value, the square of the correlation, between the observation's period number and its recorded value. That's definitely one way to measure the trend in a data series, but it's far from being the only one, and it's nowhere near the most useful.

In this case, the R^2 value is 0.077, which means that 7.7% of the variability in the observations is associated with variability in the values of the time periods (1, 2, 3, ... , 19). Another way to look at it is that the square root of the R^2 value, the correlation coefficient, is 0.277.

I would regard this as a weak relationship, but I might also bring Excel's LINEST() and F.DIST() functions to bear on the data in columns A and B. LINEST() returns an F-ratio and F.DIST() returns the probability of getting that F-ratio if the population variances are equal. Doing so in this case would inform me that I could get an R^2 of 0.077 in as many as 25% of similar samples, if the relationship between the period number and the observation were as small as 0.0 in the population. In that case, I'd probably back off my initial and solely visual impression that the time series is trended.

But there are better ways to investigate the presence of trend. One is by means of the imposingly named, but actually quite docile, statistic called the *autocorrelation function*.

Understanding the Meaning of ACFs

An autocorrelation function, usually abbreviated ACF, has a broad array of uses in predictive analytics. It is, with a couple of minor differences, the correlation between one set of observations in a time series and a subsequent set of observations in the same time series. Figure 2.9 has an example of autocorrelations.

Figure 2.9
Autocorrelations quantify the amount of dependency within the time series.

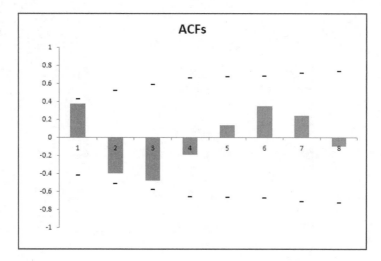

Figure 2.9 charts the ACFs that are calculated from the time series shown in Figures 2.7 and 2.8. Each data point is a different autocorrelation, and differs from the remaining data points according to the *lag* involved. The concept of a lag is an important one in time series analysis, and Figure 2.10 shows an example of the difference between a *lag 1* autocorrelation and a *lag 2* autocorrelation.

Figure 2.10 shows the autocorrelations of two different lags: the lag 1 data is in columns A through C and the lag 2 data is in columns E through G.

Consider columns B and C. They contain identical values—the same as you see in Figures 2.7 and 2.8. Cell C22 contains the correlation between the values in B2:B19 (shaded cells) and the values in C3:C20 (also shaded). It is—again, with two minor differences—the lag 1 autocorrelation because the second set of values in C3:C20 *lags* behind the first set of values in B2:B19 by one time period.

Notice that in a lag 1 you lose one pair of observations. In this example you begin with 19 observations. Working with the observations in B2:B19 and those in C3:C20, there are only 18 pairs available.

Contrast this situation with that shown in columns E through G, which represents a lag 2 autocorrelation. There, the correlation is calculated between the first 17 values in the time series and the final 17, in F2:F18 (shaded) and G4:G20 (also shaded). The Pearson correlation between those two sets of values is shown in cell G22.

Figure 2.10
The correlations and autocorrelations differ according to the length of the lags.

| G22 | ▾ | ⋮ | × | ✓ | fx | =CORREL(F2:F18,G4:G20) |

	A	B	C	D	E	F	G
1	Period (t)	Stationary Series?	Lag 1		Period (t)	Stationary Series?	Lag 2
2	1	7.8	7.8		1	7.8	7.8
3	2	4.5	4.5		2	4.5	4.5
4	3	6.1	6.1		3	6.1	6.1
5	4	8.7	8.7		4	8.7	8.7
6	5	8.2	8.2		5	8.2	8.2
7	6	6.4	6.4		6	6.4	6.4
8	7	10.1	10.1		7	10.1	10.1
9	8	8.5	8.5		8	8.5	8.5
10	9	2.9	2.9		9	2.9	2.9
11	10	3.3	3.3		10	3.3	3.3
12	11	6.0	6.0		11	6.0	6.0
13	12	9.8	9.8		12	9.8	9.8
14	13	12.0	12.0		13	12.0	12.0
15	14	9.8	9.8		14	9.8	9.8
16	15	6.8	6.8		15	6.8	6.8
17	16	3.7	3.7		16	3.7	3.7
18	17	8.4	8.4		17	8.4	8.4
19	18	11.9	11.9		18	11.9	11.9
20	19	9.3	9.3		19	9.3	9.3
21							
22		Lag 1 correlation	0.379			Lag 2 correlation	-0.453
23		Lag 1 autocorrelation	0.375			Lag 2 autocorrelation	-0.403

So we lose an additional pair of values with each additional lag. There were 18 pairs for the lag 1 correlation, and 17 pairs for the lag 2 correlation. The lag 3 analysis would involve 16 pairs, and so on.

Because each additional lag involves one fewer pair of observations, the correlations tend to become less and less accurate as measures of the relationships as the number of lags increases. You can get a visual sense of this effect from Figure 2.9. Notice the dashes above and below each charted ACF. The dashes represent two standard errors—the standard deviation of the ACFs—above and below the calculated ACF.

Those standard errors are sensitive to the number of observations involved in the calculation of each ACF: The greater the number of observations, the more exact the estimate of the ACF, and therefore the smaller the standard error. As you can see in Figure 2.9, as the size of the lags increases, the location of the two standard error indicators gets farther from zero: As the size of the lags increases, the number of pairs of observations decreases, and the distance between two standard errors above and below zero increases.

One further point, regarding true autocorrelations and standard correlations. The formula for the standard correlation, used in cells C22 and G22 in Figure 2.10, is this:

$$\sum_{i=1}^{n}(X_i - \bar{X})(Y_i - \bar{Y}) \Big/ \sqrt{\sum_{i=1}^{n}(X_i - \bar{X})^2 \sum_{i=1}^{n}(Y_i - \bar{Y})^2}$$

The true ACF is calculated with this formula:

$$\sum_{i=2}^{n}(Y_{i-1} - \bar{Y})(Y_i - \bar{Y}) \Big/ \sum_{i=1}^{n}(Y_i - \bar{Y})^2$$

Instead of calculating the deviation of each x-value from the mean of x, and the deviation of each y-value from the mean of y, the ACF formula calculates the deviation of each observation from the mean of the entire time series, in both the numerator and the denominator of the equation. These differences in the formulas for the standard Pearson correlation coefficient and that of the ACF account for the differences between the values in rows 22 and 23 in Figure 2.10.

Calculating standard Pearson correlation coefficients is easy in Excel; you just deploy the CORREL() or the PEARSON() worksheet function (the two are completely equivalent) and point it at the two data ranges you're interested in. Calculating the ACFs is much more exacting if you want to do it on the worksheet. First you have to assemble the formulas using intermediate functions such as AVERAGE(), SUMXMY2(), and DEVSQ().

Then you have to repeat that process using different range specifications—remember that the ranges get smaller by one row apiece for each additional lag. And mixed referencing such as B$2:B3 won't help you here, because as one range gets shorter from the bottom, the other range gets shorter from the top. (A complicated usage of the OFFSET() formula will do the trick but, believe me, it's not worth it.)

So it's best to rely on code to do all the repetitive work. I have included an add-in with the downloadable files for this book named ACF.xls. You can use it to calculate as many ACF lags for a given time series as you want. The code calculates the ACFs and their standard errors, and charts them. (It does the same for a closely related statistic, the partial autocorrelation function [PACF], which is indispensable in ARIMA analysis, but which has much narrower applicability in smoothing analysis. I won't be covering PACFs in this book.)

Interpreting the ACFs

Figure 2.8 shows a time series that might have a genuine, albeit slight, upward trend. Regressing the individual observations against the associated time periods results in a regression that falls short of a criterion that most people would judge significant or quantitatively meaningful.

The ACFs shown in Figure 2.9 confirm that outcome. In that figure, notice the relationship of each ACF value, represented by each charted column, to the dashes above and below the charted data series. In no case does the value exceed either the upper or the lower dashes (which, as I noted earlier, show the location of two standard errors above and below zero on the vertical axis). That means that none of the ACFs is large enough to contradict the hypothesis that the ACFs in the unobserved population are each zero, and departures from zero in this sample are just random error.

2

If one or more of the charted ACFs exceeded the two-standard-error criterion, you would have to admit the possibility that the ACFs represent real relationships between observations. A lag 1 ACF, for example, that exceeded the two-standard-error criterion would indicate the presence of a strong relationship between each observation and the one immediately following—and that's characteristic of a trended series. See Figure 2.11 for an example.

If you submit the values charted in Figure 2.11 to the ACF add-in, you get the chart shown in Figure 2.12.

Notice that the ACFs decline in value through the first seven lags, and then increase in absolute value through the remaining five lags. This pattern is consistent with trended time series: large ACF values in the shorter lags, becoming smaller as the length of the lag becomes larger.

Figure 2.11
This series is clearly trending up.

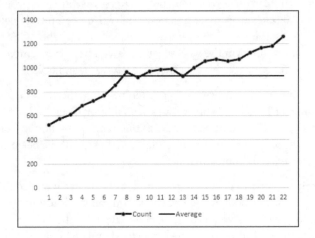

Figure 2.12
This pattern of ACFs is typical of a time series that's trended, whether up or down.

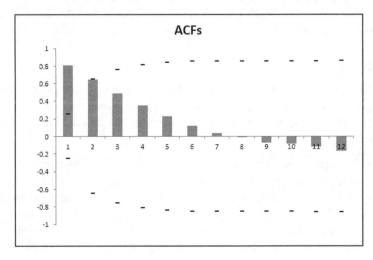

Also note that the ACF for lag 1 is approximately 0.81, whereas the two-standard-error criterion for the ACF at lag 1 is about 0.25. Even without resorting to tests of statistical significance, it's clear that the ACF of 0.81 is quite large in the context of the standard error of the lag 1 ACFs: It is more than three standard errors above zero. This constitutes pretty strong empiric evidence, above and beyond the appearance of the data series itself in Figure 2.11, that there is plenty of autocorrelation in the data set, likely due to the upward trend in the time series.

The analysis of autocorrelation is also of great value when you apply it to residuals (a *residual* is one term for the difference between a forecast value and the value actually observed for the same time period, so you also see them called *errors* or *forecast errors*). Used with residuals, the ACF (and the closely related Durbin-Watson statistic) can tell you whether the residuals are correlated, and that might help you evaluate the model that you've chosen to forecast your data set. I'll get into those uses of the ACF in Chapter 3, "Working with Trended Time Series."

> **NOTE** The Durbin-Watson statistic is a test of the lag 1 ACF.

Using the ACF Add-in

Full disclosure: The ACF add-in that comes with this book's files isn't an add-in at all. Formally, it's not an add-in because Excel doesn't save it with the .xlam extension. But I wanted you to be able to start its code running by clicking a control in the Ribbon. I also wanted you to be able to view and edit the code. And I wanted it to be compatible with versions of Excel that predate Excel 2007 and, therefore, the Ribbon.

All that added up to a file in the old .xls format with a procedure that runs when the workbook opens, to put an ACF command in the Ribbon. Even though the file is not formally an add-in, the ACF command shows up in the Add-Ins tab on the Ribbon. Therefore, I term it an *add-in* in this book, mainly to avoid creating confusion if I have to ask you to open a non-add-in from the Add-Ins tab.

With that out of the way: You can use the ACF.xls file to create correlograms, as the charts of ACFs that you've seen in Figures 2.9 and 2.12 are called. (As you'll see, the code also creates charts of PACFs, which are valuable in ARIMA analysis but much less so in smoothing applications.)

Open the file named ACF.xls and Excel responds by adding a new tab to the Ribbon, named Add-Ins. (If you already have one or more add-ins installed, you might already have the Add-Ins tab available.) You'll find the command ACF in the Add-Ins tab, in the Menu Commands group.

Then, *after* you have opened ACF.xls, open the workbook that contains the time series whose ACFs you want to calculate and chart. Only workbooks that you open after opening ACF.xls will have the ACF command available in an Add-Ins tab.

With the workbook that contains your time series open and active, click ACF in the Menu Commands group. The dialog box shown in Figure 2.13 appears.

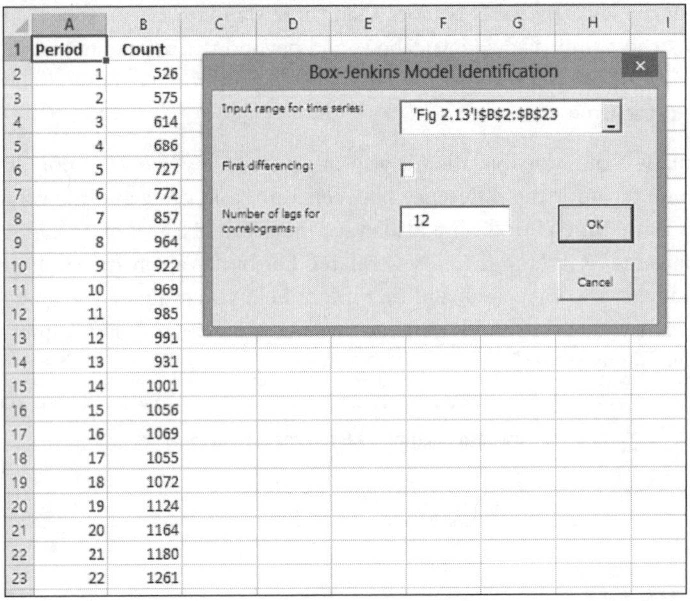

Figure 2.13
You can control the number of lags in the ACF chart from here.

When the dialog box first appears, the Input Range for Time Series box is active. Drag through your time series, or type its address into the edit box. Fill the First Differencing check box if you want Excel to stationarize the series by taking first differences—see Chapter 3 for information on the rationale for differencing.

Enter an integer greater than 1 and less than the length of your time series into the Number of Lags for Correlograms edit box. Bear in mind that the larger the number of lags, the fewer the pairs of observations that compose a given ACF. So, with the time series shown in Figure 2.11, the lag 1 ACF would be based on 21 pairs, but a lag 20 ACF would be based on only two pairs.

On the other hand, you should call for enough lags to get the information of interest. For example, if you are working with monthly data, you would want to request at least 12 lags. Twelve lags would show you the ACF between a given month in one year and the same month in the next year. Access to those ACFs would put you in a position to assess the degree of seasonality in the time series. If your ACFs spike at lag 12, and if they exceed the two-standard-error criterion, that's pretty good evidence that your time series responds to the seasonal effects of different months.

Back in the dialog box, click OK. Excel calculates the ACFs, the PACFs, and their standard errors and puts them in a new workbook. The new workbook contains a chart sheet with a correlogram for the ACFs, one for the PACFs and a worksheet named Sheet1 for the values of the ACFs, the PACFs, and their standard errors.

Testing All the ACFs at Once

If you ever took that basic-to-intermediate course in statistics that I mentioned at the beginning of this chapter, one of the topics that you probably read about is the problem with multiple t-tests. Suppose that you're testing the effectiveness of three different anti-virals against a new strain of flu. You administer them to three randomly selected groups of flu patients and measure the patients' viral loads four days later.

It appears sensible, at first, to use three t-tests to assess the statistical significance of the differences between the groups: Group 1 versus Group 2, Group 1 versus Group 3, and Group 2 versus Group 3. But if you do that, you run a higher risk of rejecting a true null hypothesis than you might think. I discuss the reasons for this effect in greater detail in *Statistical Analysis: Microsoft Excel 2013*. But here's a brief description:

Suppose that you compare two group means via a t-test, and you set your decision rules for rejecting a null hypothesis in such a way that you'll do so in at most 5% of the times that you might repeat the experiment, when in fact the null hypothesis is true. Unless the groups are of grossly different sizes *and* have grossly different variances, it's likely that the actual chance of rejecting a true null hypothesis is very close to the nominal 5% that you selected.

But now you continue your analyses and use another t-test to compare the mean of Group 1 with that of Group 3. Although you might use the same decision rules to limit the probability of rejecting a true null hypothesis to 5%, the chance that at least one of the two t-tests will do so erroneously is actually 9.8%. This is because the error rate is cumulative: The second test is mistaken in 5% of the 95% that's left over from the first test. Then, the cumulative probability is 5% plus 4.8%, or 9.8%. The third t-test makes things even dicier.

You guard against this effect by using the analysis of variance or multiple regression analysis with effect coding, instead of multiple t-tests. These procedures protect you against the cumulative error probabilities of multiple t-tests. Assuming that you get an F-ratio that meets the criterion you set for alpha—in other words, a "statistically significant" F-ratio—then subsequent multiple comparison procedures enable you to compare specific group means.

It's an analogous situation with ACFs. In a correlogram that charts the ACFs of several lags, you want to compare the size of the ACFs with the two-standard-error criteria, deciding that a given ACF is genuinely large if it exceeds two standard errors above or below zero. Again, though, those multiple comparisons combine to make the probability of at least one false positive greater than the criteria imply.

Two so-called *portmanteau* or *omnibus* tests were developed in the 1970s specifically to address the problem of multiple tests in assessing ACFs. The one developed earlier, the Box-Pierce test, turned out to underperform in simulations. A few years later the Modified Box-Pierce test, better known now as the Box-Ljung test, came along, and since the late 1970s it has been viewed as an accurate measure of the amount of randomness in a group of autocorrelations.

Figure 2.14 shows an example of the Box-Ljung test.

Figure 2.14
Excel provides you access to the chi-square distribution, required for the Box-Ljung test.

▲	A	B	C	D	E	F	G
1	Lag	ACF	N	r²/(n-k)		Q*	
2	1	0.80914	22	0.031177		42.6	=C2*(2+C2)*SUM(D2:D13)
3	2	0.647297		0.02095			
4	3	0.488689		0.012569		p	
5	4	0.355536		0.007023		0.00003	=CHISQ.DIST.RT(F2,A13)
6	5	0.227907		0.003055			
7	6	0.121133		0.000917			
8	7	0.03711		9.18E-05			
9	8	-0.00687		3.37E-06			
10	9	-0.06949		0.000371			
11	10	-0.08286		0.000572			
12	11	-0.11939		0.001296			
13	12	-0.16353		0.002674			

The Box-Ljung test returns a value often denoted as Q*. The formula for Q* is

$$Q^* = n(n+2)\sum_{k=1}^{m} r_k^2 / (n-k)$$

where

- n is the number of observations in the series that forms the basis for the ACFs.
- m is the number of ACFs that you're testing.
- k indexes the ACFs in the summation.
- r^2 is the square of each of the m ACFs.

The ACFs previously shown in Figure 2.12 are repeated, along with their lag numbers, in columns A and B in Figure 2.14. Here's how the formulas in that figure come together to yield a combined probability statement:

Cell C2 contains n, the number of original observations in the time series whose ACFs appear in column B.

Cell D2 contains this formula:

```
=B2^2/($C$2-A2)
```

In words, that's the square of the ACF in cell B2, divided by the difference between the number of original observations in C2 and the lag of the ACF in cell B2. Numerically, that works out to

```
=0.809² / (22 - 1)
```

in cell D2. By making the reference to cell C2 absolute, you can copy and paste the formula in D2 down to D13, where it becomes

```
=B13^2/($C$2-A13)
```

Or again, numerically:

```
=-0.163^2/(22-12)
```

The formula in cell F2, which is Q*, is returned by this formula:

```
=C2*(2+C2)*SUM(D2:D13)
```

And the result of the formula is `42.6`.

When the ACFs are random—that is, when the differences between the calculated ACFs and 0.0 are due to random error—then the `Q*` statistic follows a chi-square distribution with $m - p$ degrees of freedom, where m is still the number of ACFs being tested and p is the number of parameters in the model. Working with raw data, as we are here, the number of parameters in the model is 0, so the number of degrees of freedom is 13 – 0.

> **NOTE** Working with the ACFs of residuals, as will often be the case, the number of parameters depends on the model you are using to make the forecasts that result in the residuals. In that case, p equals the number of parameters in the model, and the degrees of freedom for `Q*` is less than the number of correlations being tested. An example follows shortly.

What if the ACFs are not the result of random error but instead represent real departures from a situation in which there are no relationships between observations at different lags from one another? Then `Q*` does not follow a chi-square distribution with a given number of degrees of freedom. And if you observe a `Q*` value that's sufficiently large, you must conclude either that you have observed data that are highly unusual given random relationships, or that the relationships are not random but real and replicable.

How large is sufficiently large, and how unusual is highly unusual? Those are subjective judgments, but you can bring an estimate of probability to bear on the question. Still in Figure 2.14, notice the `p` value in cell F5. It is the probability of observing a `Q*` value as great as 42.6 with 13 ACFs, under the assumption that those ACF values are all random-error departures from 0.0.

In this case, the analysis is telling you that the chances of `Q*` equal to 42.6 are approximately 3 in 100,000 if the ACFs are all 0.0 in the unobservable population. It's up to you, of course, but as far as I'm concerned that's highly unusual.

> **NOTE** Different approaches (some subtly different) to these sorts of inference are possible and plausible. What I have just outlined is the traditional frequentist orthodoxy.

The `Q*` value shown in Figure 2.14 is highly improbable given the degrees of freedom in combination with the hypothesis that in the full population, all the ACFs are 0.0. It doesn't hurt to run the Box-Ljung test if the ACFs are all well below the two-standard-error criterion, but there's not much point to doing so. It's when one or more of the ACFs barely exceeds the criterion that the Box-Ljung test is most valuable, because it can then protect you against deciding that there is autocorrelation in the series when it's just a random event. Figure 2.15 has an example of that situation.

Notice in Figure 2.15 that the ACF for lag 1 is slightly greater than the two-standard-error criterion for that lag. The ACF is 0.43 and the criterion is 0.40.

Figure 2.15
Individually, the criteria for the ACFs suggest that the lag 1 ACF is reliably different from zero.

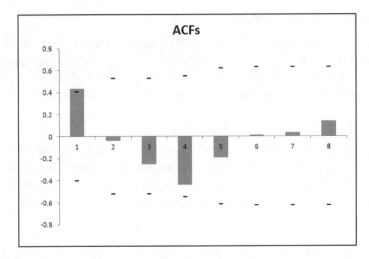

But Figure 2.16 shows what happens if you subject these ACFs to the Box-Ljung test.

If these ACFs were based on residuals that were in turn based on a single trend, then one parameter would apply, and the degrees of freedom would be adjusted accordingly. This has been done in Figure 2.16 by subtracting 1 from the number of lags, in cell A9, provided as an argument to the CHISQ.DIST.RT() function used in cell F5.

Figure 2.16
The Box-Ljung test would cause you to conclude that the larger ACFs are not reliable and replicable.

	A	B	C	D	E	F	G
1	Lag	ACF	N	r²/(n-k)		Q*	
2	1	0.433751	20	0.009902		13.2	=C2*(2+C2)*SUM(D2:D9)
3	2	-0.04129		9.47E-05			
4	3	-0.25128		0.003714		p	
5	4	-0.44008		0.012104		0.06656	=CHISQ.DIST.RT(F2,A9-1)
6	5	-0.19503		0.002536			
7	6	0.016409		1.92E-05			
8	7	0.036188		0.000101			
9	8	0.13904		0.001611			

A Q* statistic of 13.2 or larger, when compared to the chi-square distribution with 7 degrees of freedom, would occur as much as 6.7% (that is, 0.06656) of the time even if all the ACFs were 0.0 in the population. Again, it's a subjective decision, but if your probability daemon whispers to you that 6.7% is not at all uncommon, you should consider that the ACFs point to a random, horizontal process.

Testing for Seasonality in a Time Series

Just as it's useful to be able to test for the presence of trend in a time series, it's useful to test for the presence of seasonal effects in the series. The usual method for carrying out the test is very different from the use of ACFs to test for trend, discussed in earlier sections of this chapter. More typically you use least-squares analysis in conjunction with effect codes to indicate which season a given observation belongs to. Then multiple regression analysis helps you decide whether any apparent seasonality in the time series is random (you might act as though seasonality is not present) or systematic (you might decide that seasons have genuine effects on your time series and analyze it accordingly).

The remainder of this section discusses an example in which both trend and seasonality are present in the raw data observations. The example covers these tasks:

- The procedure tests for the presence of trend. When trend is found to be present and reliable, the trend is removed before checking for seasonality. The idea here is to prevent any trend that's present from interfering with our test for the presence of seasonality. Furthermore, if trend is present, we'll eventually use a model that accounts for that trend in its forecasts.

- The procedure then tests for the presence of seasonality in the residual values—that is, the values that are left over after the trend has been removed. Again, if seasonality is present, we'll choose a model that builds it into its forecasts.

You'll see much more regarding these procedures in Chapter 6, "Names, Addresses, and Formulas," which explores the logic and derivation of the formulas used in smoothing with trended and seasonal time series. In that chapter, however, the emphasis is on quantifying the effects of the trend and the seasons: What amount of change can I expect as time passes (for example, the trending effect of inflation)? And additionally, what amount of change can I expect due to the progression of the seasons (for example, the temporary increase in flu infections during the winter months)?

In contrast, the emphasis on seasonality in this section has to do with its reliability. Given that we see seasonal effects over several years of observation, can we regard them as normal and to be expected in the future, or are they more likely just random variations in the time series?

Removing Trend

Earlier sections of this chapter discussed the effects of trend on a time series, and looked at how ACFs and correlograms can indicate the presence of trend. The idea there was to diagnose trend, planning to deal with it later in some fashion, often by building it into the forecasts created by a smoothing model.

Here, though, the idea is to diagnose and quantify any trend, and then remove it from the time series so that we can test for the presence of seasonality over and above that of trend. Figure 2.17 shows a time series that is pretty clearly trended and that also might have evidence of seasonality in the observations. The data shown in Figure 2.17 shows the average number of daily hits to a hypothetical website, by quarter and by year. Clearly, as time passes, a quarter's average number of daily hits increases.

Both trend and seasonality might be driving this time series, but the problem is that they very likely combine their effects. If so, it's necessary to disaggregate the effects of the trend from the effects of the seasons. One popular way to do so is to forecast the values of the time series from the time period and then subtract the forecast values from the original series. The result is a new time series, intended to be free of trend, that can be tested for seasonality.

Figure 2.18 shows how the trend can be removed.

Figure 2.17
The trend is obvious; the spikes might also indicate seasonality.

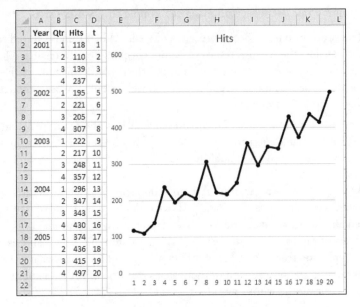

Figure 2.18
The trend in the original time series is isolated in the upper chart.

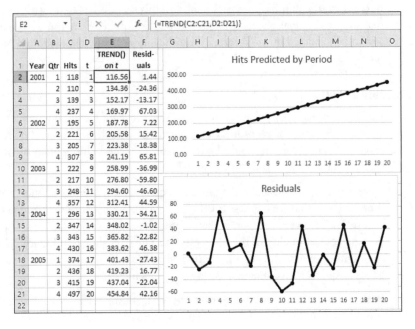

In Figure 2.18, the upper chart shows the result of using Excel's TREND() function on the same time series as is shown in Figure 2.17. You'll find much more about TREND() in later chapters. Briefly, TREND() is one of Excel's least squares regression functions. It calculates the results of a simple or multiple regression of one variable—here, average daily hits to the website—on another—here, the number of the period in the time series, shown in column D as t. (It's conventional to use the letter t to refer to a variable that numerically identifies a given point in the time series.)

Regression analysis calculates an *intercept* (also termed a *constant*) and a *regression coefficient* that, together, result in the set of predicted values or forecasts. Those predicted values are closer to the actual observations than are returned by any other intercept and coefficient. With the data in Figures 2.17 and 2.18, the intercept is 98.8 and the coefficient is 17.8. To predict the number of hits in the first period, when t equals 1, you would use this regression equation:

> $98.8 + 17.8 \times 1$

Or, using Excel's formula syntax:

> $=98.8 + 17.8*1$

Both of these equal 116.6. If you wanted the predicted hits for period 12, it's a simple modification:

> $=98.8 + 17.8*12$

or 312.4.

You can use Excel's LINEST() function to get the intercept and the coefficient, and then use them in conjunction with a predictor variable such as t to obtain the least squares predictions.

Or you can use the TREND() function, as I have in Figure 2.18. The TREND() function can be handy because it combines the results of LINEST() with entering the regression equation as a formula. In other words, given the values of the predictor variable and those of the variable to be predicted, TREND() calculates the value of the intercept and the coefficient and then applies them to the actual values of the predictor variable. That's what you see in column E of Figure 2.18. The range E2:E21 is occupied by this array formula:

```
=TREND(C2:C21,D2:D21)
```

It returns the forecast values. Notice that the forecast for quarter 1 is 116.56 and for quarter 12 it's 312.41, just as calculated earlier in this section.

Having calculated the trend in the relationship between the time period t and the number of hits, we can subtract the trend from the actual observations to get the *residuals*. The residuals are free of trend and therefore so is any seasonality that remains in the residuals.

> **NOTE**
>
> If the original time series is trended, and if the trend is not straight-line but curved, regression against a linear predictor (such as *t* in this example) will not remove all the trend. You might need to create an additional predictor such as the square of *t* and then predict from both simultaneously, first to forecast and then to remove the trend.

Still in Figure 2.18, notice column F, labeled *Residuals*. These values are the result of subtracting the predicted values in column E from the actual observations in column C. The residuals are charted against *t* in the lower chart in Figure 2.18.

It's clear that the "residualized" time series is no longer trended. It slopes generally neither up nor down. But it still could have seasonality in it. That, of course, is the purpose of removing the trend first—so that we can see either visually or via ACFs (or via another application of regression) whether there's seasonality in the detrended time series. See Figure 2.19.

Figure 2.19
These ACFs suggest a quarterly seasonal component in the residuals.

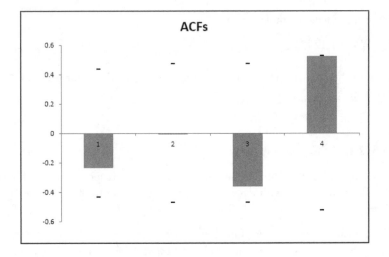

In Figure 2.19, you can tell that the ACFs for lags 1 through 3 do not approach the two-standard-error threshold. But the ACF for lag 4 does so, just barely. If you combine that result with a visual inspection of the chart of residuals in Figure 2.18, you might be convinced that a reliable quarterly effect is present in the time series, both before and after detrending. Notice that the lower chart in Figure 2.18 spikes at periods 4, 8, 12, 16, and 20. I'd be tempted to guess that the website in question sells winter clothing or equipment.

Figure 2.20 shows another way of looking at the seasonality in the series.

The first chart in Figure 2.18 shows the regression line that you get if you chart the values predicted by the regression equation against a sole predictor variable. In this case, it's the predicted hits charted against the time period. The second chart in Figure 2.18 shows the results of subtracting the forecasts from the actual average hits, charted against time period.

Figure 2.20
Here we're forecasting from the time period *and* the seasonal effects.

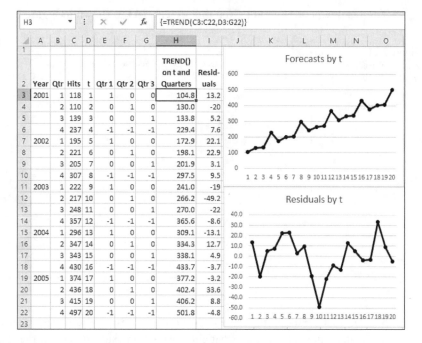

In Figure 2.20, the upper chart shows the forecasts that result from regressing daily hits against time period *and* season. With the additional information about seasons, the regression equation is able to make forecasts that reflect the seasonal regularity that Figure 2.19 suggests is present.

> **NOTE**
> Chapter 5, "Working with Seasonal Time Series," details the meaning and use of the values of the predictor variables in Figure 2.20, columns E through G. They are termed *effect codes* and enable functions such as TREND() and LINEST() to assess the effect of an observation's membership in one group (here, a fiscal quarter) versus some other group. The use of effect codes is not peculiar to Excel, although Excel does provide some tools that make them particularly easy to employ.

The lower chart in Figure 2.20 shows the residuals in column I—the values that are left after you subtract the predicted hits in column H from the observed hits in column C. There's nothing in the chart of residuals against t to suggest any trend or any seasonality in the residuals. It's reasonable to conclude, then, that subtracting the forecasts from the actual observations accounts for whatever trend and seasonality there is in the original time series.

As a further check, though, it doesn't hurt to chart the ACFs of the residual values, shown in Figure 2.20, column I. To do so, have the worksheet that shows the residual values active, and run the ACF add-in as described earlier in this chapter, in "Using the ACF Add-in." The add-in calculates the ACFs just as though they were based on the original observations instead of the residuals.

The resulting correlogram, given the present data, is shown in Figure 2.21.

Figure 2.21
A correlogram of the residuals: The ACF for lag 1 just misses the two-standard-error criterion.

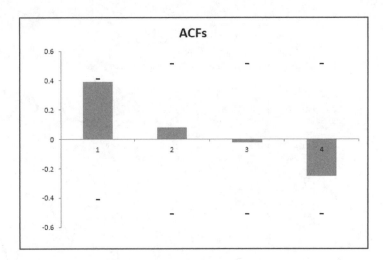

The lag 1 ACF falls a little short of two standard errors above zero. It's a subjective judgment, and mine tells me that what autocorrelation exists at lag 1 in the residuals is random error. If your judgment tells you otherwise, it's unlikely that anyone who has thought about this sort of thing would argue with you. Not seriously, anyway.

So far, the evidence we've looked at suggests the following conclusions.

A Trended Time Series

The original time series is trended. Its level increases steadily over time. You can see that in the chart in Figure 2.17. The series forecast, based on the relationship between t and the original values, is shown in Figure 2.18 and helps to confirm the apparent trend. After the forecast values are subtracted from the original observations to get its trend residuals, the trend disappears (also see Figure 2.18), so the original trend is linear, not quadratic or more complex.

A Seasonal Time Series

After the trend has been removed from the time series, a correlogram of the trend residuals (refer to Figure 2.19) indicates that a seasonal influence is still in effect. The ACF for lag 4 is slightly higher than 0.52, indistinguishable from the two-standard-error criterion. The seasonal effect appears, combined with the trend, in the forecasts shown in the upper chart in Figure 2.20—forecasts based on the combined effects of the trend of t and the vectors that indicate seasonal membership in columns E, F, and G. The lower chart in the same figure shows that both trend and the seasonality disappear from the residuals. This finding is supported by the correlogram in Figure 2.21, which shows that the large lag 4 ACF has dropped to an absolute value of 0.25 after the seasonal effects have been removed in the residuals.

Independent Residuals

I have not as yet appealed to inferential statistics in this discussion, but I'm about to do so. I've waited this long because time series often violate a crucial assumption of the inferential part of regression analysis, that the residuals are independent of one another. To look into that assumption, first we need to calculate the residuals, and we've only now reached the point where we have accounted for both trend and seasonality—and therefore have our hands on residuals that are both detrended and deseasoned. Figures 2.22 and 2.23 display those residuals, charted against other variables in the analysis to demonstrate two points:

- Subtracting the forecasts from the actual observations has removed the effects of the trend and the seasonality from the series and left a set of residuals that shows no remaining trend or evidence of seasonality.
- The residuals are independent of one another.

The first of those two points, while an important one, is not absolutely critical. Suppose that some trend, possibly curvilinear rather than straight-line, remains in the residuals when plotted against the time period. It's often possible to remove that remaining trend by adding the square of the time period figures to the set of predictor variables.

The second point in the preceding list is of crucial importance. The statistical tests that often follow or accompany a regression analysis depend on mutual independence of the values that make up the error term—that is, the residuals. If they are not independent of one another, their standard deviations, and therefore their variances, can be smaller than the statistical tests assume them to be. The test ratios then become inflated and the associated probability statements become inaccurate. Some of the assumptions usually cited as necessary for an accurate regression analysis are not terribly important in practice, or are important only to a particular aspect of the analysis such as the standard error of estimate. But the assumption of independence of errors is fundamental. If it's violated, without further investigation you really don't know where you stand.

The issue of independence of errors becomes even more critical in time series analysis such as this book explores. The measures for each time period often come from samples that are largely, even completely, the same from period to period and are *not* independent. However, it might well be that the residuals calculated by subtracting the forecasts from the actual observations have lost not only trend and seasonality, but also the dependencies. And it's worthwhile checking to see whether that has happened.

We can start by looking at the relationship between the residuals and the time period. Figure 2.22 shows the relationship between the residual values and the time period, which is how we quantified the trend in the series earlier in this chapter. The charted data series in Figure 2.22 is actually identical to one in Figure 2.20, where the emphasis of the discussion was slightly different than it is here. Notice the dotted linear trendline in Figure 2.22. If there were any linear relationship left in the residuals with the values of the time periods, the correlation would be nonzero and the trendline would be tilted. As it is, the correlation is zero and the trendline is horizontal. (This is as it must be: see the following Note.)

Figure 2.22
The trend over time in the original time series is absent from the residuals.

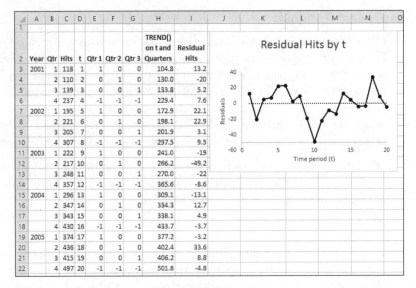

	Year	Qtr	Hits	t	Qtr 1	Qtr 2	Qtr 3	TREND() on t and Quarters	Residual Hits
2	Year	Qtr	Hits	t	Qtr 1	Qtr 2	Qtr 3	Quarters	Hits
3	2001	1	118	1	1	0	0	104.8	13.2
4		2	110	2	0	1	0	130.0	-20
5		3	139	3	0	0	1	133.8	5.2
6		4	237	4	-1	-1	-1	229.4	7.6
7	2002	1	195	5	1	0	0	172.9	22.1
8		2	221	6	0	1	0	198.1	22.9
9		3	205	7	0	0	1	201.9	3.1
10		4	307	8	-1	-1	-1	297.5	9.5
11	2003	1	222	9	1	0	0	241.0	-19
12		2	217	10	0	1	0	266.2	-49.2
13		3	248	11	0	0	1	270.0	-22
14		4	357	12	-1	-1	-1	365.6	-8.6
15	2004	1	296	13	1	0	0	309.1	-13.1
16		2	347	14	0	1	0	334.3	12.7
17		3	343	15	0	0	1	338.1	4.9
18		4	430	16	-1	-1	-1	433.7	-3.7
19	2005	1	374	17	1	0	0	377.2	-3.2
20		2	436	18	0	1	0	402.4	33.6
21		3	415	19	0	0	1	406.2	8.8
22		4	497	20	-1	-1	-1	501.8	-4.8

Residual Hits by t (chart)

Although a linear relationship will not and cannot exist, a nonlinear pattern might. In that case, we would have returned to the regression analysis and investigated the possibility that the relationship between hits and time period includes a component of a quadratic or an even higher degree. As it is, we can continue examining the residuals from the linear regression. See Figure 2.23.

Figure 2.23
The correlation between the predicted values and the residuals will always be 0.0.

	Year	Qtr	Hits	t	Qtr 1	Qtr 2	Qtr 3	TREND() on t and Quarters	Residual Hits
2	Year	Qtr	Hits	t	Qtr 1	Qtr 2	Qtr 3	Quarters	Hits
3	2001	1	118	1	1	0	0	104.8	13.2
4		2	110	2	0	1	0	130.0	-20.0
5		3	139	3	0	0	1	133.8	5.2
6		4	237	4	-1	-1	-1	229.4	7.6
7	2002	1	195	5	1	0	0	172.9	22.1
8		2	221	6	0	1	0	198.1	22.9
9		3	205	7	0	0	1	201.9	3.1
10		4	307	8	-1	-1	-1	297.5	9.5
11	2003	1	222	9	1	0	0	241.0	-19.0
12		2	217	10	0	1	0	266.2	-49.2
13		3	248	11	0	0	1	270.0	-22.0
14		4	357	12	-1	-1	-1	365.6	-8.6
15	2004	1	296	13	1	0	0	309.1	-13.1
16		2	347	14	0	1	0	334.3	12.7
17		3	343	15	0	0	1	338.1	4.9
18		4	430	16	-1	-1	-1	433.7	-3.7
19	2005	1	374	17	1	0	0	377.2	-3.2
20		2	436	18	0	1	0	402.4	33.6
21		3	415	19	0	0	1	406.2	8.8
22		4	497	20	-1	-1	-1	501.8	-4.8

Predicted by Residual Hits (chart)

The principal benefit to charting the residuals against the predicted values is to alert you if the variability in the residuals differs seriously at different ranges of the predicted values. A simplifying assumption in regression analysis is that the variability of the residuals is the same across the range of predicted values. Making that assumption, we can use the same error of estimate throughout the range of a predictor variable. As a result, confidence intervals (more frequently known in forecasting as *prediction* or *forecast intervals*) on the regression line will all have the same width. If the residuals have different variability at different levels of the forecast values, the assumption of equal spread is violated and you might want to use a log or square root transformation on the original time series. That kind of transformation can be useful for bringing unequal variances into line.

> **NOTE** The simple linear correlation between the predicted values and the residuals, or between the predictors and the residuals, will always be 0.0. Recall that linear regression calculates predicted values by choosing the intercept and coefficients that minimize the sum of squares of the residuals from a straight regression line. Every bit of variability that the observed values share with the forecast values has been wrung out of the forecasts, and everything else goes into the residuals. There is, then, no variance for the residuals to share with the predictors or the forecast values and the correlation *must* be 0.0. The point of charting the residuals against the predictors and the forecast values is not to check for independence but to look for nonlinear patterns or unequal spread.

A couple of final checks and we're through with the residuals. Recall that it's important to look for evidence of dependency in the residual values. Any remaining autocorrelation can result in misleading probability statements about the reliability of the trend and seasonal effects. Furthermore, remaining autocorrelation indicates that there is information remaining in the residuals that the current model (in this case, a quarterly trend as well as quarterly seasons) has not accounted for. Accounting for that autocorrelation, possibly with an additional predictor variable, can meaningfully improve the forecasts.

The lag 1 relationships are shown in Figure 2.24. The relationship between paired residuals for lag 1 appears to be random, so there's likely no information left in the residuals due to the period-to-period trend. The trendline does slant up, but the associated R^2 value is quite small and there's no compelling evidence for remaining autocorrelation.

The lag 4 relationships are shown in Figure 2.25. The lag 4 relationships focus on the seasonal component of the model and speak to autocorrelation between measures four periods apart. And the chart gives us little reason to be concerned about remaining autocorrelation.

> **NOTE** You might have noticed that the autocorrelations, such as they are, charted in Figures 2.24 and 2.25 have already been tested via a correlogram in Figure 2.21. It can be important to also look at the scatter plots in Figures 2.24 and 2.25 because a curvilinear relationship might exist. If so, it will show up in the scatter plot but not in the correlogram.

Figure 2.24
Regression tests of the
period-to-period trend
are probably clean.

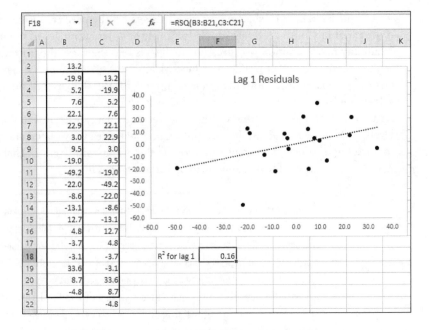

Figure 2.25
Again there's little
evidence of remaining
autocorrelation.

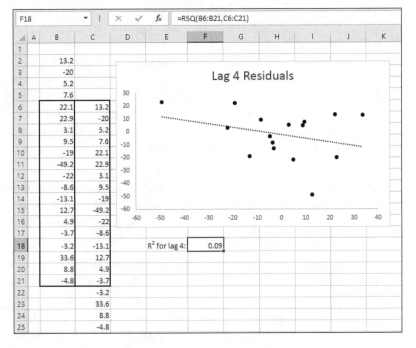

Analyzing the Regression with LINEST()

With good reason to believe that the trend and season model has wrung all the useful information out of the residuals, and that there's nothing left but random error, we can take a more confident look at the statistical tests that accompany the regression of hits on t and on the season vectors. For that purpose we rely not on the TREND() function—recall that TREND() returns the forecasts only—but on LINEST(), which returns the regression statistics. See Figure 2.26.

Figure 2.26
As used here, LINEST() simultaneously tests the time period trend and the seasonality in the time series.

J16	▾	:	✕ ✓ *fx*	=1-J15			
▲	I	J	K	L	M	N	
1							
2	Qtr 3	Qtr 2	Qtr 1	t	Intercept		
3	-24.21	-10.99	-19.16	17.03	106.94		
4	8.21	8.21	8.29	0.84	9.98		
5	0.97	21.17	#N/A	#N/A	#N/A		
6	128.62	15	#N/A	#N/A	#N/A		
7	230548.60	6721.60	#N/A	#N/A	#N/A		
8							
9							
10	Source of variation	SS	DF	MS	F	Prob. of F	
11	Regression	230548.60	4	57637.15	128.62	< 0.001	
12	Residual	6721.60	15	448.11			
13							
14	Source of variation	Prop. Of Var	DF	MS	F	Prob. of F	
15	Regression	0.97	4	0.2429	128.62	< 0.001	
16	Residual	0.03	15	0.0019			

Excel's LINEST() worksheet function can help you decide whether a trend in a time series, or the presence of seasonality in that series, or both, is a genuine phenomenon that you should retain in your forecasting model. In the example used in this chapter, and with the examination of the residuals that we've done, there's good reason to expect useful information from LINEST().

In Figure 2.26, the LINEST() function is array-entered in the range I3:M7. Specifically, you begin by selecting that range, and then typing this formula:

```
=LINEST(C3:C22,D3:G22,,TRUE)
```

After you've finished typing, hold down Ctrl and Alt as you press the Enter key. So doing, rather than just pressing Enter, signals Excel that you are entering an array formula. The array formula then shows up in the formula box surrounded by curly braces. (Leave it to Excel to supply the braces.)

The arguments to the LINEST() function as used here are these:

- The first argument, the y-values, provides the address of the variable to be predicted, in C3:C22.

- The second argument, the x-values, provides the address of the four predictor variables, D3:G22.

- The third argument is omitted, as is implied by the consecutive commas. (Whether it's ever a good idea to use this argument is the subject of considerable disagreement, much of it contentious.)

■ The fourth argument, here set to TRUE, tells Excel to return the full panoply of LINEST()'s statistics, not simply the intercept and regression coefficients.

For example, in Figure 2.26, the value in cell I5 is 0.97. That's the third row, first column of the LINEST() results, and that's where LINEST() puts the R^2 for the data you've presented to it by way of its first two arguments. To get LINEST() to supply the R^2, you must set its fourth argument to TRUE.

> **NOTE**
>
> Inconveniently, LINEST() returns the regression coefficients in reverse of the order in which the associated predictor variables are found on the worksheet. There's no good reason that LINEST() should have been designed so. That's the reason that I have supplied the predictor variable labels in both D2:G2 of Figure 2.23 and I2:L2 of Figure 2.26. Be careful with this anomaly, else you'll find yourself using the coefficient for the trend *t* with the values that indicate they occurred during the third quarter.

The R^2 value is critically important to any regression analysis. Among other things, R^2 expresses the percent of the variability in the predicted variable that is associated with variability in the combined predictor variables. Depending on how you gathered the data, you could also express this concept as "the degree to which the predictor variables cause the predicted values," or "how well the predictor variables explain the predicted variable," or "the amount of variance the predicted variable shares with the predictors." The closer that R^2 is to 1.0, the more accurately that you can predict the y-values from the x-values. But there's nothing in regression analysis itself that speaks directly to the issue of causation: again, that all depends on the context in which you gathered the data.

Still, R^2 gives you one way to gauge the statistical significance of the regression equation. By using what's termed an *F-test*, you can obtain the probability of getting an R^2 as large as the one you calculated (here, 0.97) under the assumption that the true R^2 is 0.0 and what you got was just random error.

Suppose that the trend and seasonality in the time series are just blips in a time series that lasts a couple of decades longer than the five years we've analyzed in this chapter. Suppose that over 25 years the R^2 is in fact 0.0, that there's no trend expressed by the relationship between the time period (*t*) and the quarterly hits, or between the quarterly hits and the effect codes that represent which season an observation belongs to. In that case, there's no point in using time periods and seasons to forecast hits, whether in a regression equation or a smoothing equation. If the R^2 isn't distinguishable from 0.0, you can't depend on the predictors that comprise the equation either.

Figure 2.26 shows two different ways to assess the R^2 value—that is, to help you decide whether to regard the R^2 value as genuine or unreliable. Both result in an F-test and reach the same conclusion. You might already know these tests as the *analysis of variance*, or *ANOVA*.

The range I10:N12 contains a traditional ANOVA (actually it's an ANCOVA—see "Time Series Diagnostics and the Analysis of Covariance" later in this chapter—but for present purposes we can regard it as an ANOVA). It's easily constructed from the results provided by LINEST(). Two principal sources of variation exist: variability due to regression (that's the sum of the squared deviations of the predicted values from their mean) and residual variability (the sum of the squared deviations of the residuals from their mean of zero). Those sums of squares, or *SS*, are in cells J11:J12. Notice that those values are identical to those returned by LINEST() in cells I7:J7.

The degrees of freedom (abbreviated DF) for each source of variation are given in K11:K12. The degrees of freedom for the regression equals the number of columns that contain the values of the predictor variables. In this case that's 4: one trend vector and three vectors with information about season membership. The DF for the residual is

$$N - k - 1$$

where N is the number of observations (obtained from the original data layout in Figure 2.20) and k is the number of predictor vectors: 20 observations less 4 predictor columns less 1 is 15. You can also get the DF for the residual variation from LINEST(), in cell J6 of Figure 2.26.

Traditional ANOVA now divides each sum of squares by its degrees of freedom, to get what are termed the *mean squares* in L11:L12. These are simply variances: the sum of squared deviations from the mean, divided by the degrees of freedom. When you form the ratio of the mean square regression to the mean square residual, you get an F-ratio, which in this case is 128.62 in cell M11. LINEST() saves you the trouble of calculating the mean squares and the F-ratio. You'll find the calculated F value in LINEST()'s fourth row, first column.

Lastly, you can calculate the probability of getting a sample R^2 as large as 0.97, when its true value is 0.0, with the formula

    =F.DIST.RT(M11,K11,K12)

as used in cell N11, where you present the calculated value of the F-ratio in cell M11, and the two degrees of freedom in K11:K12, to the F.DIST.RT() function. That informs you that the probability of observing an F-ratio of 128.62, with 4 and 20 degrees of freedom, when the true R^2 is 0.0, is less than 1 in 1,000. In other words, you have good grounds to go ahead with the combined trend-and-seasonal model that you've identified.

An all-but-identical analysis appears in the range I14:N16 of Figure 2.26. The only difference is that the sums of squares used in the first analysis are replaced by percentages of the total sums of squares. For example, the total sum of squares is found by adding the regression sum of squares (cell I7) to the residual sum of squares (cell J7), for a total of 237270.20.

The regression sum of squares, 230548.60, is 97.2% of the total sum of squares. Not coincidentally, that percentage is exactly equal to the R^2 value for this analysis.

The sums of squares, be they regression, residual, or total, very seldom convey any useful conceptual meaning. Measured as percentages of variability, they lose no numeric accuracy at all but gain considerable conceptual value. Thinking in terms of percentages of variability, of shared variability or R^2, helps to clear the mists that surround ANOVA and ANCOVA when you first start thinking about them. This is particularly true when you start subtracting one R^2 from another, as you do when you evaluate the predictive power of different models.

Applying the Models Comparison Approach

For example, you might ask whether the addition of the three vectors that represent seasonal membership (columns E through G in Figure 2.20) makes a meaningful difference to the accuracy of a more restricted regression, that of the website hits regressed onto the period-to-period trend. The question is an important one because a meaningful increase in the overall R^2 would depend on removing some variability from the residual sum of squares and assigning it instead to the seasonal vectors. So doing results in more accurate forecasts.

On the other hand, if the seasonal vectors do not add meaningfully to the total R^2 for the regression equation, you might as well drop those vectors. If you keep them in the equation, their mere presence in the model tends to imply that you regard them as important. Furthermore, they will lay claim to some variability that otherwise belongs to the residual component, and your interpretation of the remaining component, the period-to-period trend t, might well change accordingly.

Figure 2.27 shows how you might compare the power of a model that accounts for trend only to that of a model that accounts for both trend and seasonality (hence the term *models comparison approach*).

Figure 2.27
The models comparison for regression depends on using LINEST() at least twice.

J17							f_x	=I5-L12					
	A	B	C	D	E	F	G	H	I	J	K	L	M	N
1														
2	Year	Qtr	Hits	t	Qtr 1	Qtr 2	Qtr 3		Qtr 3	Qtr 2	Qtr 1	t	Intercept	
3	2001	1	118	1	1	0	0		-24.21	-10.99	-19.16	17.03	106.94	
4		2	110	2	0	1	0		8.21	8.21	8.29	0.84	9.98	
5		3	139	3	0	0	1		0.97	21.17	#N/A	#N/A	#N/A	
6		4	237	4	-1	-1	-1		128.62	15	#N/A	#N/A	#N/A	
7	2002	1	195	5	1	0	0		230548.60	6721.60	#N/A	#N/A	#N/A	
8		2	221	6	0	1	0							
9		3	205	7	0	0	1					t	Intercept	
10		4	307	8	-1	-1	-1					17.80	98.75	
11	2003	1	222	9	1	0	0					1.49	17.81	
12		2	217	10	0	1	0					0.89	38.34	
13		3	248	11	0	0	1					143.38	18	
14		4	357	12	-1	-1	-1					210805.41	26464.79	
15	2004	1	296	13	1	0	0							
16		2	347	14	0	1	0	Source of variation	SS	DF	MS	F	Prob. of F
17		3	343	15	0	0	1	Regression	0.08	3	0.03	14.69	< 0.001
18		4	430	16	-1	-1	-1	Residual	0.03	15	0.00		
19	2005	1	374	17	1	0	0							
20		2	436	18	0	1	0							
21		3	415	19	0	0	1							
22		4	497	20	-1	-1	-1							

The process begins by running LINEST() on the predicted variable, hits, against a larger group of predictor variables: specifically, the time period t and the three vectors that account for the seasonal membership of each of the 20 observations. That instance of LINEST() occupies the range I3:M7 in Figure 2.27 (and is identical to the instance in range I3:M7 in Figure 2.26). I'll refer to this instance as the *full model*.

A second instance of LINEST() appears in L10:M14 of Figure 2.27. That instance restricts the predictor variables to the time period only. I'll refer to this instance as the *restricted model*.

The important point to note about the two instances shown in Figure 2.27 is that the full model returns an R^2 of .97 (just as in Figure 2.26) in cell I5, whereas the restricted model returns an R^2 of .89 in cell L12. That the analysis using more predictors yields the higher R^2 is not at all surprising; that's the usual outcome of adding a predictor, even one that consists of random numbers. The question is whether the increment in the R^2 is meaningful. As always that's a subjective judgment, but we can buttress it with a little more calculation.

You'll find another analysis of variance in Figure 2.27, in the range I16:N18. The contents of its cells are as given here:

- Cell J17 contains the sum of squares regression. Despite this label, the actual value in cell J17 is the difference between the two R^2 values in the two accompanying LINEST() analysis: the R^2 for the full model less the R^2 for the restricted model, .97 − .89, or 0.08. In other words, adding three predictors in the form of the three seasonal vectors explains an additional 8% of the total sum of squares.

- Cell K17 is the *regression* degrees of freedom for the full model, 4, less the regression degrees of freedom for the restricted model, 1. The resulting degrees of freedom for the difference in the R^2 values is 3.

- Cell L17 is the difference in R^2 values divided by the difference in degrees of freedom.

- Cell J18 shows the proportion of the total variance that represents the residual sum of squares. It is 1 less the R^2 for the full model. (You can also get this value by dividing cell J7, the regression sum of squares, by the sum of cells I7 and J7, the total sum of squares. I bring this up only to badger you into thinking in terms of proportions of variability.)

- Cell K18 is the *residual* degrees of freedom for the full model.

- Cell L18 is the residual proportion of variability divided by the residual degrees of freedom.

- Cell M17 is the ratio of the regression variance to the residual variance, cell L17 divided by cell L18. This is another F-ratio, which expresses the size of the difference between two R^2 values to the full model's residual variability.

- Cell N17 states that the likelihood of observing an F-ratio as large as the one in cell M17, with 3 degrees of freedom for the numerator and 15 for the denominator, is less than 1 in 1,000, assuming that the addition of the seasonal variables makes no difference. As suggested earlier in this chapter, you could calculate that probability using =F.DIST.RT(M17,K17,K18).

Again, this probability would pass every rational person's quantitative criterion for deciding that the season vectors belong in the model.

Time Series Diagnostics and the Analysis of Covariance

If you've taken an intermediate course in statistics in the past, no doubt you recognize the analyses I've described in this chapter as very similar to the analysis of covariance, or ANCOVA, despite the fact that I referred to it in the prior section as ANOVA.

Very briefly, ANCOVA includes one or more variables that are measured on an interval scale as predictors, in addition to the vectors that represent variables measured on a categorical (or *nominal*) scale. This chapter has examined an example in which the interval variable, usually termed the *covariate*, is the time period and the categorical variables indicate which season a given observation belongs to.

There are special considerations that pertain to an ANCOVA, and I urge you to take them into account if you've studied that type of analysis (and if you haven't studied it, I urge you to do so). For example, one assumption used in ANCOVA is that the regression of the predicted variable on the covariate is the same, or *homogeneous*, across different levels of the categorical variable. This is like saying that the correlation between hits and time period is the same for observations that take place in the first quarter as it is for those in the second, third, and fourth quarters.

I did not bother with that procedural step in this chapter's discussion in part because this is a book about forecasting via smoothing, not about the different alleys you can wander down as you learn about regression analysis. Furthermore, the discussion of simultaneous analysis of trend and seasonality is secondary to the point of doing that analysis at all: deciding whether to include trend, season, or both in the model you build to smooth the data.

However, if you find yourself with a mission-critical problem in forecasting, your decisions about building the model can be equally critical. In that case you should without doubt cross all the t's, bone up on ANCOVA, and perform all the extra tests that go along with it. You'll sleep better.

Working with Trended Time Series

Various approaches to using a technique termed *exponential smoothing* for purposes of forecasting have been around for several decades. The most basic approach is called *simple exponential smoothing*. It is used in situations in which you don't see, and you don't expect to see, an ongoing upward or downward trend in your observations. The presence of seasonality in a time series, such as you see in monthly home sales and the incidence of flu, is another reason to avoid simple exponential smoothing. The bag of tricks includes special smoothing techniques, beyond simple smoothing, to deal with trending and seasonality.

This chapter reviews some of the concepts and approaches to simple exponential smoothing; if you've never encountered the technique before, you might want to take a look at a source that explains the fundamental technique in greater detail.

After reviewing simple exponential smoothing, the chapter discusses two approaches to the presence of trend in a time series: differencing and Holt's method. You would normally apply one of these two approaches after convincing yourself that trend is present, using one of the techniques discussed in Chapter 2, "Diagnosing Trend and Seasonality."

Smoothing: The Basic Idea

Suppose you've just made your drive from the tee of the 6th hole, and you're watching your golf ball curve to the right and land a good 20 yards from the center of the fairway. You resolve to spend more time at the driving range to cure that nasty slice. But in the meantime, you have to finish this hole and play another 12. What do you propose to do differently on the 7th tee?

For starters, you might want to adjust your stance so that you don't send your next drive off course to the right. And it might not hurt to arrange things so that even if the ball heads to the right or to the left of the green, it won't wind up so *far* from the center of the fairway.

This line of thought is exponential smoothing as applied to the game of golf. Applying the same thinking to forecasting, you want to do two things:

■ If your last shot was wide right, you want to aim your next drive to the left of the pin—and vice versa. (Here's another instance of the same concept, in the context of business rather than golf: If your last revenue forecast was too high, you'll adjust the next revenue forecast downward; if it was too low, you'll adjust the next one upward.)

■ Whether your prior drive was left or right of center, you want your next one to fall closer to the center of the fairway. (Again business instead of golf: If your last forecast was off by $1,000, you'll do what you can to reduce that error by, say, 30%, or by 40%, or by some other correction of your choosing.)

The Smoothing Equation's Error Correction Form

Here's the way to go about reaching those goals by way of the most basic smoothing equation:

$$\hat{y}_{t+1} = \hat{y}_t + \alpha\varepsilon_t$$

In this equation,

■ $\hat{y}_{t+1}$ is the forecast value ("y-hat") for period *t+1*—say, today's forecast for tomorrow. The caret symbol over a letter such as *y* indicates that the value represented by *y* is a forecast.

■ $\hat{y}_t$ is the current forecast value for period *t*—say, yesterday's forecast for today.

■ α is the *smoothing constant*, often referred to as *Alpha*, a value that we choose so as to make our forecasts as accurate as possible given the nature of our time series.

■ ε_t is the error in the forecast for period *t*—say, the difference between the forecast for today and the actual observation for today.

> **NOTE** In calculating a forecast's error, the forecast value is *always* subtracted from the observed value.

Suppose that the forecast for today was 110 and the actual observation taken today was 100. We subtract the forecast 110 from the observed 100 and get an error value, ε_t, of –10.

We multiply that –10 by Alpha, the smoothing constant (you'll also see the Greek letter α both in this book and elsewhere). If we chose 0.5 as our value for Alpha, we wind up with a negative 5: 0.5 * (–10).

Lastly, we add that result to our prior forecast of 110 and wind up with a forecast of 105 for tomorrow: 110 + .5 * (−10). Notice that this expression corresponds to the simple exponential smoothing formula,

$$\hat{y}_{t+1} = \hat{y}_t + \alpha \varepsilon_t$$

Also notice that the forecast for today was too high by 10, and the effect of adding a portion of the negative error is to lower the next forecast—analogous to aiming your next drive left when the last one went awry to the right. If the forecast for today had been 80 and thus too low, the error amount would have been positive instead of negative and you would have increased the next forecast by 10 instead of reducing it by 5: 80 + 0.5 * 20.

Furthermore, exponential smoothing tries to reduce the amount of error by multiplying the error amount by a fraction—that's Alpha, the smoothing constant. Here, I've set Alpha to 0.5. You can choose any value between 0.0 and 1.0 that you want. (I'll discuss one good way to decide on the value to use for Alpha later in this chapter.)

In sum, you use the forecasting formula to adjust your *next* forecast in a direction, and by an amount, that would have made the *prior* forecast more accurate.

Figure 3.1 shows how this works in practice.

Figure 3.1
Simple exponential smoothing, applied to a time series with neither trend nor seasonality.

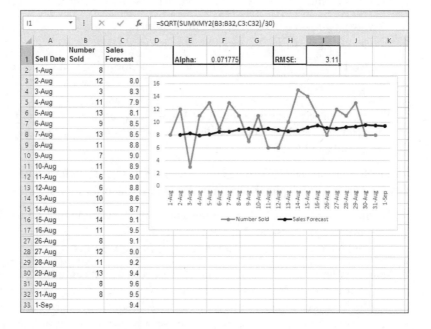

Figure 3.1 shows the daily sales of one of my books through a particular distribution channel during August 2013. The date and the number of books sold appear in columns A and B. The forecasts appear in column C. Both the actual sales and the forecast are shown in the chart.

Notice that both on the worksheet and in the chart, the actual figures begin one day before the first forecast and also end one day before the final forecast. This is because I have no prior actuals on which to base a forecast for August 1, and at close of business on August 31, I have not yet observed sales figures for September 1.

> **NOTE** You might wonder why we bother to make forecasts for periods that have already passed, and whose actual values we already have in hand. The reason is that by measuring the differences, often termed *deviations*, between all the available observations and forecasts, we can assess the overall accuracy of the forecasting method we're using. See the section "More Smoothing Terminology," later in this chapter, for more information on this sort of past-tense forecast.

The first forecast, in cell C3, is simply the first actual, in cell B2. Setting the first forecast equal to the first observation is one conventional way of initializing the forecasts. With a reasonably long baseline, and particularly using an uncomplicated technique such as simple exponential smoothing, the choice of an initial value for the first forecast makes only a trivial difference to the value of the final forecast. Although many aspects of the forecasting process are of interest, it's usually the final forecast—the number of customers tomorrow or the total revenue next quarter—that's the main point of the process.

The second forecast, in cell C4, uses this formula:

    =C3+Alpha*(B3-C3)

The worksheet formula expresses the definitional formula given earlier:

$$\hat{y}_{t+1} = \hat{y}_t + \alpha \varepsilon_t$$

That is, the forecast for period *t+1*, or August 3, equals the forecast for period *t*, or August 2, in cell C3, plus Alpha times the difference between the actual and the forecast for August 2, in cells B3 and C3.

The formula in cell C4 is copied down through row 33. Each forecast is therefore the sum of the prior forecast plus Alpha times the error in the prior forecast.

I defined the range name *Alpha* on the worksheet shown in Figure 3.1 to refer to cell F1. That makes it very easy to change the value of Alpha—by simply changing the value in cell F1—and observing the effect on the accuracy of the forecasts.

Which brings us to the RMSE in cell I1, 3.11. The abbreviation RMSE stands for root mean square error. We take the difference between each observed value in the range B3:B32 and the associated forecast in C3:C32 (the *errors*), square each error and divide by the number of pairs (the *mean square*), and take the square root of the result (the *root*). The smaller the RMSE, the more accurate overall the forecasts.

Using Excel's Solver to Choose Alpha

You can deploy Excel's Solver so as to select the optimum value for Alpha. Given the proper instructions, Solver tries out many different values for Alpha and stops only when it has found the value of Alpha that minimizes RMSE. Assuming that the Solver add-in is installed on your system and has been made available to Excel, take these steps (which are based on the layout shown in Figure 3.1):

1. With the worksheet shown in Figure 3.1 active, enter some value between 0.0 and 1.0 in cell F1. When you do so, you are doubtless changing Alpha from the optimum value to some suboptimal value. The RMSE in cell I1 increases in response.

2. Select cell I1. This is the cell you want Solver to minimize.

3. Click the Ribbon's Data tab, and then click Solver in the Analysis group.

4. The Solver dialog box, Solver Parameters, appears (see Figure 3.2). Leave the Objective Cell at I1.

5. Click the Min radio button. This instructs Solver to minimize the value in I1.

6. In the By Changing Variable Cells box, type the name `Alpha` (or enter its address—in this example, that's F1).

7. Click the Add button to the right of the Constraints list box. Use the Add Constraint dialog box to set cell F1 (or Alpha, if you prefer) to be less than or equal to 1.0. Click Add.

8. Again use the Add Constraint dialog box to set cell F1 to be greater than or equal to 0.0. Click OK.

9. Choose GRG Nonlinear as the Solving Method.

10. The Solver Parameters dialog box should now appear as shown in Figure 3.2. Click Solve.

3

Figure 3.2
Your version of Solver might appear somewhat different, but the functionality is largely the same across different versions.

Solver now iterates through different possible values for Alpha until it reaches the one that results in the smallest value for the RMSE. At that point it stops and lets you know that it's found a solution (or, with other data, that it has not and can't be expected to).

Choose to keep the Solver results. When you once again have full control over the worksheet in Figure 3.1, notice that Solver has set Alpha to 0.071775 (assuming that you have followed the list of steps just given). With this data set, the RMSE is minimized to 3.11 when Alpha, the smoothing constant, is set to 0.071775. And when RMSE is minimized, the accuracy of the forecasts is maximized.

> **NOTE** I've just described a very basic use of Solver to deal with a fairly simple problem. Chapter 4, "Initializing Forecasts," goes into greater detail regarding Solver options such as Multistart that allow you to deal with more complex situations.

The Equation's Smoothing Form

The preceding section discussed simple smoothing's forecast equation in its error correction form: the prior forecast plus Alpha times the prior forecast error. This form of the equation emphasizes Alpha's role in moving the *prior* forecast in a direction and by an amount that would have reduced the forecast error.

There is another, algebraically equivalent form of that forecasting equation called its *smoothing form*. Here it is:

$$\hat{y}_{t+1} = \alpha y_t + (1 - \alpha)\hat{y}_t$$

That is, the forecast at period *t* for period *t+1* is Alpha times the actual observation at period *t*, plus 1 minus Alpha times the forecast for period *t*. Another way of putting this is to note that the forecast is a weighted average of the prior actual and the prior forecast. The weight applied to the observed value at time *t* is of course Alpha.

> **NOTE** The quantity $(1 - \alpha)$ is actually what is referred to as the *damping factor* by Excel's Data Analysis add-in's Exponential Smoothing tool. That tool chooses to ask you for $(1 - \alpha)$ instead of α, doubtless for reasons that seemed good at the time.

The smoothing form of the equation is useful because it expresses more clearly than does the error correction form that each forecast is a mix of the prior actual and the prior forecast, and the nature of that mix is determined by Alpha—a quantity that is entirely under your control and subject to optimization using Solver. If you build your own forecasts using a simple smoothing formula, the two forms of the equation are completely equivalent. Use the one you feel more comfortable with.

For years, users of smoothing analysis preferred the error correction forms of the various smoothing equations. The reason was that personal computers had not yet replaced paper-and-pencil and hand calculators. Particularly in the cases of trended and seasonal time series, the error correction forms involved fewer calculations and therefore were less prone to arithmetic errors. You still see both forms used in the literature, and it's partly for that reason that Chapter 6, "Names, Addresses, and Formulas," details the derivation of the more complex, but still equivalent, smoothing and error correction forms.

The discussion of simple exponential smoothing in this section has been as brief as I could make it while still covering the basics of the smoothing technique as you would implement it in Excel. Understanding simple exponential smoothing is important to understanding the more complicated techniques designed for use with trended series and series with seasonality. Therefore, if you have difficulty following the material on trends and seasons, I urge you to first review a more basic text on exponential smoothing. My book *Predictive Analytics: Microsoft Excel*, also published by Pearson, discusses such basics of exponential smoothing as the role of exponentiation, setting other options in Solver, the smoothing and the error correction forms of the forecasting equation, and so on.

About the Smoothing Approaches to Forecasting

Let's get the bad news out of the way right now: There's no one way to forecast using smoothing—there is a finite but large number of ways. How you go about it, regardless of the software platform you want to use, depends on several issues, discussed in the next three sections.

A Time Series' Pattern

Is your set of baseline observations horizontal? This is the simplest case, and your main concern is the current level of the series (for example, amount of rainfall today, number of surgeries performed this month, or traffic fatalities this week). If you have a horizontal baseline, you usually use the method that this chapter has briefly discussed, simple exponential smoothing.

If it's not clearly horizontal, does your baseline display a trend, whether up or down? Then you have to account for both the current level of the series *and* its current slope. The family of smoothing techniques includes a couple of approaches to deal with a trended baseline. Both approaches are named for their developers. Brown's method is used much less frequently than is Holt's method, which is sometimes called *double exponential smoothing* because it employs two smoothing constants instead of just one. (You'll also see this method termed *Holt's linear exponential smoothing*.) This book focuses on Holt's method, rather than Brown's, for trended time series.

What about seasonality? A season is a regularly recurring portion of a longer period, most typically the four seasons in a year. But there are also four quarters in a fiscal year that don't necessarily correspond to spring, summer, fall, and winter. In a much smaller compass, weeks have weekends, when traffic accidents tend to spike, and even a hospital's day has three shifts. Some incidents are more likely to occur during a given shift than during another.

If seasonality exerts its effects on your time series, you need to account for the level of the series, possibly a trend in the series, and the regular rise and fall in the series that's independent of level and trend and has to do principally with the turn of the seasons. In the family of smoothing methods, you generally see the *simple seasonal smoothing* method applied to time series that react to seasons but that are otherwise horizontal. The usual smoothing approach used when a time series has both trend and seasonality is the Holt-Winters method. The Holt-Winters method is sometimes termed *triple exponential smoothing* because it uses one smoothing constant for the level of the series, another for the trend, and another for the seasonal effects.

Those three issues—level, trend, and seasonality—together make up what you might think of as the *pattern* of a time series. As you'll see, we account for each of them in a similar fashion if it's present in the time series. We choose *smoothing constants* to help us focus on the signal and soft-pedal the noise, and we choose one smoothing constant for level, one for trend, and one for seasonality.

Additive and Multiplicative Models

When we establish a trend in a time series, or when we identify an amount that the series rises or falls according to which season it's in, we can add or subtract some amount from a current observation. This helps to make the best forecast for the series in the next time period. We might add 4 inches of precipitation to the annual level if we're forecasting rain and snow during the fall and winter months, and subtract a similar amount for the spring and summer months. This is termed an *additive seasonal model*.

But there are many situations in which the amount of change to a series, due to trend or to seasonality, is not well described by an additive model. In the early years of the twentieth century, the Dow Jones Industrial Average traded in what today we would think of as a ridiculously narrow range—between 30 and 90 from 1900 to 1925. A 60-point swing in a single day was virtually unheard of in an era when the Dow varied around a long-term average of around 60. A 5-point swing, perhaps due to an annual Santa Claus rally, was rare but not wholly unexpected.

Today, of course, a 5-point swing is news only because it's vanishingly small in the context of a Dow centered around 17,000 or 18,000. A century back we might have added 5 points to our forecast so as to account for an anticipated seasonal rally. We couldn't do that today because rallies and corrections are measured in hundreds and thousands of points on the Dow.

When the amount of an anticipated rise or fall in a time series depends on the level of the time series, we generally prefer a *multiplicative model* to an additive model. We multiply the current value of quarterly snow tire revenue by, say, 125% in the fall and winter, and by 75% in the spring and summer. Rather than adding a constant amount (be it positive or negative) to a current value in order to account for a trend or season, we multiply by an amount greater than or less than 1.0 to keep the adjustment at a sensible amount, given the current level of the time series.

> **NOTE** Along these lines, it's a good idea to bear in mind that trends don't go on forever. They *cycle* in a way that's reminiscent of the turning of the seasons, but on an irregular basis. Theorists have introduced *damped trend* models to help account for this behavior, and Chapter 7, "Multiplicative and Damped Models," provides examples of these methods.

In sum, you need to decide whether an additive or a multiplicative model results in more accurate forecasts of your time series, regardless of whether that time series is or is not trended, and displays seasonality or fails to do so. The choice of an additive or a multiplicative model adds another layer of complexity to quantitative forecasting.

Initializing Values

Yet another source of complexity in forecasting via smoothing is the choice of how to establish initial values. You can see the problem most easily in simple smoothing, in which one of the components of the next forecast depends on the most recent forecast. At the end of Day 1, you want to base your forecast for Day 2 in part on your forecast for Day 1. But there is no Day 0 when you made a forecast for Day 1. Every baseline has a starting period, before which there is neither a prior observation nor a prior forecast. You need both.

There are many approaches to this problem. The simplest, which you saw at work earlier in the "Using Excel's Solver to Choose Alpha" section, is to take the value of the first actual observation to be the value of the first forecast. And this is quite often a reasonable, useful approach, especially when you're working with a lengthy baseline in an untrended, non-seasonal series. In that case, by the time you get to the final forecast, the effect of a bad choice of an initial forecast has been swallowed up by the effect of all the subsequent observations.

Other approaches to initializing forecasts include *backcasting*, which involves turning the baseline around and forecasting to Day 0 (and in some situations to Day −1, Day −2, and so on). This is another reasonable approach in many cases and is a staple of Box-Jenkins ARIMA (autoregressive integrated moving averages) analysis. Along similar lines, it's possible to regress the observations against the number of the time period when the observation is made. Then you might take the regression equation's prediction for Period 1 as that period's forecast.

In some cases you might want to use Solver to optimize an initial forecast, in a process similar to the one described earlier in this chapter to optimize Alpha. I have much more to say about that approach in Chapter 4.

And in trended and seasonal series, some practitioners recommend averaging early values to get useful and sensible initial values. Certainly, when a baseline is complicated by trend and seasonality, it can take more careful estimates to arrive at good initial values. The more complex time series tend to suffer more forecast inaccuracy due to bad initialization than do simple horizontal time series.

Each of the issues mentioned in this section—stationary versus trended versus seasonal patterns, additive versus seasonal models, and initialization procedures—is further discussed and detailed in later chapters of this book.

Initializing Versus Validation

Those who are new to the use of smoothing in predictive analytics sometimes confuse the purposes and calculations used to initialize the forecasts with the purposes and calculations used to validate smoothing's results. That happens because both initialization and validation involve treating the first few observations in a time series differently than the remaining observations.

The purpose of initialization is to bootstrap the forecasts of the level and trend in a time series. The whole basis of the smoothing approach relies on making use of the prior forecast: either in a weighted average (the smoothing form of the equation) or to adjust the error in the prior forecast (the error correction form of the equation).

At the outset of the time series, there is no naturally occurring forecast to use in the first calculated forecast. Therefore, we resort to other methods to get the forecasts going, including these popular methods:

■ The average of the first few observations

■ The first observation itself

■ A predicted value based on regressing the first few observations onto their time periods

■ Backcasting, by reversing the order of the first few observations

The purpose of initialization, then, is to provide a substitute for the forecast that would take place at Period 0, were it not for the absence of any actual observations before Period 1. Notice that the typical methods for providing that substitute rely on at least one and often several of the first observations in the time series.

Validation also makes use of the first few observations in the time series, but its purpose is entirely different. You have probably heard of and perhaps used a technique called cross-validation. Regression analysis uses it where possible. The idea is to calculate a regression equation using a random subset, perhaps half, of the data that's available. You can then apply that regression equation to the remaining cases, in the hope and expectation that the accuracy of the forecasts is not too much less than the accuracy you found in the original regression.

Smoothing employs a similar technique. The idea is to develop your model using one portion of your time series. You use a tool such as Excel's Solver to adjust the values of the smoothing constants to return the smallest RMSE possible given that data.

Then use the same values of the smoothing constants to get forecasts for the remaining observations and check the RMSE for that portion of the time series.

> **NOTE** The first of these two time series subsets, which you use to optimize the smoothing constants, is often termed the *training set*. The second subset is then the *test set*. The idea is that you use the first set to train your model to use the optimized values for the constants, and the second set to test those values with different observations. Other terms that some people use include *in sample* for the training set and *out of sample* for the test set.

It's typical to use a quarter to a third of the observations in the original time series as the training set.

It makes little difference whether the training set comes from the start of the time series, from its end, or from somewhere in the middle. (Nevertheless, it's easier to start the training set with the first observation in the time series.) But it's important that the observations in the training and in the test sets be sequential and consecutive, just as they're found in the full time series.

Terminology Problems

With all these choice points confronting you—trend or no-trend, seasonal or nonseasonal, additive or multiplicative, choice of initialization method—it's little wonder that no two sources of information are likely to give you the same guidance regarding forecasting method.

Complicating matters even further is the fact that the terminology and symbols are not standardized. (I'm honestly surprised by this situation, given that it's been more than 50 years since Winters's first journal article on accounting for seasonality in Holt's linear exponential smoothing methods.)

Consider the *level* of a series: what is taken to be the series' starting value, or, in a regression context, the regression equation's intercept. In books, journal articles, and professional or academic postings on the Web, I've seen that concept represented as B_0, B_1, L_T, and S_T.

What's worse, there's little real consensus on the symbols used for the trend and season smoothing constants in Holt-Winters seasonal smoothing, which I discuss in some detail in later chapters. Although nearly all writers I've found agree on α as the smoothing constant for the series' level, you find both β and γ used for the slope and, for the seasonal smoothing constant, you find different writers referring to it as δ, as β, and as γ, in such combinations as the following:

- α level, γ slope, δ seasonal
- α level, β slope, γ seasonal
- α level, γ slope, β seasonal

So if you want to benchmark any of the sample forecasts that I discuss in this book against procedures you locate in other sources, I urge you to take special care to interpret carefully the symbols you find here as well as those used in other references. (It's particularly discouraging to find that the National Institute of Standards and Technology, a division of the U.S. Department of Commerce, uses symbols in its discussion of seasonal smoothing in an utterly idiosyncratic fashion.)

More Smoothing Terminology

Symbols such as those used for smoothing constants aren't the only source of confusion in the smoothing arena. Some of the terminology can lead you astray. Now that this chapter has discussed some of the basic concepts regarding the smoothing of trended series, it's helpful to get more clarity regarding the terms.

Slope and Trend

Generally, *slope* and *trend* are used interchangeably in the literature on smoothing. Both refer to the rate of change in observations from one period to another, usually the next. A very few writers use *trend* to refer to the expected value of a series at a given period, but the expected value is what most references, including this book, term the *level* of the series.

Smoothing Constant and Damping Factor

Some use the term *damping factor* to refer to the value of 1 minus the smoothing constant. So if the smoothing constant is 0.3, the damping factor is 0.7. As I noted earlier in this chapter, in the section "The Equation's Smoothing Form," the Exponential Smoothing tool in Excel's Data Analysis add-in asks that you provide the damping factor rather than the smoothing constant.

Another instance of confusion caused by this terminology is that in recent years, *damped trend models* have attracted considerable attention as a way to prevent a trended series from running away with itself. I discuss damped models in Chapter 7. Briefly, however, the idea is to use a *damping constant* as an exponent in the forecasting equation. The result is that the constant trend in a forecast horizon that extends well past the final actual observation is damped, or bent from an initially sharp angle back toward the horizontal. This is how many growth curves behave, particularly those that track the performance of new products whose sales can take off at first and then gradually subside.

The damping factor that Excel's Data Analysis add-in asks you to supply has nothing to do with damped trend models in general or with the damping constant in particular.

Dealing with Trend: Holt's Linear Exponential Smoothing

What if you must deal with a time series that's *trended*—that is, one that displays a persistent tendency to increase or decrease its level as time passes? Figure 3.3 shows an example of a trended time series.

Figure 3.3
This time series as a trend, or *slope*, which can be quantified.

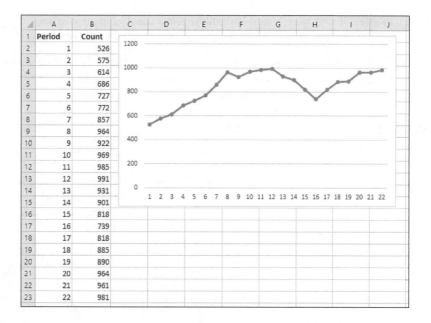

Period	Count
1	526
2	575
3	614
4	686
5	727
6	772
7	857
8	964
9	922
10	969
11	985
12	991
13	931
14	901
15	818
16	739
17	818
18	885
19	890
20	964
21	961
22	981

It's pretty obvious that the time series in Figure 3.3 has an upward trend. (Refer to Chapter 2 for information on how to determine the presence of trend empirically instead of just subjectively.) What happens if you use simple exponential smoothing with a time series such as this one, with a trend? See Figure 3.4.

Figure 3.4
The forecasts lag behind the actual observations.

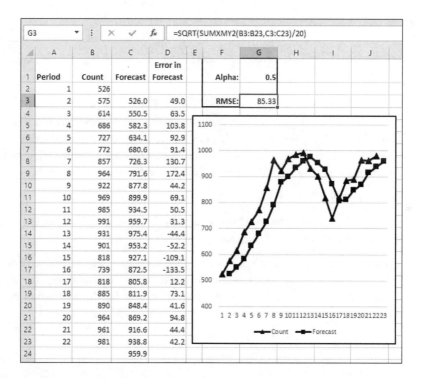

G3 fx =SQRT(SUMXMY2(B3:B23,C3:C23)/20)

Period	Count	Forecast	Error in Forecast		Alpha:	0.5
1	526					
2	575	526.0	49.0		RMSE:	85.33
3	614	550.5	63.5			
4	686	582.3	103.8			
5	727	634.1	92.9			
6	772	680.6	91.4			
7	857	726.3	130.7			
8	964	791.6	172.4			
9	922	877.8	44.2			
10	969	899.9	69.1			
11	985	934.5	50.5			
12	991	959.7	31.3			
13	931	975.4	-44.4			
14	901	953.2	-52.2			
15	818	927.1	-109.1			
16	739	872.5	-133.5			
17	818	805.8	12.2			
18	885	811.9	73.1			
19	890	848.4	41.6			
20	964	869.2	94.8			
21	961	916.6	44.4			
22	981	938.8	42.2			
		959.9				

Figure 3.4 shows one possible result of using simple exponential smoothing on a trended time series. The forecasts aren't bad, but they *consistently* lag one period behind the actuals.

For Figure 3.4, I pulled the value of Alpha out of my hat. Figure 3.5 shows what often happens if you use simple exponential smoothing on a trended time series and deploy Solver to minimize the RMSE by adjusting Alpha.

Figure 3.5
Solver has set Alpha to 1.0.

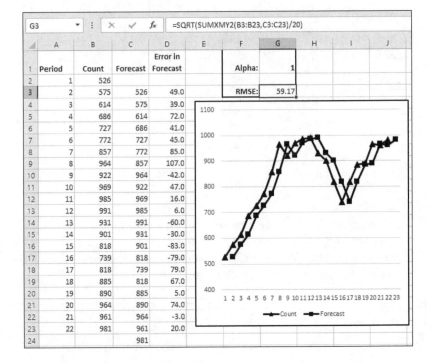

The forecasts in Figure 3.5 are somewhat better than those shown in Figure 3.4 (as measured by RMSE), but with an Alpha of 1.0 we have what's termed *naïve forecasting*: Each forecast is exactly equal to the prior actual observation. A quick review of the simple exponential smoothing formula (in its smoothing form) shows why this is so:

$$\hat{y}_{t+1} = \alpha y_t + (1 - \alpha)\hat{y}_t$$

If Alpha is 1, then 1 minus Alpha is zero. In that case, each forecast is 1 times the prior actual, plus 0 times the prior forecast.

There can be occasions when naïve forecasting is precisely what you want. Those occasions do not include trended time series. Simple exponential smoothing attends *only* to the prior actual observation and the prior forecast. It ignores any difference between an actual that's one period back and an actual that's two periods back.

> **NOTE**
> Those last two sentences constitute an overstatement. In simple exponential smoothing, the forecast for time t uses the forecast for time $t–1$. And the forecast for time $t–1$ uses the forecast for time $t–2$. And so on. More precisely—and more insipidly—simple exponential smoothing pays *direct* attention only to the prior actual observation and the prior forecast.

The difference between the observation made at $t–2$ and the one made at $t–1$ is the most current estimate available of the time series' slope. Suppose you're taking monthly observations. In that case, from June 1 to June 29, your most current available estimate of the slope of the time series is the difference between the observation for May and the observation for April. By bringing the slope into the mix, you can improve the accuracy of your forecasts beyond what's available from knowing only the level of the time series.

Two principal methods of dealing with the trend exist: differencing and smoothing.

Dealing with Trend by Differencing

One important method of dealing with a trended time series is to *detrend* it. There are several reasons to detrend a trended time series. For example, if the series is not only trended but seasonal, you want to disaggregate the effect of the trend from the effects of the seasons, and that becomes feasible after the trend has been removed.

One useful way to detrend a time series is to *difference* it. To difference a time series is to subtract the observation made at period $t–1$ from the observation made at period t; stated differently, subtract Wednesday's actual from Thursday's actual, Tuesday's actual from Wednesday's, Monday's actual from Tuesday's, and so on.

In most cases, the series that you wind up with is untrended and therefore stationary. Figure 3.6 shows an example of a trended series and its differences.

The differences shown in Figure 3.6 are termed *first differences*. It can happen that the differences between adjacent observations, such as those in Figure 3.6, don't form a stationary series. (This tends to happen when your original observations form a trended series that describes not a straight line but a curve, in which the differences themselves increase or decrease over time.) In this sort of case, you might need to take *second differences*, or the differences between first differences, in order to arrive at a stationary, horizontal series.

When you have arrived at a stationary series to work with—and in most cases that will be your original series' first differences—you can proceed with simple smoothing to get forecasts *of the differences*. You're getting ready to forecast not the actual values, but the difference between one observation and the next: How much do I expect the next observation to differ from this one, and in which direction?

Add those forecast differences back into the original series to get forecasts of the original series. For example, if your forecast of differences indicates that Wednesday's observation will be 10 points higher than Tuesday's, you can add 10 points to Tuesday's actual to get Wednesday's forecast.

Figure 3.6
The series of differences is horizontal.

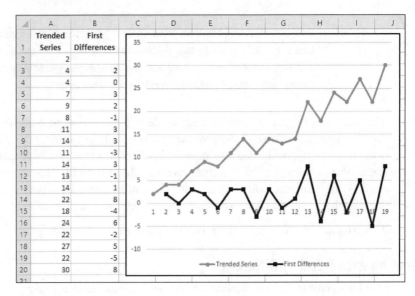

Figure 3.7 shows how this works.

Figure 3.7
This approach forecasts a trended series indirectly, by way of its stationary differences.

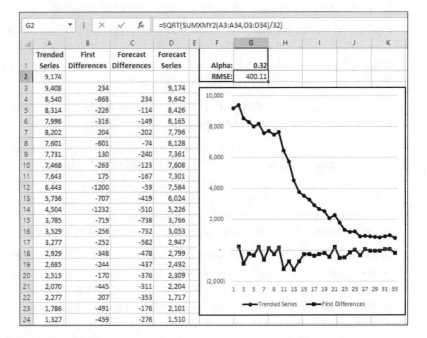

In Figure 3.7, the original values appear in column A. (I've chosen a time series with a negative trend just to make it clear that these methods work equally well with declining levels as with increasing levels.) The first differences of this trended time series are in column B, with this formula in cell B3:

```
=A3-A2
```

That formula is copied and pasted down through the end of the series in Column A (lack of space forces me to end the series at row 24 in Figure 3.7). The result is a new series of values, in cells B3:B34, which are shorn of the effect of the decreasing trend and represent only the size and direction of the difference from period to period. So, an original series with a perfectly steady downward trend—such as 16, 14, 12, 10, and so on—would yield a perfectly horizontal set of first differences: –2, –2, –2, and so on.

More typical, because only artificial time series have perfectly smooth trends, is the series of first differences shown at the bottom of the chart in Figure 3.7. The differences between some pairs of original observations are greater than others, and so the charted differences bounce around a bit. But you can tell from simply eyeballing this set of data that the differences form a stationary, or horizontal, series.

Forecasting the Differences

Because you now have a stationary series in the form of the first differences, you can apply simple exponential smoothing to that series so as to create forecast differences. The process is the same as discussed earlier in the section "Smoothing: The Basic Idea." The first forecast difference, in cell C4 of Figure 3.7, is set equal to the first observed difference, the value of 234 in cell B3. Then the second forecast difference, in cell C5, is found with this formula:

```
=(Alpha*B4)+(1-Alpha)*C4
```

That is, Alpha times the previous observed difference, plus (1 – Alpha) times the previous forecast difference. That formula is copied and pasted down through the end of the series of observed differences. That formula uses the smoothing form of the equation. Here's the same forecast difference, using the error correction form:

```
=C4+Alpha*(B4-C4)
```

In words, the new forecast difference is the prior forecast difference in C4, plus Alpha times the error in the forecast, B4 – C4. Note that both the smoothing form and the error correction form return the same result, 113.8 (or, rounded, -114 as shown in cell C5 of Figure 3.7).

Consider the distinction between an observed difference, such as the one in cell B4, and its associated forecast difference in cell C4. In B4, you have the actually observed difference between the original values in cells A4 and A3. In cell C4, you have the forecast difference between the same two original values. The model for the data assumes that there is some error in the actual difference, just as there is some error in the values that result in the difference. The hope is that the smoothing process removes some of that error and leads to more accurate forecasts than does something such as naïve forecasting.

> **NOTE**
>
> The term *error* in this context is used broadly. It can refer to actual error, such as an error in transcribing or entering data, or measurement error due to the difficulty in quantifying values that are well out into the tails of a normal distribution. In cases such as those, something has actually gone wrong, as the term *error* connotes. But it can also mean the sort of discrepancy that comes about when a random event such as a meteor strike disrupts what our model's level and trend tell us should happen next. Nothing has gone wrong, no one has made a mistake, but the model is nevertheless in error.

In that case, if smoothing has indeed removed some of the error in the forecast differences, you can think to yourself that you observed a difference of, say, –226 in cell B5, but you forecast a difference of –114 in cell C5. You *could* restore the actual original value of the series in A5 by adding the original value of 8540 in A4 to the observed difference of –226 in cell B5, resulting in 8314—the originally observed value.

Instead—and this is the point of this procedure—you can add the *forecast* difference of –114 to 8540, and get a forecast value of the trended series of 8426 in cell D5. The remaining forecasts of the original series follow the same pattern: add the original value to its forecast difference from the subsequent period.

With an initial estimate of the forecasts in hand, you can deploy Solver just as before to optimize the value of Alpha: to find the value that minimizes the RMSE between the observed values in column A and the forecast values in column D. The resulting Alpha is 0.32, as shown in Figure 3.7, and the resulting RMSE between the original values and the forecast values is a touch over 400.

> **NOTE**
>
> Be sure you see that Alpha is used to optimize the forecast differences, whereas the RMSE is calculated using the original values in column A and the forecast values in column D.

The process of differencing a trended series to obtain a stationary one, then dealing with the untrended differences, and finally integrating the forecasts back into the original series is fundamental to such approaches to time series analysis as Box-Jenkins ARIMA modeling. But there's another useful way to deal with a trended time series, known as *linear exponential smoothing*, or *Holt's method*. The next section discusses that method. (Don't confuse Holt's method with the Holt-Winters method, which additionally accounts for seasonality and is covered in Chapter 5, "Working with Seasonal Time Series.")

Using Holt's Linear Exponential Smoothing

Simple exponential smoothing, described and discussed earlier in this chapter, concerns itself solely with the *level* of the time series. And so do you: Your whole purpose in making a forecast is to estimate the level of next quarter's revenues, or next week's level of a patient's low-density serum cholesterol, or the level of next year's rainfall.

But by attending to more than just a time series' level, by attending to its *trend* as well as its level, you can often make a better forecast of its level than otherwise.

> **NOTE**
>
> The term "trend" as used in this context can cause some confusion. We normally think of a trend as a phenomenon that lasts for an appreciable period of time. For example, we think of an economy characterized by constantly increasing unemployment as the result of a long-term trend, even though the measures often are taken weekly.
>
> But in the sort of smoothing discussed in this section, a trend can be as short as a day (often only an hour in some manufacturing situations). If 2010's reported level is $100,000 and 2011's reported level is $150,000, the trend as of 2011 is $50,000. A single time series might have many different trends between individual data points. At the other extreme, it might have one trend only, if each of the first differences were a constant value—that is, a time series such as 1, 4, 7, 10, 13, and so on.

Forecasting a Level

The preceding section showed how the process of differencing observations deals with trend by performing a biopsy on the original series, by isolating the individual differences between observations, by forecasting the levels of those differences via simple exponential smoothing, and finally by integrating the forecast differences back into the time series.

In contrast, Holt's linear exponential smoothing deals with trend by leaving the period-to-period differences in place, and by smoothing both the level of the original trended series *and* the differences (these differences are usually termed *trends* in the context of Holt's method). One constant, Alpha, is used to smooth the level. Another constant, which most writers call Gamma, is used to smooth the trends. Holt's forecast of the next period's observation is the sum of the level estimate and the trend estimate. If the current level is 100 and the current trend is 3, the forecast of the next period's value is 103.

I show the mechanics of estimating the trend in the next section; this section discusses the estimate of the series level.

> **NOTE**
>
> Earlier in this chapter, a rant complained about inconsistent names for the smoothing constants. I use Gamma for the trend's smoothing constant partly because my sense is that more authors use Gamma than use its alternatives. Further, Gamma is closer to Alpha in the classical Greek alphabet than are alternatives such as Delta, which is often used in more complicated seasonal situations. I avoid Beta because it's often used to represent an intercept (β_0) and a coefficient (β_1) in regression analysis, which Chapter 4 shows to be intimately connected to smoothing. Furthermore, the letter *b* is typically used to represent the series trend, so to avoid confusion I prefer not to use β to represent the trend's smoothing constant.

3

Recall that simple exponential smoothing sets the next forecast of the time series' level as a weighted average of the current observation and the forecast of the current period. Similarly, Holt's linear smoothing sets the next period's level as a weighted average of the current observed value of the series and the forecast of its current value.

Using symbols, the formula to forecast the level of the series is similar to the formula used in simple exponential smoothing:

$$\hat{l}_t = \alpha y_t + (1 - \alpha)\hat{y}_t$$

That is, the forecast level for period t is Alpha times the observation made at time t, plus (1 minus Alpha) times the series forecast for period t. Notice that the actual observation is shown as y_t, whereas the forecast observation is shown as $\hat{y}_t$.

Simple exponential smoothing forecasts $\hat{y}_{t+1}$ only, and it does so directly with one equation per period. In contrast, Holt's method forecasts a level *and* a trend, which combine to produce $\hat{y}_{t+1}$, the forecast for the next period. The preceding formula forecasts the level portion only, symbolized as $\hat{l}_t$.

Bear in mind that the forecast of period t is the sum of the estimated level and the estimated slope from period $t–1$. In that case an equivalent formula, one which also shows up in the literature, is as follows:

$$\hat{l}_t = \alpha y_t + (1 - \alpha)\left(\hat{l}_{t-1} + \hat{b}_{t-1}\right)$$

This version of the formula for the series level shows explicitly how to arrive at the forecast for period t, or $\hat{y}_t$: by adding the forecast level for period $t–1$ (or $\hat{l}_{t-1}$) to the forecast trend for period $t–1$ (or $\hat{b}_{t-1}$).

Before I move on from the level forecast to the trend forecast, I want to note that it's here that generic smoothing formulas, such as the two just given for the level, start to become ambiguous. Those ambiguities, combined with the lack of standardization of the symbols I noted earlier in this chapter, can make it very difficult to interpret the formulas. And that's one reason that I regard Excel as such a useful application for smoothing and other quantitative techniques.

For example, one popular source of information on smoothing gives this formula for the estimate of the series' level:

$$l_t = \alpha y_t + (1 - \alpha)(l_{t-1} + b_{t-1})$$

This formula is nearly identical to the one I gave earlier for the smoothing form of the level equation in Holt's method. It's missing the carets over the symbols *l* and *b*, but that's a trivial difference. The problem is that you can't be sure what *t* refers to. Compare the latter formula to the next, also given earlier in this section:

$$\hat{l}_t = \alpha y_t + (1 - \alpha)\hat{y}_t$$

Setting aside the issue of the carets, the difference between the two formulas is that the first calls out the sum of the level and the trend at period $t–1$, and one refers to the sum of those two terms, $\hat{y}_t$. And that notation is ambiguous. You can't tell from looking at it whether it's the forecast value of the series made at period t for period $t+1$, or the forecast value of the series made at period $t-1$ for period t.

Of course, given the context of this discussion, it's pretty clear that $\hat{y}_t$ refers to the forecast of the series value at period t, made at period $t-1$. But the point is that it's ambiguous. The literature on smoothing is characterized by an unusually high rate of typographical errors. (I counted eight such errors in a 14-page stretch of a hardbound textbook retailing for more than $120, all in either formulas or their results.) So without prior knowledge it's hard to tell whether an apparent problem in a formula is just an ambiguity to be resolved or an outright error.

By way of comparison, here's the same formula in Excel's syntax, for use in row 3 of the worksheet in Figure 3.8:

```
=Alpha*B3+(1-Alpha)*F2
```

Figure 3.8
You can pick up the forecast portion of the formula from either cell F2 or cell C3.

	A	B	C	D	E	F	G	H	I
		Observed, Trended	Forecast of Current			Forecast of Next			
1	Period	Series	Period	Forecast Level	Forecast Trend	Period		Alpha:	0.1
2	1	9,174		9,174.0	0	9,174.0		Gamma:	0.1
3	2	9,408	9,174.0	9,197.4	2.3	9,199.7			

D3 — fx =Alpha*B3+(1-Alpha)*F2

There's no ambiguity in that formula. By looking at the formula in the worksheet, you can tell that cell B3 contains the current actual observation. You can tell what (1 – Alpha) is multiplying simply by looking at cell F2—and while you're at it, you can select cell F2 and see that F2 is the sum of D2 and E2, the prior period's level and trend.

Symbolic formulas work well when you want to implement them in C or VBA or some other coding language that gets expressed in SAS or R. They're not so useful when your purpose is to understand or otherwise assess a predictive model.

Forecasting a Trend

Here's the symbolic formula for the forecast trend in Holt's trend for smoothing (the symbol γ is pronounced "gamma"):

$$\hat{b}_{t+1} = \gamma\left(\hat{l}_t - \hat{l}_{t-1}\right) + (1-\gamma)\hat{b}_t$$

The formula for the forecast trend is analogous, if not precisely parallel, to the formula for the forecast level. The trend that's forecast for time $t-1$, symbolized as $\hat{b}_{t+1}$, is Gamma times the difference between the forecast levels $\hat{l}$ at times t and $t-1$, plus (1 – Gamma) times the trend forecast for period t, or $\hat{b}_t$.

Here's how the formula might be applied in row 3 of an Excel worksheet:

```
=Gamma*(D3-D2)+(1-Gamma)*E3
```

For both forecasts, the level and the trend, Holt's method does the following:

■ It multiplies a *constant* times a *current value*. For the level forecast for period *t+1*, that's Alpha times the current actual observation, y_t, which is our best estimate of the current level of the time series. For the trend forecast for period *t+1*, that's Gamma times the difference between the current forecast level $\hat{l}_t$ and the prior forecast level $\hat{l}_{t-1}$. That difference between two consecutive levels is as close as we can come to an actual observation of the value of the current trend.

■ It multiplies *1 minus the constant* times a *prior forecast*. For the level at period *t+1*, that's (1 − Alpha) times the forecast of the series for period *t*, or $\hat{l}_t + \hat{b}_t$. For the trend at period *t+1*, that's (1 − Gamma) times the forecast of the trend for period *t*, or $\hat{b}_t$.

Let's put some meat on the formulas' bones.

Forecasting the Next Level and the Next Trend

Here's another look at the formula to forecast a series' next level, at period *t+1*:

$$\hat{l}_{t+1} = \alpha y_t + (1 - \alpha)\hat{y}_t$$

It's similar to the forecast formula used in simple exponential smoothing, but there's a difference. In simple smoothing, the term $\hat{y}_t$, the forecast for period *t*, is not a forecast of level but a forecast of the series—what Holt's method would call the level plus the trend. Figure 3.9 shows this difference more objectively.

Figure 3.9
The next level forecast depends partly on the prior series forecast.

	A	B	C	D	E	F	G	H	I
1	Period	Observed, Trended Series	Forecast of Current Period	Forecast Level	Forecast Trend	Forecast of Next Period		Alpha:	0.1
2	1	9,174		9,174.0	0	9,174.0		Gamma:	0.1
3	2	9,408	9,174.0	9,197.4	2.3	9,199.7			

Figure 3.9 illustrates the following points:

■ The names Alpha and Gamma are defined and refer to the cells I1 and I2.

■ After the actual value for the first period has been obtained—but before the actual value for the second period—the forecast *level* of the series in cell D2 is taken to be the actual measured level, in cell B2. In cell E2, the forecast *trend* is taken to be zero, that is, a horizontal slope. (More on this matter is found in the "Initializing Values" section earlier in this chapter. Bear in mind that the absence of observations prior to Period 1 means that we must use special calculations to forecast into Period 2.)

- The series forecast (that is, the forecast of the value of the series to be observed in the next period) appears in cell F2. It is the sum of the level forecast in cell D2 and the trend forecast on cell E2.

- The forecast for Period 2 in cell F2 is repeated for convenience in cell C3, where it is used in the calculation of the forecasts for Period 3.

After you have observed the actual result for Period 2, you have a long enough baseline of existing observations that you can calculate actual forecasts. You need not act as though a credible forecast for the next period is the first observation, 9174, plus an assumed slope of zero. Here's how things work out during Period 2, after its actual value has been observed (and it's how things work out for all subsequent periods as well):

- The actual observation for Period 2, 9408, appears in cell B3.

- The forecast made at the end of Period 1 is carried forward from cell F2 into cell C3. Cell C3 contains this formula:

      =F2

- The level forecast for the *next* period, Period 3, appears in cell D3, using this formula:

      =Alpha*B3+(1-Alpha)*C3

  The formula for the forecast level follows the familiar pattern: Alpha times the current observation in B3, plus (1 – Alpha) times the forecast of the current period in C3.

- The trend forecast for the next period appears in cell E3. It's calculated with this formula:

      =Gamma*(D3-D2)+(1-Gamma)*E2

  Again we're working with a variation on the same basic pattern. A current value is multiplied by a constant, Gamma. The current value is the difference between two consecutive estimates of the series' level, found in cells D2 and D3. The difference is the current value of the trend. Then the prior estimate of the trend in cell E2 is multiplied by (1 – Gamma), and the two products are summed. The result is the forecast of the trend in cell E3.

- The forecast for the series as of the next period, Period 3, appears in cell F3. It is simply the sum of the level forecast for Period 3 in cell D3 and the trend forecast for Period 3 in cell E3. Cell F3 therefore contains this formula:

      =D3+E3

Extending the Forecast

Suppose that your full series of actual observations extended from cell A2 to cell A34. With the formulas in row 3 as given in the preceding list, you can copy from B3:F3 and paste into B4:F34. One handy way of doing that is to select B3:F3 and then double-click the selection handle, the small dark box in the lower-right corner of cell F3. Excel copies the formulas in B3:F3 as far down as there is data in an adjacent column—here, that's column A.

The result of copying the formulas from row 3 into rows 4 through 34 appears in Figure 3.10.

Figure 3.10
You can almost certainly improve on these forecasts.

I3	▼	:	×	✓	f_x	=SQRT(SUMXMY2(B3:B34,C3:C34)/32)		

	A	B	C	D	E	F	G	H	I
1	Period	Observed, Trended Series	Forecast of Current Period	Forecast Level	Forecast Trend	Forecast of Next Period		Alpha:	0.1
2	1	9,174		9,174.0	0	9,174.0		Gamma:	0.1
3	2	9,408	9,174.0	9,197.4	2.3	9,199.7		RMSE:	1670.563
4	3	8,540	9,199.7	9,133.8	-4.3	9,129.5			
5	4	8,314	9,129.5	9,048.0	-12.4	9,035.5			
6	5	7,998	9,035.5	8,931.8	-22.8	8,909.0			
7	6	8,202	8,909.0	8,838.3	-29.9	8,808.4			
8	7	7,601	8,808.4	8,687.7	-41.9	8,645.8			
9	8	7,731	8,645.8	8,554.3	-51.1	8,503.2			
10	9	7,468	8,503.2	8,399.7	-61.4	8,338.3			
11	10	7,643	8,338.3	8,268.7	-68.4	8,200.3			
32	31	890	-436.7	-304.0	-342.8	-646.8			
33	32	968	-646.8	-485.4	-326.7	-812.0			
34	33	791	-812.0	-651.7	-310.6	-962.4			

Rows 12 through 31 in Figure 3.10 are hidden to save space. You can unhide these rows in the downloaded copy of the workbook for this chapter. Take these steps:

1. Activate the worksheet for Figure 3.10.

2. Make a multiple selection of the visible rows 11 and 32.

3. Click the Format button in the Cells group on the Ribbon's Home tab.

4. Choose Hide & Unhide.

5. Click Unhide Rows.

A slightly quicker sequence is to right-click one of the row headers after step 2, and choose Unhide from the shortcut menu.

Optimizing the Constants

Although the results in Figure 3.10 are accurate, you can do better. The problem is that they are based on the arbitrary values for Alpha and Gamma, 0.1, in cells I1 and I2. You can deploy Solver again to optimize them. One of the many features of Solver that distinguish it from the rudimentary Goal Seek tool is that you can direct Solver to modify more than one Variable cell in pursuit of its optimal solution for the Target cell. See Figure 3.11.

In Figure 3.11, both Alpha and Gamma (cells I1 and I2 in Figure 3.10) are specified as Variable cells. Solver changes both values as it works to minimize the RMSE, found in the Target cell, I3.

Also notice that constraints have been placed on both Alpha and Gamma, to keep each of them between 0.0 and 1.0.

Figure 3.11
Notice that both Alpha and Gamma are used as Variable cells.

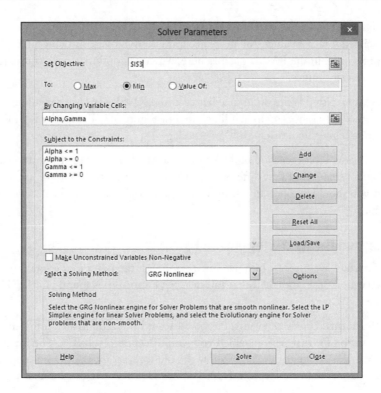

Clicking Solve in Figure 3.11 results in the much lower RMSE shown in Figure 3.12.

Figure 3.12
The RMSE in cell I3 has fallen from 1671 to 384.

	I3		× ✓	f_x	=SQRT(SUMXMY2(B3:B34,C3:C34)/32)			
	A	B	C	D	E	F	G	H	I
1	Period	Observed, Trended Series	Forecast of Current Period	Forecast Level	Forecast Trend	Forecast of Next Period		Alpha:	0.94769
2	1	9,174		9,174.0	0	9,174.0		Gamma:	0.284488
3	2	9,408	9,174.0	9,395.8	63.1	9,458.8		RMSE:	383.661
4	3	8,540	9,458.8	8,588.1	-184.6	8,403.4			
5	4	8,314	8,403.4	8,318.7	-208.7	8,109.9			
6	5	7,998	8,109.9	8,003.9	-238.9	7,764.9			
7	6	8,202	7,764.9	8,179.1	-121.1	8,058.0			
8	7	7,601	8,058.0	7,624.9	-244.3	7,380.6			
9	8	7,731	7,380.6	7,712.7	-149.8	7,562.8			
10	9	7,468	7,562.8	7,473.0	-175.4	7,297.6			
11	10	7,643	7,297.6	7,624.9	-82.3	7,542.7			
32	31	890	739.7	882.1	-35.6	846.6			
33	32	968	846.6	961.6	-2.8	958.8			
34	33	791	958.8	799.8	-48.1	751.7			

The RMSE in cell I3 has fallen almost 1300 units from Figure 3.10 to Figure 3.12, solely as a function of changing the values of Alpha and Gamma. Recall that the lower the RMSE, which depends on the size of the squared errors between the actual observations and their associated forecast values, the more accurate the forecasts. But you can expect a dramatic improvement in the RMSE, such as here, when you optimize your constants from their initial, arbitrary values.

More interesting is the difference between the RMSE for Holt's method as compared to the smoothed differences approach illustrated in Figure 3.7. There, the RMSE was 400, about 16 units higher than using Holt's method.

In this case, Holt's method of dealing with a trended series turns out to be a bit more accurate than smoothing first differences. That's not always true, and for any important application you should be open to testing various approaches against the data set that you have in hand.

Going Beyond the Next-Step-Ahead Forecast

So far you have forecast into just one period past the point that contains the final actual observation. In Figure 3.12 that forecast, for Period 34, is found in cell F34 and has the value 751.7.

In the normal course of events, Period 34 would roll around and you would get an actual observation for that period, which you would record in cell B35. Then you would enter the formula =F34 in cell C35, to show the old forecast for the present period. Similarly you would copy the formulas from D34:F34 into D35:F35 to get a forecast for Period 35.

But you're not there yet, and meanwhile your colleagues want forecasts, not just for Period 34 but for Periods 35 through 38 as well.

Using Holt's method, *forecasts for periods following the final one-step-ahead period are assumed to have a constant level and trend.*

In the sample data set last shown in Figure 3.11, that means that the level of the series is frozen at its final estimated level of 751.7, shown in cell D34 for Period 33.

The final trend estimate, –48.1 in cell E34 for Period 33, is also frozen but it continues to take effect in subsequent forecasts. Figure 3.13 shows how this comes together.

At the end of Period 33, you have the forecast for Period 34, in cell F34. As with earlier periods, you carry it forward into cell C35.

But because you have run out of actual observations, you can calculate neither a new level forecast nor a new trend forecast. Therefore, the assumption is that the level is frozen at 751.7. The trend estimate, although also frozen at –48.1, is added repeatedly to the prior forecast to result in the next forecast—in Figure 3.13, that is done through Period 38.

Figure 3.13
The forecast for Period 34 has been found in Period 33 and appears in cells F34 and C35.

I3		:	×	✓	fx	=SQRT(SUMXMY2(B3:B34,C3:C34)/32)			

	A	B	C	D	E	F	G	H	I
		Observed, Trended	Forecast of Current	Forecast	Forecast	Forecast of Next			
1	Period	Series	Period	Level	Trend	Period		Alpha:	0.94769
2	1	9,174		9,174.0	0	9,174.0		Gamma:	0.284488
3	2	9,408	9,174.0	9,395.8	63.1	9,458.8		RMSE:	383.661
4	3	8,540	9,458.8	8,588.1	-184.6	8,403.4			
5	4	8,314	8,403.4	8,318.7	-208.7	8,109.9			
6	5	7,998	8,109.9	8,003.9	-238.9	7,764.9			
7	6	8,202	7,764.9	8,179.1	-121.1	8,058.0			
8	7	7,601	8,058.0	7,624.9	-244.3	7,380.6			
9	8	7,731	7,380.6	7,712.7	-149.8	7,562.8			
10	9	7,468	7,562.8	7,473.0	-175.4	7,297.6			
11	10	7,643	7,297.6	7,624.9	-82.3	7,542.7			
32	31	890	739.7	882.1	-35.6	846.6			
33	32	968	846.6	961.6	-2.8	958.8			
34	33	791	958.8	799.8	-48.1	751.7			
35	34		751.7	=F34					
36	35		703.6	=C35+$E$34					
37	36		655.6	=C36+$E$34					
38	37		607.5	=C37+$E$34					
39	38		559.4	=C38+$E$34					

3

The formulas used in Figure 3.13 for cells C36:C39 appear in cells D36:D39. As you can see, each formula simply adds the last estimated trend figure, –48.1, to the prior series forecast.

The result is a straight line, beginning at the forecast for the first period following the final actual observation. You can see the result in the final five periods shown in Figure 3.14.

There's good news and bad news associated with the straight-line result. The good news is that if a trend is present in the actual observations—and if not then there's no point to using Holt's method at all—you're taking note of that trend in the forecasts that extend well beyond your final actual observation.

The bad news is that all kinds of assumptions are packed into the simple act of extending a current trend several periods into the future. You're assuming that the level remains constant into Period 35, into Period 36, into Period 37, and so on. You're assuming that the trend remains constant through the same periods. At a much more fundamental level, you're assuming that the nature of the measurements that form your existing time series will remain in place during your forecast horizon. What if you're forecasting the number of people who have hypertension and the American Society of Cardiology decides to redefine the systolic and diastolic indicators of high blood pressure?

No matter how careful and sophisticated the forecasting techniques you apply, the farther you stretch your forecast the more likely it is to break. Be sure to take a look at the material in Chapter 7 concerning damped trend models, which can help you avoid having a trend run away with itself as it leaves the actual observations behind.

Figure 3.14
The direction of the fore-casts is determined by the last and the next-to-last actuals.

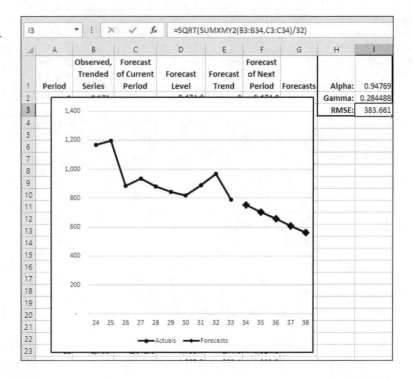

Validating the Results

As long as I'm playing Cassandra here, we might as well take a look at a validation of the results of the time series used in Figures 3.7 through 3.14. I described the procedure's bare bones earlier in this chapter, in "Initializing Versus Validation." Figure 3.15 provides a springboard for discussing the details.

In Figure 3.15 the values in the time series are the same as in earlier figures. However, the level and trend smoothing constants are chosen by Solver to minimize the RMSE figure in cell I4, which has this formula:

```
=SQRT(SUMXMY2(B3:B12,C3:C12)/10)
```

Figure 3.15 changes the way that Figure 3.12 handles matters. Solver used the smoothing constants in Figure 3.12 to minimize the RMSE calculated on the time series and forecasts, from B3:C3 to B34:C34.

In Figure 3.15, Solver altered the smoothing constants to minimize the RMSE in cell I4, which is based not on the entire time series but on what I chose as a training set, in B3:C3 to B12:C12. The RMSE formula in cell I4 is this:

```
=SQRT(SUMXMY2(B3:B12,C3:C12)/10)
```

My reasons for choosing the 2nd through the 11th periods for the training set were largely subjective. The full time series contains only 33 observations and 32 forecasts. A training set of 8 periods (25%) seemed a bit short, and I didn't want the training set to eat too far into the test set—so I settled on 10 periods.

Figure 3.15
These forecasts are based on a training set and a test set.

I4			× ✓ fx	=SQRT(SUMXMY2(B3:B12,C3:C12)/10)					

	A	B	C	D	E	F	G	H	I	J
1	Period	Observed, Trended Series	Forecast of Current Period	Forecast Level	Forecast Trend	Forecast of Next Period		Based on Training Set Only		
2	1	9,174		9,174.0	0	9,174.0		Alpha:	0.467	
3	2	9,408	9,174.0	9,283.2	34.6	9,317.8		Gamma:	0.317	
4	3	8,540	9,317.8	8,954.7	-80.4	8,874.3		RMSE:	471.845	Training Set
5	4	8,314	8,874.3	8,612.7	-163.3	8,449.4				
6	5	7,998	8,449.4	8,238.7	-230.0	8,008.6				
7	6	8,202	8,008.6	8,098.9	-201.4	7,897.5				
8	7	7,601	7,897.5	7,759.1	-245.3	7,513.8				
9	8	7,731	7,513.8	7,615.2	-213.2	7,402.0				
10	9	7,468	7,402.0	7,432.8	-203.4	7,229.4				
11	10	7,643	7,229.4	7,422.5	-142.2	7,280.3				
12	11	6,443	7,280.3	6,889.4	-266.1	6,623.3				
13	12	5,736	6,623.3	6,209.1	-397.3	5,811.8		RMSE:	497.704	Test Set
14	13	4,504	5,811.8	5,201.2	-590.7	4,610.6		RMSE:	489.769	Full Series
15	14	3,785	4,610.6	4,225.2	-712.8	3,512.4				
16	15	3,529	3,512.4	3,520.1	-710.3	2,809.8				
17	16	3,277	2,809.8	3,027.9	-641.2	2,386.7				
18	17	2,929	2,386.7	2,639.9	-561.0	2,078.9				
19	18	2,685	2,078.9	2,361.8	-471.4	1,890.4				
20	19	2,515	1,890.4	2,182.0	-379.0	1,803.0				
21	20	2,070	1,803.0	1,927.6	-339.5	1,588.1				
22	21	2,277	1,588.1	1,909.7	-237.7	1,672.0				
23	22	1,786	1,672.0	1,725.2	-220.8	1,504.4				

Minimizing the RMSE for the 2nd through 11th periods, Solver returned the values in cells I2 and I3 of Figure 3.15. Notice that the RMSE in cell I4 (471.8), averaged across 10 pairs of observations and forecasts, is somewhat larger than the RMSE in Figure 3.12 (383.7), averaged across 32 pairs of observations.

But Figure 3.15 has another RMSE in cell I13 (497.7), which is based on periods 12 through 33. That value is quite close to the RMSE for the training set (471.8). The small difference between the RMSEs tends to support the notion that the smoothing constants in cells I2 and I3 in Figure 3.15 will continue to be useful as you acquire more and more actual observations.

Contrast that outcome with the one shown in Figure 3.16.

Figure 3.16 uses the smoothing constants that were optimized in Figure 3.12, using the full set of observations and forecasts in B3:C34. However, Figure 3.16 shows RMSEs for both the training set and the test set. It also shows the RMSE for the full set in cell I13; notice it is the same as the RMSE in Figure 3.12, as well it should be.

However, in Figure 3.16, the RMSE for the training set (527.2, in cell I4) is considerably larger than the RMSE for the test set (296.2, in cell I13). That suggests that Solver's choice of the smoothing constants was influenced more heavily by the final 22 observations (which we have now taken to be a test set) than by the first 10 observations (now regarded as a training set).

Figure 3.16

The smoothing constants were optimized using the full time series, and then were applied to the training and test sets.

	I4		▼	:	×	✓	*fx*	=SQRT(SUMXMY2(B3:B12,C3:C12)/10)		

▲	A	B	C	D	E	F	G	H	I	J
1	Period	Observed, Trended Series	Forecast of Current Period	Forecast Level	Forecast Trend	Forecast of Next Period		Based on Full Series		
2	1	9,174		9,174.0	0	9,174.0		Alpha:	0.948	
3	2	9,408	9,174.0	9,395.8	63.1	9,458.8		Gamma:	0.284	
4	3	8,540	9,458.8	8,588.1	-184.6	8,403.4		RMSE:	527.242	Training Set
5	4	8,314	8,403.4	8,318.7	-208.7	8,109.9				
6	5	7,998	8,109.9	8,003.9	-238.9	7,764.9				
7	6	8,202	7,764.9	8,179.1	-121.1	8,058.0				
8	7	7,601	8,058.0	7,624.9	-244.3	7,380.6				
9	8	7,731	7,380.6	7,712.7	-149.8	7,562.8				
10	9	7,468	7,562.8	7,473.0	-175.4	7,297.6				
11	10	7,643	7,297.6	7,624.9	-82.3	7,542.7				
12	11	6,443	7,542.7	6,500.5	-378.7	6,121.8				
13	12	5,736	6,121.8	5,756.2	-482.8	5,273.4		RMSE:	296.221	Test Set
14	13	4,504	5,273.4	4,544.2	-690.2	3,854.1		RMSE:	383.661	Full Series
15	14	3,785	3,854.1	3,788.6	-708.8	3,079.8				
16	15	3,529	3,079.8	3,505.5	-587.7	2,917.8				
17	16	3,277	2,917.8	3,258.2	-490.9	2,767.3				
18	17	2,929	2,767.3	2,920.5	-447.3	2,473.3				
19	18	2,685	2,473.3	2,673.9	-390.2	2,283.7				
20	19	2,515	2,283.7	2,502.9	-327.8	2,175.1				
21	20	2,070	2,175.1	2,075.5	-356.2	1,719.3				
22	21	2,277	1,719.3	2,247.8	-205.8	2,042.0				
23	22	1,786	2,042.0	1,799.4	-274.8	1,524.6				

In that case, there's some reason to suspect that as more data arrives, the RMSE will react by growing back to the level of the training set in Figure 3.16—that is, the 500s or higher. Figure 3.17 provides some added insight into this issue.

Figure 3.17

The smoothing constants were optimized using the full time series, and then were applied to the training and test sets.

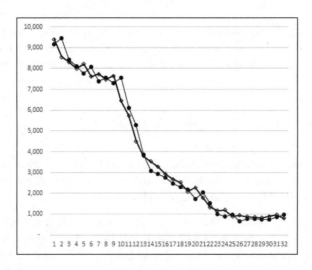

Notice in Figure 3.17 that the forecasts track the actuals much more closely toward what is now the end of the time series than they do at the beginning, where the training set is found. If new data changes the direction of the trend, it's quite possible that the overall RMSE found in cell I13 will increase and approach the level found for the training set.

My own tendency would be to monitor the time series and forecasts closely for at least 10 more periods, to see whether the status quo holds or the time series takes a new direction with consequences for the overall RMSE.

With this chapter's material on handling trended time series in mind, it's time to move on to more sensitive methods for initializing forecasts than we've discussed so far.

3

Initializing Forecasts

$$4$$

If you want to avoid making a complete guess at forecasting the first few values of a time series, you have to have a *baseline*. That baseline should be a series of actual observations, derived from some sort of empirical process. The baseline gives you something to work with.

In practice, you arrive at that ideal after you've had some experience with whatever it is you want to forecast. Perhaps that is corporate revenues; perhaps it's a hospital's daily admissions for a particular virus; it might be something less weighty, such as that new first baseman's batting average. It frequently happens that you start measuring something, and after a while the periodic measurements become more and more interesting or useful. Then the next step is often to ask for a forecast.

In that sort of situation, you have at least a handful of actual results—a baseline you can forecast from. The same is true, or nearly so, if you're extrapolating from a closely related phenomenon. Suppose that you manufacture a product and have several years of its revenue history. You consider expanding your operations by producing a new product, one that's closely related to the existing line but different in some important respect. It wouldn't be outrageous to expect the new product to return, say, 50% of the existing product's revenues during the first few months it's on the market. Then you could use the existing product's revenues, cut in half, as a baseline for forecasting the new product's performance.

It's even possible, albeit precarious, to start with a baseline of just one observation. You'd prefer a much longer baseline, of course, but the formulas for simple exponential smoothing allow you to calculate a Period 2 forecast with only one observation at hand. Whether it's wise to do so is normally a question of the importance of making early decisions based on the forecasts. The longer you can wait, the less rickety your structure.

Other initialization methods exist, some of them clever and intuitively appealing. As you saw in Chapter 3, "Working with Trended Time Series," the level of a time series is not the only variable that you might need to initialize. You might need to initialize the trend if the time series is not stationary and horizontal. And if the time series exhibits seasonality, you might need to initialize the seasonal effects. Furthermore, the way you go about initialization can depend on whether the model you adopt is additive or multiplicative. (Most of this book assumes additive models, largely because additive models tend to result in clearer discussions of other points than do multiplicative models. See Chapter 7, "Multiplicative and Damped Trend Models," for information on using multiplicative models.)

So the issue of initialization is a complicated one. This chapter and sections of subsequent chapters are intended to offer some disentangling.

Setting Initial Values

Particularly with very short time series, the choice of the initial value or values can exert a powerful influence on the forecast values, and therefore on their accuracy as predictors of the actual values. Figure 4.1 shows one example of how this comes about.

Figure 4.1
The value chosen for the initial forecast can influence the entire set of forecasts.

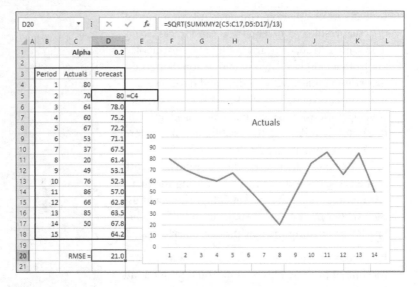

The same set of actual observations appears twice in Figures 4.1 and 4.2. The series is not trended and therefore simple exponential smoothing is a reasonable approach to generating forecasts. The same value for Alpha, the smoothing constant, is used in both examples.

Figure 4.2 shows the forecasts from Figure 4.1 along with another method to initialize them.

Figure 4.2
Using an average as the initial forecast is likely to improve accuracy.

| D20 | ▾ | ⋮ | ✕ | ✓ | *fx* | =SQRT(SUMXMY2(C5:C17,D5:D17)/13) |

◢ A	B	C	D	E	F	G	H	I	J
1		Alpha	0.2				Alpha	0.2	
2									
3	Period	Actuals	Forecast			Period	Actuals	Forecast	
4	1	80				1	80		
5	2	70	80	=C4		2	70	68.2	=AVERAGE(H4:H8)
6	3	64	78.0			3	64	68.6	
7	4	60	75.2			4	60	67.6	
8	5	67	72.2			5	67	66.1	
9	6	53	71.1			6	53	66.3	
10	7	37	67.5			7	37	63.6	
11	8	20	61.4			8	20	58.3	
12	9	49	53.1			9	49	50.6	
13	10	76	52.3			10	76	50.3	
14	11	86	57.0			11	86	55.5	
15	12	66	62.8			12	66	61.6	
16	13	85	63.5			13	85	62.5	
17	14	50	67.8			14	50	67.0	
18	15		64.2			15		63.6	
19									
20		RMSE =	21.0				RMSE =	19.3	

The only difference between the two examples in Figure 4.2 is in the values that are selected for the first forecast. Those values appear in cells D5 and I5 of Figure 4.2. (The formulas for the initial forecasts appear in E5 and J5.)

The first example in Figure 4.2 uses a typical choice for the first forecast: the first actual. It's worth noting again here that the subsequent forecasts use the following formula instead (it is the smoothing form of the forecast formula):

$$\hat{y}_{t+1} = \alpha y_t + (1 - \alpha)\hat{y}_t$$

In words, the forecast for Period *t+1* equals Alpha times the actual observation for Period *t*, plus (1 – Alpha) times the forecast for Period *t*. Suppose that we want a forecast for Period 1. Then, according to the formula, we need an actual observation for Period 0 as well as a forecast for Period 0, presumably made at Period –1. Because no Period 0 exists (else we'd call it Period 1), we can't rely on the normal simple exponential smoothing formula for Period 1. Some other approach is needed to *initialize* the forecasts.

A few such approaches exist, and I'll describe several of them in this chapter. The approach illustrated in the range B3:D18 of Figure 4.2 is easy to apply and simple enough that it's used in many introductions to simple exponential smoothing. It provides no forecast at all for Period 1.

This approach takes as the forecast for Period 2 the actual observed value for Period 1. Period 3 and subsequent periods can be forecast using the formula given earlier in this section, because Period 2 will then have both an observed value y_2 and a forecast value $\hat{y}_2$ (which equals the actual value observed at Period 1). The initial forecast value in cell I5, 68.2, is calculated by taking the average of the first five actual values. The overall forecast accuracy is better than it is when only the first actual value is used as the initial forecast, as is done in B3:D18.

Taking the average of the first five values brings the initial forecast more closely in line with those actuals, and therefore the resulting forecasts are more accurate. Notice that the RMSE for the analysis in G3:I18 is smaller than the RMSE for that in B3:D18.

In Figure 4.2, the, initial forecast in cell I5 is the average of five values, but nowhere is it written or suggested that five values is the correct number to use. You won't find the correct number anywhere because there is no correct number. I just pulled "five" out of my hat. I am congenitally suspicious of anything as arbitrary as that.

But it's the difference between the initial forecast and the subsequent actuals that can really make a difference to the RMSE, not simply the choice of the number of actuals to include in the average. See Figure 4.3.

4

Figure 4.3
A real outlier such as that in cell N5 can reduce the accuracy of the forecasts substantially.

I20 =SQRT(SUMXMY2(H5:H17,I5:I17)/13)

	B	C	D	E	G	H	I	J	L	M	N	O
1		Alpha	0.2			Alpha	0.2			Alpha	0.2	
2												
3	Period	Actuals	Forecast		Period	Actuals	Forecast		Period	Actuals	Forecast	
4	1	80			1	80			1	150		
5	2	70	80	=C4	2	70	68.2	=AVERAGE(H4:H8)	2	70	150	=M4
6	3	64	78.0		3	64	68.6		3	64	134.0	
7	4	60	75.2		4	60	67.6		4	60	120.0	
8	5	67	72.2		5	67	66.1		5	67	108.0	
9	6	53	71.1		6	53	66.3		6	53	99.8	
10	7	37	67.5		7	37	63.6		7	37	90.4	
11	8	20	61.4		8	20	58.3		8	20	79.8	
12	9	49	53.1		9	49	50.6		9	49	67.8	
13	10	76	52.3		10	76	50.3		10	76	64.0	
14	11	86	57.0		11	86	55.5		11	86	66.4	
15	12	66	62.8		12	66	61.6		12	66	70.3	
16	13	85	63.5		13	85	62.5		13	85	69.5	
17	14	50	67.8		14	50	67.0		14	50	72.6	
18	15		64.2		15		63.6		15		68.1	
19												
20		RMSE =	21.0			RMSE =	19.3			RMSE =	45.4	

The range L3:N18 in Figure 4.3 shows what can happen if you use a single point estimate for your initial forecast, as in cell N5, and that estimate is well outside the range occupied by the other actuals. Notice that the RMSE in cell N20 is more than twice as large as the other two measures in cells D20 and I20.

The pattern of the actuals in M4:M17 is not at all unusual, including the large outlier in cell M4. For example, that's precisely the sort of pattern you get when a new product such as a book hits the market. Many retailers make large initial buys in order to get the product into stock. Unless the retailers' own sales forecasts were unduly pessimistic, sales by the manufacturer to the retailers then tail off as the retailers attempt to reach a just-in-time inventory position. But the relatively high initial value is still there, and if you base your initial forecast on that value alone, you're courting trouble.

This example is meant to emphasize the desirability of having not only a choice of more than one method of initialization, but also a familiarity with the nature of the time series or closely related time series.

That said, let's move on to other approaches to initializing forecasts in simple exponential smoothing, and subsequently move on to other, more complex models.

Getting an Initial Forecast with Backcasting

Backcasting is a way of forecasting in reverse. The process seems simple enough, and in fact it is, but it's also robust and is used in more sophisticated contexts than simple smoothing, such as Box-Jenkins ARIMA techniques. The basic idea is to put the time series in reverse chronological order and then forecast backward to Period 0 instead of forward to, say, Period 15.

Figure 4.4 shows the first step in backcasting.

Figure 4.4
You can use the backcast to Period 0 as the initial forecast for Period 1.

Period	Actual		Period	Actual
1	80		14	50
2	70		13	85
3	64		12	66
4	60		11	86
5	67		10	76
6	53		9	49
7	37		8	20
8	20		7	37
9	49		6	53
10	76		5	67
11	86		4	60
12	66		3	64
13	85		2	70
14	50		1	80
			0	

4

In Figure 4.4, the original time series is shown in the range B2:C16. You'd like to backcast into Period 0 so that you can get an estimate of the time series' value one period before the actual recording started.

It's helpful to think of a backcast as a forecast of the series in reverse. So the range E2:F17 in Figure 4.4 reverses the order of the series. (It's also helpful to have period identifiers such as those in columns B and E, which you can use as a sort key.) Just copy your existing time series, including period identifiers, to a new location, and sort the range using the period identifier as a declining sort key.

If necessary, add a row for Period 0 to the newly sorted time series, as is done in E17:F17 in Figure 4.4.

Establish a smoothing constant for your backcast. I've done that in cell G1 of Figure 4.5.

Figure 4.5
The name that has been given to the cell G1 appears in the Formula Bar's Name Box.

AlphaBack			× ✓ fx	0		
A	B	C	D	E	F	G
1					Alpha (Backcast)	0.00
2	Period	Actual		Period	Actual	Backcast
3	1	80		14	50	
4	2	70		13	85	50.0
5	3	64		12	66	85.0
6	4	60		11	86	66.0
7	5	67		10	76	86.0
8	6	53		9	49	76.0
9	7	37		8	20	49.0
10	8	20		7	37	20.0
11	9	49		6	53	37.0
12	10	76		5	67	53.0
13	11	86		4	60	67.0
14	12	66		3	64	60.0
15	13	85		2	70	64.0
16	14	50		1	80	70.0
17				0		80.0
18						
19						
20					RMSE =	18.8

To help keep things straight, I've given the name `AlphaBack` to the smoothing constant for the backcast, found in cell G1.

Next, enter the formulas for the backcasts into column G. No estimate as yet exists for Period 14—that's our eventual goal—so leave cell G3 blank. Enter this formula in cell G4:

```
=F3
```

That formula conforms to the approach you've seen used earlier in this book: setting the first forecast equal to the first actual observation. The formula for G5 will also look familiar:

```
=(AlphaBack*E4)+(1-AlphaBack)*F4
```

It multiplies the prior actual by the smoothing constant (here named `AlphaBack`), and adds the product of (1 – `AlphaBack`) and the prior forecast. The formula in cell G5 can be copied and pasted down into G6:G17. The cell G17 will hold the optimized backcast for Period 0 after Solver has finished its work.

Now establish a formula for RMSE. In Figure 4.5, it's in G20:

```
=SQRT(SUMXMY2(F4:F16,G4:G16)/13)
```

Lastly, optimize the smoothing constant `AlphaBack` in order to minimize the RMSE. Take these steps:

1. Select cell G20, or wherever you've put the RMSE formula.
2. In the Analysis group of the Ribbon's Data tab, click Solver.
3. Use G20 as the Objective cell, and click the Min radio button.
4. Enter G1 as the Variable Cell.
5. Establish 0 and 1 as limits on cell G1 in the Constraints section. (You can review how to complete this step in the instructions for Figure 3.2, in Chapter 3.)
6. Make sure that GRG Nonlinear is selected as the Solving Method.
7. Click Options, select the GRG Nonlinear tab, and make sure that the Use Multistart box is checked. You can also check the Require Bounds on Variables check box.
8. Click OK to return to the Solver Parameters dialog box, and click Solve.

> **NOTE**
>
> As far as I can tell from the documentation and from experience, the Require Bounds on Variables check box is a belt-and-suspenders issue. Suppose that you check that box and that you have established one or more cells as a constraint on the main Solver dialog box. If all the constraint cells have been given both an upper and a lower bound (as in step 5 of the preceding list), then Solver will proceed to search for a solution. If not all the constraint cells have both an upper and a lower bound, Solver stops with a warning message.
>
> If you haven't specified any constraints, the Require Bounds check box has no effect.
>
> If you've been reasonably careful about setting up your constraints, though, and have provided both upper and lower bounds, you've put on the belt. Filling the check box is tantamount to adding a pair of suspenders. I suppose that if you need to establish many constraints, one or more might slip through missing an upper or lower bound. In that case, filling the check box could save you some grief.
>
> I discuss the reasons to use Multistart at all in the section "About Multistart and Solver," later in this chapter.

In fairly short order you should have a solution to the problem that you handed over to Solver. Using the data supplied for Figures 4.4 and 4.5, Solver returns an optimum value of 0.0471, the smoothing constant, which minimizes the value of RMSE.

In turn, that value for the smoothing constant returns a value of 76.3 as the backcast for Period 0. See Figure 4.6.

Figure 4.6
Cell K1 is named Alpha.

	K20	▾	:	×	✓	*fx*	=SQRT(SUMXMY2(J4:J17,K4:K17)/14)	

	D	E	F	G	H	I	J	K	L
1			Alpha (Backcast)	0.0471			Alpha (Forecast)	0.305645	
2		Period	Actual	Backcast		Period	Actual	Forecast	
3		14	50			0	76.3		
4		13	85	50.0		1	80	76.3	=J3
5		12	66	81.6		2	70	77.4	
6		11	86	63.5		3	64	75.1	
7		10	76	82.5		4	70	71.7	
8		9	49	72.9		5	67	71.2	
9		8	20	47.1		6	53	69.9	
10		7	37	19.4		7	57	64.8	
11		6	53	35.6		8	53	62.4	
12		5	67	50.8		9	57	59.5	
13		4	60	64.1		10	76	58.7	
14		3	64	57.4		11	86	64.0	
15		2	70	61.1		12	66	70.7	
16		1	80	66.8		13	85	69.3	
17		0		76.3		14	50	74.1	
18						15		66.7	
19									
20			RMSE =	18.6			RMSE =	12.8	

Figure 4.6 restores the original time series, in ascending chronological order, in the range I2:K18. Notice that the restored time series includes both the fictional Period 0 and the upcoming Period 15, which we want to forecast now that we have used backcasting to initialize a forecast for Period 1.

As Figure 4.6 illustrates, you can plug the backcast value of 76.3 from cell G17 into cell J3, the third row of the Actual column, giving you an estimate of what an actual value for Period 0 would have been had you been able to observe and record it. You can use it to initialize the forecasts in cell K4, by way of the simple linking formula =J3.

You'll also need an RMSE formula for the forecast. In Figure 4.6 that formula, in cell K20, is as follows:

```
=SQRT(SUMXMY2(J4:J17,K4:K17)/14)
```

Finally, use Solver to minimize the value of Alpha for the RMSE in K20. The procedure is closely analogous to the steps just given for the backcast. Just change the Objective cell to K20 and the Variable cell to K1 (named Alpha for this example).

Getting an Initial Forecast with Optimization

Both this chapter and Chapter 3 have described the use of Solver to help identify an optimal value for Alpha. In that method, Solver uses a search algorithm to determine the value of Alpha that minimizes the sum of the squared differences between actual observations and their associated forecasts.

Since roughly 2004, some writers have discussed using the same approach, not just to identify Alpha but also to select the initial forecasts in various types of smoothing (including simple exponential smoothing, Holt's method, and the Holt-Winters seasonal smoothing).

At first glance this approach appears to have great intuitive appeal. All methods that involve exponential smoothing rely on three inputs to generate useful forecasts: the time series or baseline itself, the value of the smoothing constant, and the selection of a value for the initial forecast. The data series itself is a given: It's your empirical source of information, and you change any of its values at your professional peril.

Using an optimization engine, in conjunction with a method such as RMSE of measuring the amount of error in the collective forecasts, is an accepted way to objectively determine Alpha (some continue to counsel more subjective criteria, using grounds that seem to me difficult to justify).

Why not use the same approach to selecting an initial forecast? Recall that the initial forecast can't be calculated in the same way as subsequent forecasts, for lack of an observation at Period 0. Other approaches, such as backcasting, or taking the value of the first observation as the value of the first forecast, have some justifiable rationale. But Figure 4.2, among others, shows that the same time series and the same Alpha can return different forecasts, depending on different ways, each sensible, of estimating the initial forecast.

Initial Forecast in Simple Exponential Smoothing

If it makes sense to use Solver to find the value of Alpha that results in the smallest RMSE, perhaps it makes sense to find the best value of the initial forecast using the same method. Figure 4.7 shows how you might set up the process.

With the skeleton for the analysis in place as shown in Figure 4.7, take these steps:

1. Enter 0.9 in cell D1. That value is well away from an optimized value for Alpha, but it's within the limits of 0.0 and 1.0.

2. Name cell D1 as Alpha if you want. If you're using the version of Figure 4.7 that you can download from the publisher's website, D1 already has the name Alpha, its scope limited to the worksheet named Figure 4.7.

Figure 4.7
Periods 0 and 15 are
unpopulated. Period 0 is
imaginary and 15 hasn't
occurred yet.

	A	B	C	D
		Alpha	▾	⋮ × ✓ ƒₓ
			Alpha	
1				
2		Period	Actual	Forecast
3		0		
4		1	80	
5		2	70	
6		3	64	
7		4	70	
8		5	67	
9		6	53	
10		7	57	
11		8	53	
12		9	57	
13		10	76	
14		11	86	
15		12	66	
16		13	85	
17		14	50	
18		15		
19				
20			RMSE =	

3. Enter values for the Period 0 actual and forecast. As shown in Figure 4.8, I used 300 and 100, for no particular reason, but you can choose whatever values you want. It wouldn't hurt to keep them at roughly the same order of magnitude as the actual observations.

4. Enter the following formula in cell D4, copy it, and paste it down into cell D17.
   `=(Alpha*C3)+(1-Alpha)*D3`

   In D17, the formula's references to C3 and D3 should have adjusted to C16 and D16. And if you haven't named cell D1 as Alpha, replace the formula's reference to Alpha with $D$1, making sure to use the dollar signs so that the reference is absolute as it's pasted into rows 4 through 17.

5. Enter the following formula in cell D20:
   `=SQRT(SUMXMY2(C4:C17,D4:D17)/14)`

   You probably recognize that as the formula for RMSE. Your worksheet should now have the entries shown in Figure 4.8.

Figure 4.8

Consider using Data Validation, on the Ribbon's Data tab, to restrict the possible range of values in D1 to between 0.0 and 1.0, in case someone tinkers with your work.

	A	B	C	D	E	F	G	H
D20				=SQRT(SUMXMY2(C4:C17,D4:D17)/14)				
1			Alpha	0.9				
2		Period	Actual	Forecast				
3		0	300	100				
4		1	80	280.000				
5		2	70	100.000				
6		3	64	73.000				
7		4	70	64.900				
8		5	67	69.490				
9		6	53	67.249				
10		7	57	54.425				
11		8	53	56.742				
12		9	57	53.374				
13		10	76	56.637				
14		11	86	74.064				
15		12	66	84.806				
16		13	85	67.881				
17		14	50	83.288				
18		15		53.329				
19								
20			RMSE =	55.756				

6. With cell D20 selected, click Solver in the Data tab's Analysis group. Use the settings for the main Solver Parameters and the Solver Options dialog boxes as shown in Figures 4.9 and 4.10.

When you have supplied the settings in Figure 4.9, click Options. The All Methods tab appears. You can accept its default settings. Click the GRG Nonlinear tab to get to the settings shown in Figure 4.10.

I suggest that you be sure to use the settings shown in Figure 4.10. I discuss the effect of the Multistart option later in this chapter, in "About Multistart and Solver." And because you're asking Solver to work with two values (Alpha, and the forecast at Period 0), as shown in Figure 4.9, it might well help to allow Solver to go through as many as 100 locations in its search for the optimum combination of values to minimize the RMSE. Therefore, set the Population Size to 100. It's likely to take longer, on the order of a minute or two with two Variable cells, but the extra time can pay dividends.

> **NOTE** According to the Solver documentation, Population Size refers to the number of local solutions that Solver tests with Multistart. In that case, the number is a sample, not a population. I find the Solver documentation generally accurate and helpful, but don't be thrown by its occasionally inconsistent and misleading terminology.

Figure 4.9
If you did not define the name Alpha for cell D1, use $D$1 in its place.

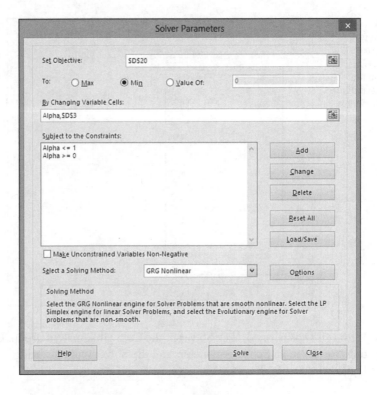

Figure 4.10
These settings pertain to the GRG Nonlinear solution type.

Using the settings shown in Figure 4.10, click OK to return to the Solver Parameters dialog box, and then click Solve to start Solver. When Solver reaches a solution and displays a message to that effect, choose to keep Solver's results and click OK. You should see the results shown in Figure 4.11.

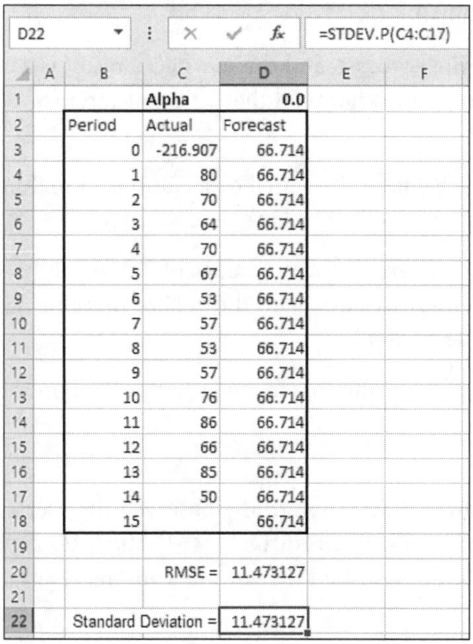

Figure 4.11
Simultaneously optimizing Alpha and the initial forecast results in a constant forecast value.

	A	B	C	D	E	F
		D22	▼ : × ✓ f_x	=STDEV.P(C4:C17)		
1			Alpha	0.0		
2		Period	Actual	Forecast		
3		0	-216.907	66.714		
4		1	80	66.714		
5		2	70	66.714		
6		3	64	66.714		
7		4	70	66.714		
8		5	67	66.714		
9		6	53	66.714		
10		7	57	66.714		
11		8	53	66.714		
12		9	57	66.714		
13		10	76	66.714		
14		11	86	66.714		
15		12	66	66.714		
16		13	85	66.714		
17		14	50	66.714		
18		15		66.714		
19						
20			RMSE =	11.473127		
21						
22		Standard Deviation =	11.473127			

What's happened here? Solver has determined that a value of 0.0 for Alpha, the smoothing constant, combined with a forecast of 66.714, constant for the full 15 periods, results in a minimum RMSE value of 11.47. That's not a useful outcome, so let's dig a little more deeply into it. First, why the constant forecast?

The reason is pretty clear after you have another look at the smoothing formula used in simple exponential smoothing:

$$\hat{y}_{t+1} = \alpha y_t + (1 - \alpha)\hat{y}_t$$

Solver has set the value of Alpha to 0. That removes the influence of the observation for period t from the formula, which therefore simplifies to this:

$$\hat{y}_{t+1} = (1 - \alpha)\hat{y}_t$$

And therefore to this (remember, Alpha equals zero):

$$\hat{y}_{t+1} = \hat{y}_t$$

In words, each forecast equals the forecast for the prior period: the forecast for the 10th period equals the forecast for the 9th, the forecast for the 5th equals that for the 4th, and—most pertinent for this discussion—the forecast for the Period 1 equals the "forecast" for Period 0. (I put "forecast" in quotes because Period 0's is not a true forecast. It's provided by Solver, but at this point we're acting as though it's based on an actual observation and calculated by the smoothing formula.)

So each forecast equals its prior forecast, and the inevitable result is a constant forecast through the forecast horizon. Now, where did that constant forecast value, 66.714, come from?

First, 66.714 equals the mean value of the actual observations in the time series, in the range C4:C17 in Figure 4.11. As you'll see, that's no coincidence.

Second, bear in mind that Solver arrived at the values of 0.0 for Alpha, and arrived at the mean of the actuals for the forecast values, with the goal of minimizing RMSE. The minimum RMSE that Solver achieved is 11.47.

As an illuminating exercise, try entering this formula somewhere on the worksheet with the data shown in Figure 4.11:

```
=STDEV.P(C4:C17)
```

That formula returns the standard deviation of the observed time series, treated as a population rather than a sample. The formula returns 11.473, *exactly the same value as the RMSE for the optimized forecasts.* (You can also find that formula and its result in Figure 4.11, cell D22.)

As I said, there's more than simple coincidence going on here. Have a look at one of the definitional formulas for the population standard deviation:

$$\sqrt{\sum_{i=1}^{N}(x_i - \mu)^2 / N}$$

The formula says to do the following:

1. Subtract the mean of all the values from each of the values.
2. Square each difference.
3. Total the squared differences.
4. Divide by the number of values.
5. Take the square root of the result of step 4.

This is precisely what the formula for RMSE does. Here it is once again in Excel syntax and using cell references as shown in Figure 4.11:

```
=SQRT(SUMXMY2(C4:C17,D4:D17)/14)
```

The fragment SUMXMY2(C4:C17,D4:D17) takes care of steps 1 through 3. Of course, the values themselves are in C4:C17 and the mean of the values is in D4:D17 after Solver has minimized RMSE. Dividing by 14 is step 4, and the SQRT function is step 5.

One of the reasons that statistical analysis relies so heavily on the mean and the standard deviation (and its close cousin the variance, which is the square of the standard deviation) is that the mean minimizes the squared differences from a value in a population. That is, if you subtract the mean from each value, square the differences, and total them, the result is smaller than if you subtracted *any other value* from each of the observed values.

> **NOTE** This characteristic of the mean and the variance leads to the term *least squares* in regression analysis, the analysis of variance, and any other statistical technique based on the general linear model. It is intimately related to the notion of and rationale for degrees of freedom. I discuss these concepts in greater detail in *Statistical Analysis: Microsoft Excel 2013* (Que, 2013).

Therefore, the RMSE (in this context, that's just another name for standard deviation) can take on a minimum value only when the number that's subtracted from each of the observations is precisely the mean of those observations. As it iterates through possible solutions to this problem, Solver (or any other well designed and implemented optimization routine) eventually reaches two conditions:

- Alpha, the smoothing constant, is tentatively set to zero. Due to the way in which the smoothing formula is constructed, this causes all the forecasts to equal the first forecast.
- The first "forecast," the value in cell D3 of Figure 4.11, is set tentatively to 66.714. As it happens, that value is the mean of the original observations, and therefore satisfies the criterion of minimizing the sum of its squared differences with each of the original observations.

And when I wrote "as it happens" in the preceding paragraph, that's exactly what I meant. You have not set Solver the task of calculating a standard deviation, nor of calculating the mean of the actual observations. You have set it the task of minimizing the RMSE and, as it happens, you minimize the RMSE only when the forecasts are a single constant value and when that value is the mean of the actuals. For Alpha, the smoothing constant, to equal zero is one precondition to minimizing RMSE in this case. The other precondition is for the Period 0 forecast to equal the mean of the actuals.

> **NOTE** Another way of thinking about the fact that the standard deviation of the actual observations equals the RMSE is to note that when Alpha is zero, all the forecasts are constant—in this case, 66.714. When you subtract a constant from each value in a set of observations, the standard deviation of the resulting values is precisely the same as the standard deviation of the original values.

This stuff is not perfectly intuitive. But if you work and think your way through it a time or two, I think you'll find that, like ghee, it clarifies nicely. A good test of your grasp of this material is to ask yourself whether it matters if you include cell C3 along with D3 and Alpha in Solver's Variable cells, and if so, why? Or if not, why not?

Initial Forecasts with Holt's Method

Matters are similar if you optimize smoothing constants and initial forecasts for a time series with trend. Recall from Chapter 3 that one of your options with a trended time series is to use Holt's method, in which you smooth both the level of the series and its trend (also known as *slope*) from period to period.

You use one smoothing constant, Alpha, for the level and a different one, Gamma, for the trend. The issues pertaining to optimizing the smoothing constants for a trended series are similar to the issues involved with simple smoothing and stationary series. Chapter 3 discusses them.

The issues involved in optimizing the initial forecasts for both the series' level and its trend are also similar to those involved with the initial forecast for a stationary series, discussed in the preceding section.

> **NOTE**
>
> This section includes an example for you to use, so that if you wish you can try out Holt's method in the context of optimized initial forecasts. When, as here, you have four variable or changing cells (level forecast, Alpha, trend forecast, and Gamma), Solver can take much longer than you might expect to reach a solution. For example, on a one-year-old, not especially swift laptop, it took more than two hours for the example to complete its run—just so you know.
>
> I'm sure that I could have speeded things up with Solver's options, by adjusting the convergence and constraint precision or by limiting the number of subproblems, and I suppose I should do so. But I'm supposed to be writing a book, not benchmarking software.

Figure 4.12 has the skeleton for the analysis, along with a trended data series.

With a worksheet that looks like Figure 4.12 active, take these steps:

1. Establish the range name Alpha to refer to cell I1 and Gamma to refer to cell I2. You can use the Formula bar's Name box if you want to scope the names to the entire workbook. Or you can use the Define Name tool on the Formulas tab if you want to restrict the names' scope to a specific worksheet.

2. Enter 0.0 in cell D2, to establish a starting point for Solver's search for a Period 0 level.

3. Enter 0.0 in cell E2, as a starting point for the trend.

4. Enter this formula in cell F2, to return the forecast for Period 1 as of Period 0:
   ```
   =D2+E2
   ```
   It's not strictly necessary to display the forecast in both row 2 and row 3, but doing so helps clarify when each forecast can be made and which period the forecast applies to.

5. Enter the following formula in cell C3:
   ```
   =F2
   ```

Figure 4.12
Compared to simple smoothing, a trended series needs an additional column and an additional smoothing constant.

	A	B	C	D	E	F	G	H	I
		Observed, Trended Series	Forecast of Current Period	Forecast Level	Forecast Trend	Forecast of Next Period			
1	Period							Alpha:	
2	0							Gamma:	
3	1	262						RMSE:	
4	2	253							
5	3	293							
6	4	381							
7	5	439							
8	6	392							
9	7	407							
10	8	432							
11	9	444							
12	10	405							
13	11	586							
14	12	617							
15	13	638							
16	14	571							
17	15	644							
18	16	785							
19	17	837							
20	18	622							
21	19	855							
22	20	962							

Entering that formula in cell C3 helps to show that the forecast can be made at the end of Period 0 and that the forecast value pertains to Period 1.

6. Here's the formula for cell D3:

```
=Alpha*B3+(1-Alpha)*C3
```

This formula estimates the *level* portion of the next forecast. You can recognize it as the level smoothing constant Alpha times the current actual observation for Period 1, plus (1 – Alpha) times the prior forecast of the current period.

7. Enter this formula in cell E3:

```
=Gamma*(D3-D2)+(1-Gamma)*E2
```

The formula estimates the *trend* portion of the next forecast. Multiply the current trend (the current level in D3 less the prior level in D2) by the trend smoothing constant Gamma. Add to that quantity the product of (1 – Gamma) and the prior forecast trend of the current period.

8. The forecast for the next period is the total of its forecast level and its forecast trend. In cell F3, add them together with this formula:

```
=D3+E3
```

9. Make a multiple selection of C3:F3. Drag it down into, for this example, C22:F22. If you want to establish all the formulas for the first true forecast, drag the multiple selection down through C23:F23.

10. Enter the value 0.5 in cell I1.

11. Enter the value 0.5 in cell I2.

12. Enter this formula in cell I3:

```
=SQRT(SUMXMY2(B3:B22,C3:C22)/20)
```

Be sure to adjust the two range addresses and the divisor of 20 if you supply a longer or shorter time series in column B.

Your worksheet should now have the entries shown in Figure 4.13.

Figure 4.13
Solver can report your starting values for Objective and Variable cells, so you need not record them separately.

	A	B	C	D	E	F	G	H	I
		Observed, Trended Series	Forecast of Current Period	Forecast Level	Forecast Trend	Forecast of Next Period			
1	Period							Alpha:	0.5
2	0			0.0	0.0	0.0		Gamma:	0.5
3	1	262	0.0	131.0	65.5	196.5		RMSE:	113.2196
4	2	253	196.5	224.8	79.6	304.4			
5	3	293	304.4	298.7	76.8	375.5			
6	4	381	375.5	378.2	78.2	456.4			
7	5	439	456.4	447.7	73.8	521.5			
8	6	392	521.5	456.8	41.4	498.2			
9	7	407	498.2	452.6	18.6	471.2			
10	8	432	471.2	451.6	8.8	460.4			
11	9	444	460.4	452.2	4.7	456.9			
12	10	405	456.9	431.0	-8.3	422.7			
13	11	586	422.7	504.4	32.6	536.9			
14	12	617	536.9	577.0	52.6	629.5			
15	13	638	629.5	633.8	54.7	688.5			
16	14	571	688.5	629.7	25.3	655.1			
17	15	644	655.1	649.5	22.6	672.1			
18	16	785	672.1	728.5	50.8	779.3			
19	17	837	779.3	808.2	65.2	873.4			
20	18	622	873.4	747.7	2.4	750.1			
21	19	855	750.1	802.5	28.6	831.1			
22	20	962	831.1	896.6	61.3	957.9			

The formula bar shows: I3 =SQRT(SUMXMY2(B3:B22,C3:C22)/20)

Click Solver in the Data tab's Analysis group. Make entries in the Solver Parameters dialog box as shown in Figure 4.14.

Click Options. You can accept the defaults on the All Methods tab of the Options dialog box, but you should make sure that the GRG Nonlinear tab appears as in Figure 4.15.

Click OK to return to Solver Parameters, and then click Solve to start Solver.

> **NOTE**
> If you run out of patience, your keyboard's Esc key is a reliable way to stop Solver's execution and exit to the main Excel interface in an orderly way.

Figure 4.14
Constraints on the initial forecasts are not absolutely necessary but might help speed the solution.

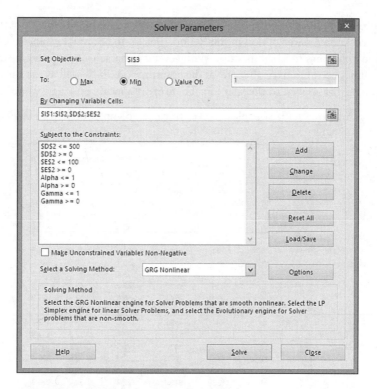

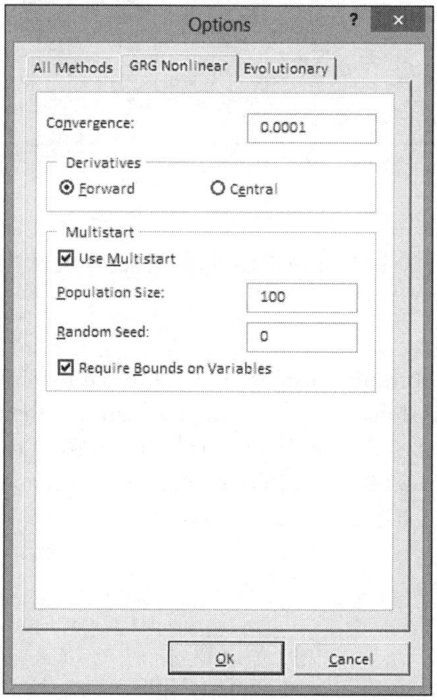

Figure 4.15
The Population Size criterion refers to the number of starting points that the Multistart option will use.

I recommend that when Solver is done—and that might possibly be tomorrow morning—you click the Answer option in the Reports box on the Solver Results dialog box that appears when Solver has finished its work. With several Variable cells and an Objective cell to worry about, it's useful to have a record of their starting values, as well as the values of Solver's Options that applied to the solution. That report appears on a new worksheet.

The results you get if you allow Solver to run to completion appear in Figure 4.16.

Figure 4.16
Notice that Solver has set Alpha to zero.

	I3	▼	:	×	✓	fx	=SQRT(SUMXMY2(B3:B35,C3:C35)/20)		
▲	A	B	C	D	E	F	G	H	I
1	Period	Observed, Trended Series	Forecast of Current Period	Forecast Level	Forecast Trend	Forecast of Next Period		Alpha:	0
2	0			199.0	32.6	231.6		Gamma:	0.827081
3	1	262	231.6	231.6	32.6	264.2		RMSE	67.10504
4	2	253	264.2	264.2	32.6	296.8			
5	3	293	296.8	296.8	32.6	329.4			
6	4	381	329.4	329.4	32.6	362.0			
7	5	439	362.0	362.0	32.6	394.6			
8	6	392	394.6	394.6	32.6	427.2			
9	7	407	427.2	427.2	32.6	459.8			
10	8	432	459.8	459.8	32.6	492.4			
11	9	444	492.4	492.4	32.6	525.0			
12	10	405	525.0	525.0	32.6	557.5			
13	11	586	557.5	557.5	32.6	590.1			
14	12	617	590.1	590.1	32.6	622.7			
15	13	638	622.7	622.7	32.6	655.3			
16	14	571	655.3	655.3	32.6	687.9			
17	15	644	687.9	687.9	32.6	720.5			
18	16	785	720.5	720.5	32.6	753.1			
19	17	837	753.1	753.1	32.6	785.7			
20	18	622	785.7	785.7	32.6	818.3			
21	19	855	818.3	818.3	32.6	850.9			
22	20	962	850.9	850.9	32.6	883.5			

There are several points of interest in Figure 4.16 that I discuss next.

Alpha Is Zero

In the process of setting the smoothing constants and the initial forecasts to values that minimize RMSE, Solver has set Alpha, the smoothing constant for the time series' level, to zero. I discussed the implications of that setting in earlier sections of this chapter, but here's how it applies to a trended time series with Holt's method. One version of the Holt formula for level as it was introduced in Chapter 3 is this:

$$\hat{l}_t = \alpha y_t + (1 - \alpha)\left(\hat{l}_{t-1} + \hat{b}_{t-1}\right)$$

So, for example, the level for Period 5 is estimated as Alpha times the observation at Period 5, plus (1 – Alpha) times the forecast of Period 5 at Period 4. The forecast of Period 5 is the sum of the estimated level ($\hat{l}_{t-1}$) and the estimated trend ($\hat{b}_{t-1}$), both for Period 4. (Compare this general formula with the specific version in cell D7 of Figure 4.16.)

If Alpha is zero, the general formula reduces to this:

$$\hat{l}_t = (1 - \alpha)(\hat{l}_{t-1} + \hat{b}_{t-1})$$

And, even more simply, to this:

$$\hat{l}_t = \hat{l}_{t-1} + \hat{b}_{t-1}$$

That is, when Alpha equals zero, each level forecast equals the prior series forecast. And because the prior series forecast is simply the sum of the prior level and the prior trend, the only figure that causes the forecast level to change from period to period is the associated trend.

Gamma Is Irrelevant

Again, recall that the general formula for the trend forecast is as follows:

$$\hat{b}_t = \gamma(\hat{l}_t - \hat{l}_{t-1}) + (1 - \gamma)\hat{b}_{t-1}$$

As expressed on the worksheet for the trend forecast made in Period 1, the general formula works out to this Excel formula (see cell E3 in Figure 4.16):

```
=Gamma*(D3-D2)+(1-Gamma)*E2
```

In Figure 4.16, Solver has assigned the value 32.6 to the trend at Period 0. The forecast for Period 1 is just the Period 0 level plus the Period 0 trend. The formula for the trend forecast subtracts the level for Period 0 from the level for Period 1, and the result is precisely the trend forecast at Period 0, which is 32.6. So, when Alpha is zero, the difference between two consecutive level forecasts, such as D2 and D3, must always be precisely the value in E2, the optimized forecast of initial trend.

Tautologically, then, the formula for the forecast trend—again, given that Alpha is zero—must result in a constant value throughout the periods. The trend is calculated from the difference between two consecutive levels, and the difference between the levels is determined by the trend. Here, the trend's constant value is 32.6.

And the value of Gamma, given that it's between 0.0 and 1.0, therefore becomes irrelevant. Suppose that Solver decides that the optimum Gamma is 0.25. Then the Excel formula for the Gamma forecast is as follows:

```
= .25 * 36.2 + .75 * 36.2
```

Or, if Gamma is 0.4, then the forecast is this

```
= 0.4 * 36.2 + 0.6 * 36.2
```

No matter Gamma's value, the forecast trend is the same throughout the time series—again, given that Alpha is zero.

Bear in mind that this situation results from the way in which Holt's method behaves when Alpha equals 0. It's not directly due to the way in which the forecast is initialized. Nevertheless, the situation inevitably arises if the initialization method—here, optimization—used for the constants and for the forecast results in an Alpha of 0.

Optimizing Initial Forecasts Equals Linear Regression

In Figure 14.17 I have added an instance of LINEST() to the results of Holt's method.

Figure 4.17
The coefficient and the intercept from regression analysis equal the optimized trend and level from Holt's method.

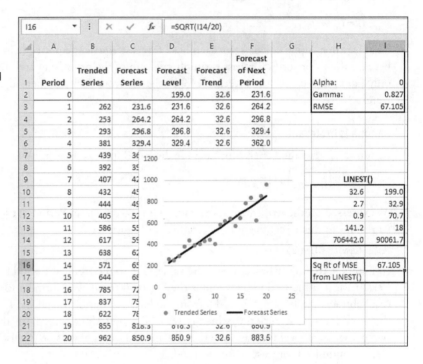

The LINEST() function is how Excel returns an analysis of the relationship between a predicted variable (here, the time series itself in column B of Figure 4.17) and a predictor variable (here, the numbered periods in column A). The function must be array-entered with Ctrl+Shift+Enter if it is to return the full set of possible results in a worksheet range.

In Figure 4.17, the LINEST() function returns the regression coefficient in cell H10, and the regression intercept in cell I10. You use those two statistics to predict, or forecast, a value of the outcome variable from a value of the predictor variable. At Period 1, then, the regression equation would be as follows:

= 199.0 + (36.2 * 1)

At Period 2, the regression equation would be this:

= 199.0 + (36.2 * 2)

And so on through, if you want, Period 100. Notice that—again, when Alpha equals 0—the regression intercept of 199.0 equals the initial level estimate, as selected by Solver in the context of Holt's smoothing method as applied to this data set. And the regression coefficient of 36.2 equals the initial trend estimate, also as selected by Solver when it optimized the constants and initial forecasts for this data.

Understanding the Relationship Between Holt's Method and Linear Regression

One of the characteristics of linear regression analysis via least squares is that the regression equation minimizes the sum of the squared differences between the actual and the predicted observations. Those predicted observations describe a straight line in ordinary linear regression. Linear regression analysis calculates the elevation (also known as the *constant* or *intercept*) and the slope of that straight line, and is able to report, very quickly, the intercept and slope of the line that minimizes the sum of the squared differences. If the calculated regression line has an intercept of, say, 10 and a slope of 2, *no other straight line*, with a different slope or different intercept, can return a smaller sum of squared distances between the observed data points and the regression line.

I have included a chart in Figure 4.17 showing both the actual observations in the time series and the associated values forecast using Holt's method, with both the smoothing constants and the initial forecasts optimized by Solver. Notice that the line described by the forecasts is perfectly straight. Furthermore, if you were to right-click on one of the chart's actual observations and choose to add a linear trendline to the chart, you would find that the trendline appears in precisely the same location as the charted forecasts.

> **NOTE** "Trendline" is Excel's term for the more typical term "regression line."

Suppose that, under Holt's method, you use Solver to optimize the values of Alpha, Gamma, and the two initial estimates of the level and trend. Suppose further that, when it finds that it has minimized the RMSE, Solver returns a value of zero for Alpha. As you've seen, that outcome returns forecasts that describe a straight (and horizontal) line.

That's *precisely* what linear regression analysis does—again, via a different route, by minimizing the sum of the squared differences between the actual observations and the regression line (also called the *line of best fit*).

So it might seem that there's little point to using Solver, or any other optimization engine, to determine the best values for the initial forecasts of the level and the trend. You can get there lots faster by using regression analysis, and in the context of Excel that means using LINEST() or, if all you're after is the forecasts, TREND(). After using regression to determine the best initial forecasts, you can deploy Solver to get the best values of the smoothing constant(s).

> **NOTE** This outcome—that is, the equivalent results of using Solver and of using `LINEST()`—is largely due to the use of RMSE as the measure of the accuracy of the forecasts. As I've illustrated them in this chapter, both methods seek to minimize the sum of the squared deviations of the forecasts from the actuals. That is the standard way to quantify the accuracy of the forecasts, but it's not the only way. Other measures include the mean absolute deviation (MAD) and the mean absolute percent error (MAPE). Because these are very different measures of goodness of fit, it is highly unlikely that using them along with Solver would produce the same results as using RMSE—or, as you've seen, using least squares regression.

Except that's true only if Alpha equals zero. What if the optimization process, when used with both smoothing constants *and* the initial forecast estimates, manages to get RMSE *below* what regression analysis would return? That can happen if the best fit regression line turns out to be curved instead of straight.

If Alpha is nonzero, the value of Gamma becomes relevant once again (refer to the prior section titled "Gamma Is Irrelevant"). If so, the trendline described by the forecasts might be curved. Because the curved line minimizes the RMSE, a straight line cannot do so, and a straight line is what basic linear regression gets you.

> **NOTE** Multiple regression can get you a curved regression line. This is typically done by raising the predictor variable to a series of powers and using the results to augment the original set of predictors. So in addition to a column of X values as predictors of a column of Y values, you also supply X^2, X^3, and so on as additional predictors. So doing normally results in a curved line of best fit. See the "Initializing with Regression" section later in this chapter for an example.

Therefore it's a good idea to at least eyeball your observations in a chart that shows the observations against the period number. Figure 4.18 has an example.

In Figure 4.18, the actual values suggest not the straight line of the sort shown in Figure 4.17, but a curved line that rises steeply before tailing off beginning at Period 13.

> **NOTE** I have included a second order regression trendline, indicated by a series of dots, in Figure 4.18 to indicate the general form of the curve of the actuals. A second order polynomial includes both the original predictor and the square of that predictor. This formula, array-entered in an 18-row by 1-column range, would return to the worksheet the values that define the trendline:
>
> `=TREND(B3:B20,A3:A20^{1,2})`

The fact that the actual values roughly describe a curve means that the straight regression line calculated by `LINEST()` cannot minimize the squared differences as much as they're minimized by Holt's method.

Figure 4.18
With this curvilinear time series, Solver returns a nonzero value for Alpha.

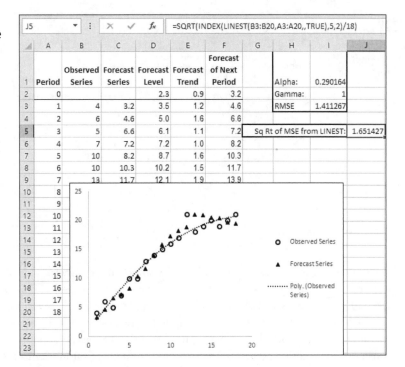

Notice that Solver minimizes RMSE to a value of 1.411, as shown in cell I3. Figure 4.18 also shows in cell J5 the square root of the result of dividing the number of observations into the error sum of squares from LINEST(). This was also done in Figure 4.17, cell I12; there, regression and Holt's method with optimization agreed on the amount of error in prediction, 67.105.

In contrast, in Figure 4.18, the RMSE of 1.411 is smaller than that returned by linear regression, 1.651. The linear regression approach is limited by the straight regression line and cannot get the sum of the squared errors smaller than Holt's method can, with its curved line of forecasts.

Finally, Figure 4.19 shows how optimizing the initial forecasts as well as the smoothing constants can return a more accurate overall forecast than optimizing only the smoothing constants (given that the actual observations follow a curved path rather than a straight line).

Compare the inputs and outcomes in Figure 4.19 with those in Figure 4.18. The actual observations are the same in both cases. The initial forecasts in Figure 4.18 were generated using Solver. The initial forecasts in Figure 4.19 were initialized by one of the simple methods described at the beginning of this chapter: The first forecast level is taken to be equal to the first actual observation, and the first forecast trend is taken to be zero. After those initial forecasts were set, Alpha and Gamma were optimized with Solver so as to minimize RMSE.

Figure 4.19
Optimized initial forecasts can be an improvement over other methods of initializing the forecasts.

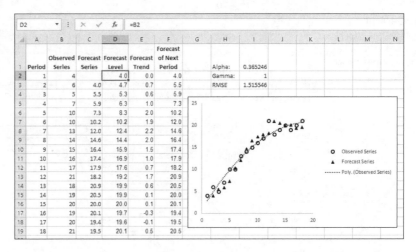

Period	Observed Series	Forecast Series	Forecast Level	Forecast Trend	Forecast of Next Period
1	4		4.0	0.0	4.0
2	6	4.0	4.7	0.7	5.5
3	5	5.5	5.3	0.6	5.9
4	7	5.9	6.3	1.0	7.3
5	10	7.3	8.3	2.0	10.2
6	10	10.2	10.2	1.9	12.0
7	13	12.0	12.4	2.2	14.6
8	14	14.6	14.4	2.0	16.4
9	15	16.4	15.9	1.5	17.4
10	16	17.4	16.9	1.0	17.9
11	17	17.9	17.6	0.7	18.2
12	21	18.2	19.2	1.7	20.9
13	18	20.9	19.9	0.6	20.5
14	19	20.5	19.9	0.1	20.0
15	20	20.0	20.0	0.1	20.1
16	19	20.1	19.7	-0.3	19.4
17	20	19.4	19.6	-0.1	19.5
18	21	19.5	20.1	0.5	20.5

Alpha: 0.365246
Gamma: 1
RMSE 1.515546

In Figure 4.18, as already discussed, both the smoothing constants and the initial forecasts were optimized using Solver. The RMSE is smaller in Figure 4.18. The forecast for Period 18 is 20.1 in Figure 4.18 (where it's obscured by the chart) and 20.5 in Figure 4.19. It's for you to decide whether those are meaningful differences, but it's clear that by the RMSE criterion, optimizing both the constants and the initial forecasts is superior to optimizing the constants only—at least when the actuals describe a curve rather than a straight line.

About Multistart and Solver

Multistart is an option that was introduced in the Excel Solver in Excel 2010. It applies to the GRG Nonlinear solution, which is the method that most users of Excel's Solver prefer for problems that involve a nonlinear relationship between the values of the Variable cells and those of the Objective cell.

If you choose the Multistart option, Solver begins by selecting several points along the continuum described by the Variable cells—in the context of Holt's method, the Variable cells are often the smoothing constants and could include the initial estimates of the level and trend forecasts. Solver then moves up and down the continuum seeking a better outcome in the Objective cell—as discussed in this chapter, that's the RMSE. For example, moving in one direction from a particular location on that continuum might mean increasing the value of the level smoothing constant, with some consequence for the RMSE.

If the continuum isn't a perfectly smooth one, Solver could be fooled if it started its search at one location only. If Solver searched up the continuum without improving the Objective cell, and got the same result when it looked down the continuum, it might decide that it couldn't improve on the current location and that the Variable cells were therefore optimized.

However, starting at a different location might bring about a very different result. What if the actual starting location is at the bottom of a local valley along the continuum? Suppose you were mysteriously plucked from your chair and deposited in the middle of Aspen, Colorado. You would look around, would see that you were surrounded by mountains, and might conclude that you were at the lowest point available. In fact, your elevation is 8,000 feet, and if you climbed one of those fourteeners you could head down to sea level. But because you don't have a Multistart option, you have no way of finding that out. You're stuck there in Aspen at 8,000 feet, and you can't peer over the mountaintops to see that you could minimize your altitude by using some other starting point.

The Multistart option tends to help Solver avoid this sort of problem, particularly if you're in a position to establish bounds (also termed *constraints* in the Solver Parameters dialog box) on the Variable cells. If Solver looks in one location for a best solution, then skips to another point and checks there, and then tries yet another, it's less likely to get trapped into a solution that's best locally but not best globally. It's less likely to get stuck at 8,000 feet in Aspen when sea level in San Francisco is just beyond the next mountain.

A brief complaint about terminology: When, at the end of a search, Solver reports that it "has converged in probability to a global solution," it means nothing of the sort. It means that the solution it has reached is the best of the local solutions it found.

I can't help saying that I have a lot more respect for Solver itself than I do for the way its developers express themselves.

Initializing with Regression

Holt theorists aren't through with you yet. Another approach to initializing the forecasts is via regression. At least one well-known writer on the topic suggests regressing the actuals onto the number of the time period. Then take the resulting intercept and slope from the regression equation and use them as the initial forecasts for the level and the trend, respectively.

The first time I read that suggestion it struck me as eminently sensible. Then I realized that I'd been there and done that. So have you. It's simply what's illustrated in Figure 4.17 from a different point of view, and also as discussed briefly in an earlier section of this chapter, "Optimizing Initial Forecasts Equals Linear Regression."

I grant that it can be a lot faster to get to the optimized initial forecasts using a regression analysis than by way of optimization's trial and error. And there might be nothing wrong with that approach, depending on the nature of your data. As Figure 4.17 shows, with a straight regression line and an Alpha of 0.0, you can initialize the forecasts to the same values as by using Solver to optimize them. In that figure, compare cells D2 and I10, and cells E2 and H10.

Arranging for Curvilinear Regression

But what if you have a curved, rather than a straight-line, time series to work with? See Figure 4.20.

Figure 4.20
This is the same time series as in Figure 4.17, with the last few observations altered to bend the line down.

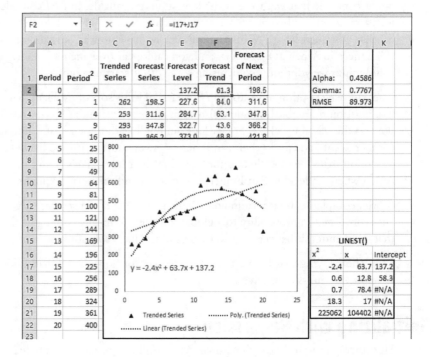

To alter the nature of the time series shown in Figure 4.17, I have reduced the values of the final five observations. With that change, a straight regression line is no longer adequate to describe the observed data. You need a curved regression line instead.

In Figure 4.20, I show that distinction with the two charted trendlines, each represented by a sequence of dots. The straight trendline is the standard linear trendline, the default when you tell Excel to insert a trendline in a chart. The curved trendline is a "second order polynomial" trendline—that is, it regresses the predicted variable against the combination of the predictor variable and the predictor variable raised to the second power.

Notice that the curved polynomial trendline appears to do a better job of representing the actual values (shown as triangular markers) than does the linear trendline.

You can call for the trendline by charting the predicted variable (the values in the range C3:C22) against the predictor variable (the values in the range A3:A22). Then right-click the charted data series and choose Add Trendline from the shortcut menu. A Format Trendline dialog box appears, with the Trendline Options pane visible. Choose Linear to get the linear trendline; to get the curved, quadratic trendline, choose Polynomial and set the Order to 2.

Also notice the LINEST() function in the range I17:K21 of Figure 4.20. The figures in its first row are, reading left to right, the regression equation's coefficient for the squared Period number, then for the Period number itself, and then the regression equation's intercept.

> **NOTE** Keep in mind that LINEST() unaccountably returns the regression coefficients in reverse of the order in which they're found on the worksheet. If X is to the *left* of X^2 on the worksheet, then X is to the *right* of X^2 in the LINEST() results. The intercept is always to the right of the coefficients in the array of results.

Following the notion of using the intercept as the initial level estimate in Holt's method, you'll see that the value in cell K17 is identical to the value in cell E2.

> **NOTE** It can help to bear in mind that the regression equation's intercept (here, 137.2) identifies the value where the regression line crosses the vertical Y axis. Notice from the chart in Figure 4.20 that the curved, polynomial trendline would cross the Y axis at about 137. And the Y axis crosses the X axis at Period 0—precisely the period during which we're calculating a level forecast for Period 1.

Further, the value in cell F2, the initial trend forecast of 61.3, is equal to the sum of the regression coefficients in cells I17 and J17.

Deriving the Regression Equation

As the prior section noted, to create the polynomial regression line or equation, you need to add at least one variable: the square of the original predictor variable. Adding its square gets you to a quadratic trend, adding its cube gets you a cubic trend, and so on. (I've seldom found that I need more than the quadratic trend, but it does happen.)

One way to get a polynomial trendline and equation is with the chart, and by requesting that Excel display the equation on the chart. When you do so, Excel automatically generates the additional predictor variable or variables. In the case of the second order polynomial, just the one additional variable, the square of the original predictor, is needed. When you call for the polynomial equation to be displayed on the chart, you need not provide it explicitly on the worksheet. Excel handles that in the background.

It usually happens, though, that you want more information about the regression equation than just the regression coefficients and intercept in the form of a chart label. In that case, the best approach is to create the additional predictor variable explicitly on the worksheet and use it, plus the original predictor and the predicted variable, as inputs to LINEST()

to get the regression equation. You can also use those variables in conjunction with the TREND() function to get the predicted values. See Figure 4.21.

Figure 4.21
The TREND() function helps you save a step in calculating the predicted values.

M3			×	✓	ƒx	{=TREND(C3:C22,A3:A22^{1,2})}						

	A	B	C	D	E	F	G	H	I	J	K	L	M
1	Period	Period^2	Trended Series	Forecast Series	Forecast Level	Forecast Trend	Forecast of Next Period		Alpha:	0.4586			TREND() Function
2	0	0			137.2	61.3	198.5		Gamma:	0.7767			
3	1	1	262	198.5	227.6	84.0	311.6		RMSE	89.973			198.5
4	2	4	253	311.6	284.7	63.1	347.8						255.1
5	3	9	293	347.8	322.7	43.6	366.2			LINEST()			306.9
6	4	16	381	366.2	373.0	48.8	421.8		-2.4	63.7	137.2		354.0
7	5	25	439	421.8	429.7	54.9	484.6		0.6	12.8	58.3		396.3
8	6	36	392	484.6	442.2	21.9	464.1		0.7	78.4	#N/A		433.8
9	7	49	407	464.1	437.9	1.6	439.5		18.3	17	#N/A		466.6
10	8	64	432	439.5	436.1	-1.1	435.0		225062.1	104401.6	#N/A		494.7
11	9	81	444	435.0	439.1	2.1	441.3						517.9
12	10	100	405	441.3	424.6	-10.8	413.8						536.4
13	11	121	586	413.8	492.8	50.5	543.3						550.2
14	12	144	617	543.3	577.1	76.8	653.9						559.1
15	13	169	638	653.9	646.6	71.1	717.7						563.4
16	14	196	571	717.7	650.4	18.9	669.3						562.8
17	15	225	644	669.3	657.7	9.8	667.5						557.5
18	16	256	685	667.5	675.6	16.1	691.6						547.5
19	17	289	537	691.6	620.7	-39.0	581.7						532.7
20	18	324	422	581.7	508.5	-95.9	412.6						513.1
21	19	361	555	412.6	477.9	-45.2	432.7						488.7
22	20	400	332	432.7	386.5	-81.0	305.5						459.6

Notice first that Figure 4.21, like Figure 4.20, adds a variable to the original predictor in column A; the values in column B are the squares of the values in column A. So both predictors are present on the worksheet.

The LINEST() function in the range I6:K10 (as well as the instance of LINEST() in I17:K21 of Figure 4.20) takes advantage of the additional variable as a predictor. To enter it requires only three steps:

1. Select a five-row, three-column range such as I6:K10.
2. Type, but do not enter as yet, this formula:

   =LINEST(C3:C22,A3:B22,,TRUE)

   (Notice that the second argument, the X values, now specifies columns A *and* B.)
3. Array-enter the formula by holding down Ctrl and Shift as you press Enter.

Notice that the result array has three columns, not two, so as to accommodate the second predictor variable.

You can use the results in I6:K6 to calculate what a polynomial regression equation predicts as the result for each individual value of Period. To get the prediction for the third time period, for example, you could use this equation:

   =K6+J6*A5+I6*B5

In words, that equation adds the intercept (K6) to the regression coefficient for Period (J6) times Period (A5), and then adds the regression coefficient for Period Squared (I6) times Period Squared (B5). The result, 306.9, is what the polynomial regression (*not* Holt's method) would predict for this time series at the third time period.

> **NOTE**
>
> You could be less explicit and avoid entering the square of the Period number on the worksheet. Instead, use Excel's array constant capability in your LINEST() function's arguments. In the second step of the prior list, use this formula instead of the one given:
>
> =LINEST(C3:C22,A3:A22^{1,2},,TRUE)
>
> The string ^{1,2} tells Excel to raise the values in A3:A22 to the first power, and to create (in memory, not on the worksheet) an adjacent column vector with the squares of the values in A3:A22.

Also as in Figure 4.21, you can get the actual predicted values for the polynomial prediction by using the TREND() function. LINEST() and TREND() are closely related, but are not quite the same. LINEST() returns the regression equation's intercept and coefficients so that you can apply them to the underlying data to get actual predictions. It also returns summary information about applying the equation, such as R^2, the F ratio, and sums of squares.

In contrast, TREND() returns only the results of applying the equation to the underlying data—in other words, the predictions themselves. With those in hand, you can compare and contrast regression forecasts with those from smoothing. In Figure 4.21, the TREND() results are returned with these steps:

1. Select the range M3:M22.
2. Type this formula:

   =TREND(C3:C22,A3:B22)

   Or, if you prefer to use the array constant, use this formula:

   =TREND(C3:C22,A3:A22^{1,2})

3. Array-enter the formula with Ctrl+Shift+Enter.

Confirming the Regression Equation

If you want it, Excel will display on the chart the equation that's behind the polynomial trendline. At the bottom of the Trendline Options pane is a Display Equation on Chart check box. Fill it to see the equation on the chart. To see it properly, you might have to click and drag the equation, which is really just a label, to an empty section of the chart's plot area.

The predictor variable in this sort of situation is frequently, but not always, a set of sequential integers that identify the time period, such as those in the range A3:A22 in Figure 4.20. On occasion you will find yourself using some other identifier for the time period such as Year (that is, 1980, 1984, and so on). In that case, be sure to have Excel create an XY (Scatter) chart rather than some other type, such as a Line chart.

A Line chart's horizontal axis is a category axis, not a value axis. So when you request a trendline in a Line chart, the values on the horizontal axis, regardless of their appearance as labels on the chart, are treated as 1, 2, 3,..., 9 rather than, for example, 1980, 1984, 1988,..., 2012. That means that the equation as it appears on the chart will differ from the equation as it's returned by LINEST(). That inconsistent outcome has resulted in more ill-informed complaints to web groups about inaccurate polynomial regression in Excel than I care to count; I got to the mid-30s before I sickened of the task.

To avoid the apparent inconsistency, be sure to call for an XY (Scatter) chart rather than a chart with categories on the horizontal axis, such as a Line or a Column chart.

Deciding to Use Polynomial Regression

The entire point of the preceding section, "Initializing with Regression," is to outline the issues that help you decide whether to use regression analysis to calculate initial estimates of forecasts based on Holt's linear smoothing. You have other options, including backcasting and single-point estimates. Your best decision rule concerning how to initialize forecasts in a time series is probably a measure of forecast accuracy such as RMSE.

And the same might be true of choosing between a straight and a quadratic regression line to arrive at initial forecasts. But it can take a while before you get a difference in RMSEs that's large enough, and sufficiently long lasting, to settle confidently on one type of equation in preference to another.

This book largely steers clear of discussing statistical inference. The techniques discussed here tend to be largely nonparametric. But not when it comes to *diagnosing* differential effects. Although I recommend that you resort to statistical inference sparingly in forecasting situations, it can be your best bet for deciding whether to add another variable to a regression equation.

One good way to decide between a straight-line regression and a polynomial such as a quadratic is often termed the *models comparison* approach. Briefly, the idea is to calculate results using a simpler model, and then calculate results using a more complex model. It is then possible to quantify the difference between the two models and compare the difference to a distribution whose characteristics are well understood. That comparison might enable you to judge whether a difference is likely to stand up as more actuals come in.

Suppose that the difference is an unlikely one in the known distribution, and that it's large enough to be unlikely as a random event. In that case we can reject the notions that the more complex model makes no genuine difference to the outcome, and that any observed difference was just sampling error. Instead we can conclude that the more complex model did in fact make a difference and we should use it going forward.

Figure 4.22 shows how this might work out in practice with the data used in Figures 4.20 and 4.21.

Figure 4.22
The range I20:M22 contains an old-style analysis of variance.

I21 f_x =I17-I11

Period	Period²	Trended Series	Forecast Series	Forecast Level	Forecast Trend	Forecast of Next Period		I	J	K	L	M
0	0			137.2	61.3	198.5		Alpha:	0.458559			
1	1	262	198.5	227.6	84.0	311.6		Gamma:	0.776739			
2	4	253	311.6	284.7	63.1	347.8		RMSE	89.97299			
3	9	293	347.8	322.7	43.6	366.2						
4	16	381	366.2	373.0	48.8	421.8		LINEST()				
5	25	439	421.8	429.7	54.9	484.6		13.7	320.4			
6	36	392	484.6	442.2	21.9	464.1		4.1	49.4			
7	49	407	464.1	437.9	1.6	439.5		0.4	106.4			
8	64	432	439.5	436.1	-1.1	435.0		11.1	18			
9	81	444	435.0	439.1	2.1	441.3		125609.7	203854.0			
10	100	405	441.3	424.6	-10.8	413.8						
11	121	586	413.8	492.8	50.5	543.3		-2.4	63.7	137.2		
12	144	617	543.3	577.1	76.8	653.9		0.6	12.8	58.3		
13	169	638	653.9	646.6	71.1	717.7		0.7	78.4	#N/A		
14	196	571	717.7	650.4	18.9	669.3		18.3	17	#N/A		
15	225	644	669.3	657.7	9.8	667.5		225062.1	104401.6	#N/A		
16	256	685	667.5	675.6	16.1	691.6						
17	289	537	691.6	620.7	-39.0	581.7						
18	324	422	581.7	508.5	-95.9	412.6		Sum of Squares	df	Mean Square	F	Prob of F
19	361	555	412.6	477.9	-45.2	432.7		99,452.39	1	99,452.39	16.194	0.001
20	400	332	432.7	386.5	-81.0	305.5		104,401.64	17	6,141.27		

Figure 4.22 contains two instances of LINEST() results: one that uses time period only as a predictor (see the range I7:J11), and one that uses both time period and the square of time period as predictors (see the range I13:K17).

Cell I11 contains the sum of squares due to the regression of the predicted variable on the single predictor variable, Period. This number is a measure of the amount of variation in the predicted variable that can be accounted for by the predictor variable.

Cell I17 contains the sum of squares due to the regression of the predicted variable on both Period and the square of Period. It's a measure of the amount of variability in the predicted variable that the predictor variable together with its square can account for.

If we subtract the value in cell I11 from that in cell I17, we can determine the incremental sum of squares due to adding the second predictor. It is in fact the sum of squares for the second predictor *after* the influence of the first predictor has been accounted for. The result of the subtraction of I11 from I17 is in cell I21.

We have a useful residual sum of squares from the LINEST() analysis in cell J17. It is the appropriate error term to test whether the incremental sum of squares in I21 can be judged a reliable increment—reliable, that is, in the sense of whether we can expect a sizable increment due to the second predictor variable if we repeat this analysis at some future time.

The remainder of the range I20:M22 is the familiar analysis of variance (ANOVA) table. The quadratic source in row 21 has 1 degree of freedom. The error term has 17 degrees of freedom: 20 observations, less 1 for the straight-line predictor, less 1 for the quadratic, less 1 for the grand mean, results in 17 degrees of freedom for the residual. The mean squares are the sums of squares divided by their degrees of freedom, and the F ratio is the ratio of the mean squares.

An F ratio of 16.19 with 1 and 17 degrees of freedom occurs by chance, when the variances of the increment and the residual are equal in the population, less than once in 1,000 samples. You could therefore adopt the hypothesis that the relationship between the predicted variable on one hand and time period and its square on the other is reliable. In that case you can confidently use the quadratic equation to estimate your initial forecasts.

I have used the traditional sums-of-squares approach in this example. Just as a matter of personal preference, I usually work with proportions of variance instead of sums of squares. If you're of a like mind, you could substitute this formula in cell I21:

```
=I15-I9
```

to get the difference between the R^2 values for the two analyses. Then this formula in cell I22

```
=1-I15
```

gives you the proportion of variance in the second model that is residual. The remainder of the analysis is unchanged.

4

Working with Seasonal Time Series

Matters get incrementally more complicated when you have a time series that's characterized in part by seasonality: the tendency of its level to rise and fall in accordance with the passing of the seasons. We use the term *season* in a more general sense than its everyday meaning of the year's four seasons. In the context of predictive analytics, a season can be a day if patterns repeat weekly, or a year in terms of presidential election cycles, or just about anything in between. An eight-hour shift in a hospital can represent a season.

This chapter takes a look at how to decompose a time series so that you can see how its seasonality operates apart from its trend (if any). As you might expect from the material in Chapters 3 and 4, several approaches are available to you.

Simple Seasonal Averages

The use of simple seasonal averages to model a time series can sometimes provide you with a fairly crude model for the data. But the approach pays attention to the seasons in the data set, and it can easily be much more accurate as a forecasting technique than simple exponential smoothing when the seasonality is pronounced. Certainly it serves as a useful introduction to some of the procedures used with time series that are both seasonal *and* trended, so have a look at the example in Figure 5.1.

The data and chart shown in Figure 5.1 represent the average number of daily hits to a website that caters to fans of the National Football League. Each observation in column D represents the average number of hits per day in each of four quarters across a five-year time span.

Figure 5.1
With a horizontal model, simple averages result in forecasts that are no more than seasonal means.

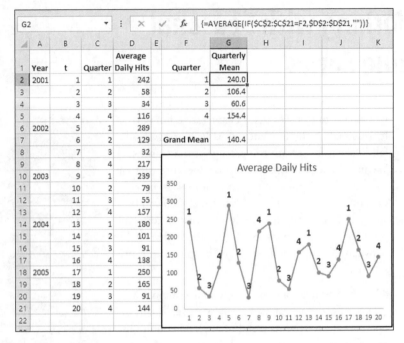

Identifying a Seasonal Pattern

You can tell from the averages in the range G2:G5 that a distinct quarterly effect is taking place. The largest average number of hits occurs during fall and winter, when the main 16 games and the playoffs are scheduled. Interest, as measured by average daily hits, declines during the spring and summer months.

> **NOTE**
>
> The averages are easy to calculate whether or not you feel comfortable with array formulas. To get the mean of all five instances of Quarter 1, for example, you can use this array formula in cell G2 of Figure 5.1:
>
> =AVERAGE(IF($C$2:$C$21=F2,$D$2:$D$21,""))
>
> Array-enter it with Ctrl+Shift+Enter. Or you can use the AVERAGEIF() function,
>
> =AVERAGEIF(C2:C21,F2,D2:D21)
>
> which you can enter in the normal way, pressing the Enter key. In general, I prefer the array formula approach because it gives me scope for greater control over the functions and criteria involved.

The charted data series includes data labels showing which quarter each data point belongs to. The chart echoes the message of the averages in G2:G5: Quarters 1 and 4 repeatedly get the most hits. There's clear seasonality in this data set.

Calculating Seasonal Indexes

After you've decided that a time series has a seasonal component, you'd like to quantify the size of the effect. The averages shown in Figure 5.2 represent how the simple-averages method goes about that task.

Figure 5.2
Combine the grand mean with the seasonal averages to get the seasonal indexes.

	A	B	C	D	E	F	G	H
							f_x	=G2-$G$7
	Year	Quarter	t	Daily Hits		Quarter	Quarterly Mean	
1	2001	1	1	242		1	240.0	
2		2	2	58		2	106.4	
3		3	3	34		3	60.6	Forecasts
4		4	4	116		4	154.4	
5	2002	1	5	289				
6		2	6	129		Grand Mean	140.35	
7		3	7	32				
8		4	8	217		Additive Seasonal Indexes		
9	2003	1	9	239			99.65	
10		2	10	79			-33.95	
11		3	11	55			-79.75	
12		4	12	157			14.05	
13	2004	1	13	180				
14		2	14	101		Seasonally adjusted data for 2005		
15		3	15	91			150.4	
16		4	16	138			199.0	
17	2005	1	17	250			170.8	
18		2	18	165			130.0	
19		3	19	91				
20		4	20	144				

In Figure 5.2, you get additive seasonal indexes in the range G10:G13 by subtracting the grand mean in cell G7 from each seasonal average in G2:G5. The result is the "effect" of being in Quarter 1, that of being in Quarter 2, and so on. If a given month is in Quarter 1, you expect it to have 99.65 more average daily hits than the grand mean of 140.35 hits per day.

This information gives you a sense of how important it is to be in a given season. Suppose that you own the web site in question and you want to sell advertising space on it. You can surely ask a higher price of advertisers during the first and fourth quarters than during the second and third. More to the point, you can likely charge twice as much during the first quarter than during either the second or the third.

With the seasonal indexes in hand, you're also in a position to calculate seasonal adjustments. For example, still in Figure 5.2, the seasonally adjusted values for each quarter in 2005 appear in G16:G19. They're calculated by subtracting the index from the associated quarterly measurement.

5

> **NOTE** Traditionally, the term *seasonal index* refers to the increase or decrease in the level of a series that's associated with each season. The synonymous term *seasonal effect* has appeared in the literature in recent years. Because you'll see both terms, I've used them both in this book. It's a small matter; just bear in mind that the two terms have the same meaning.

Notice that in the normal course of events from 2001 to 2005, you expect the second quarter's results to lag behind the first quarter's results by 133.6 (that is, 99.65 minus –33.95). But in both 2004 and 2005, the seasonally adjusted results for the second quarter exceed those for the first quarter. That outcome might well prompt you to ask what has changed in the final two years that reverses the relationship between the seasonally adjusted results for the first two quarters. (I don't pursue that issue here. I bring it up to suggest that you often want to have a look at both the observed and the seasonally adjusted figures.)

Forecasting from Simple Seasonal Averages: No Trend

Although the method of simple averages is—as I said earlier—crude, it can be much more accurate than the more sophisticated alternative of exponential smoothing, particularly when the seasonal effects are pronounced and reliable.

When the time series is untrended, as is the case with the example this section has discussed, the simple seasonal forecasts are nothing more than the seasonal averages. When the series is not trending either up or down, your best estimate of the value for the next season is that season's historic average. See Figure 5.3.

Figure 5.3
Combine the grand mean with the seasonal averages to get the seasonal indexes.

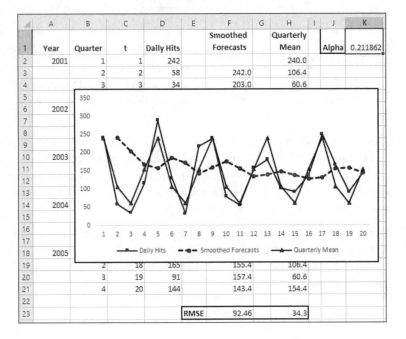

	A	B	C	D	E	F	G	H	I	J	K
1	Year	Quarter	t	Daily Hits		Smoothed Forecasts		Quarterly Mean		Alpha	0.211862
2	2001	1	1	242				240.0			
3		2	2	58		242.0		106.4			
4		3	3	34		203.0		60.6			
5											
6	2002										
7											
8											
9											
10	2003										
11											
12											
13											
14	2004										
15											
16											
17											
18	2005										
19		2	18	165		155.4		106.4			
20		3	19	91		157.4		60.6			
21		4	20	144		143.4		154.4			
22											
23					RMSE	92.46		34.3			

In the chart in Figure 5.3, the dashed line represents the forecasts from simple smoothing. The two solid lines represent the actual seasonal observations and the seasonal averages. Notice that the seasonal averages track the actual seasonal observations quite closely—much more closely than do the smoothed forecasts. You can see how much more closely from the two RMSEs in cells F23 and H23. The RMSE for the seasonal averages is just a little more than a third of the RMSE for the smoothed forecasts.

You can chalk that up to the size of the seasonal effects as well as their consistency:

■ Suppose, for example, that the difference between the average first and second quarters were 35.0 instead of 133.6 (which is the difference between cells G2 and G3 in Figure 5.2). Then, in a smoothing context, the actual value for Quarter 1 would be a much better predictor of the value for Quarter 2 than is the case with this time series. And exponential smoothing can rely heavily on the value of the current observation for its forecast of the next period. If the smoothing constant is set at 1.0, exponential smoothing resolves to naïve forecasting and the forecast always equals the prior actual.

■ The fact that the size of each seasonal swing is so consistent from quarter to quarter means that the simple seasonal averages are reliable forecasts: No actual quarterly observation departs very far from the overall seasonal average.

Simple Seasonal Averages with Trend

The use of simple seasonal averages with a trended series has some real drawbacks, and I'm tempted to suggest that we ignore it and move on to meatier topics. But it's possible that you'll run into situations in which someone has used this method and then it won't hurt to know both how it works and why there are better choices.

Any method of dealing with seasonality in a trended series must deal with the fundamental problem of disentangling the effect of the trend from that of the seasonality. Seasonality tends to obscure trend, and vice versa. See Figure 5.4.

The fact that the trend in the series is upward over time means that simply averaging each season's observations, as was done in the no-trend case, confounds the general trend with the seasonal variation. The usual idea is to account for the trend separately from the seasonal effects. You could quantify the trend and subtract its effect from the observed data. The result is an untrended series that retains the seasonal variation. It could be handled in the same fashion as I illustrated earlier in this chapter.

5

Figure 5.4
The presence of trend complicates the calculation of seasonal effects.

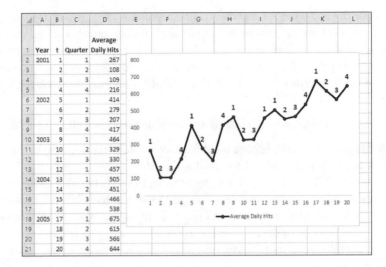

	A	B	C	D	E	F	G	H	I	J	K	L
1	Year	t	Quarter	Average Daily Hits								
2	2001	1	1	267								
3		2	2	108								
4		3	3	109								
5		4	4	216								
6	2002	5	1	414								
7		6	2	279								
8		7	3	207								
9		8	4	417								
10	2003	9	1	464								
11		10	2	329								
12		11	3	330								
13		12	1	457								
14	2004	13	1	505								
15		14	2	451								
16		15	3	466								
17		16	4	538								
18	2005	17	1	675								
19		18	2	615								
20		19	3	566								
21		20	4	644								

Calculating the Mean for Each Year

One way to detrend the data (and other ways will doubtless occur to you) is to calculate the trend based on yearly averages rather than quarterly data. The idea is that the yearly average is insensitive to the seasonal effects. That is, if you subtract a year's mean from the value for each of its quarters, the sum (and thus the average) of the four quarterly effects is precisely zero. So a trend calculated using the yearly averages is unaffected by the seasonal variations. This calculation appears in Figure 5.5.

Figure 5.5
This method now imposes linear regression on the simple averages.

I3   fx   {=LINEST(H3:H7,G3:G7,,TRUE)}

	A	B	C	D	E	F	G	H	I	J
1										
2	Year	t	Quarter	Average Daily Hits		Year	Year Number	Average Daily Hits	LINEST() Function	
3	2001	1	1	267		2001	1	175.00	106.08	84.63
4		2	2	108		2002	2	329.25	7.79	25.84
5		3	3	109		2003	3	395.00	0.98	24.64
6		4	4	216		2004	4	490.00	185.38	3
7	2002	5	1	414		2005	5	625.00	112519.06	1820.89
8		6	2	279						
9		7	3	207				Quarter		
10		8	4	417		Year	1	2	3	4
11	2003	9	1	464		2001	267	108	109	216
12		10	2	329		2002	414	279	207	417
13		11	3	330		2003	464	329	330	457
14		12	4	457		2004	505	451	466	538
15	2004	13	1	505		2005	675	615	566	644
16		14	2	451						
17		15	3	466				Quarterly Adjustments		
18		16	4	538		Mean	465.0	356.4	335.6	454.4
19	2005	17	1	675		Trend	0	26.5	53.0	79.6
20		18	2	615		Adjusted				
21		19	3	566		Mean	465.0	329.9	282.6	374.8
22		20	4	644						
23							Adjusted Grand Mean	363.1		

The first step in detrending the data is to get the average daily hits for each year. That's done in the range H3:H7 in Figure 5.5. The formula in cell H3, for example, is =AVERAGE(D3:D6).

Calculating the Trend Based on Annual Means

With the yearly averages in hand, you're in a position to calculate their trend. That's managed by using LINEST() in the range I3:J7, using this array formula:

```
=LINEST(H3:H7,G3:G7,,TRUE)
```

> **NOTE** If you don't supply x-values as the second argument to LINEST(), Excel supplies default x-values for you. The defaults are simply the consecutive integers beginning with 1 and ending with the number of y-values that you call for in the first argument. In this example, the default x-values are identical to those specified on the worksheet in G3:G7, so you could use =LINEST(H3:H7,,,TRUE). This formula uses two defaults, for the x-values and the constant, represented by the three consecutive commas.

The point of this exercise is to quantify the year-to-year trend, and LINEST() does that for you in cell I3. That cell contains the regression coefficient for the x-values. Multiply 106.08 by 1; then by 2; then by 3, 4, and 5; and add to each result the intercept of 84.63. Although that gets you annual forecasts, the important point for this procedure is the value of the coefficient 106.08, which quantifies the annual trend.

> **NOTE** The step I just discussed is the source of my misgivings about the entire approach that this section describes. You typically have a small number of encompassing periods—in this example, that's years—to run through the regression. Regression's results tend to be terribly unstable when, as here, they're based on a small number of observations. And yet this procedure relies on those results heavily in order to detrend the time series.

Prorating the Trend Across Seasons

The simple-averages method of dealing with a trended, seasonal series such as this one continues by *dividing the trend by the number of periods in the encompassing period* to get a per-period trend. Here, the number of periods per year is four—we're working with quarterly data—so we divide 106.08 by 4 to estimate the trend per quarter at 26.5.

The procedure uses that periodic trend by subtracting it from the average periodic result. The purpose is to remove the effect of the annual trend from the seasonal effects. First, though, we need to calculate the average result across all five years for Period 1, for Period 2 and so on. To do that, it helps to rearrange the list of actual quarterly hits, shown in the range D3:D22 of Figure 5.5, into a matrix of five years by four quarters, shown in the range G11:J15. Notice that the values in that matrix correspond to the list in column D.

With the data arranged in that fashion, it's easy to calculate the average quarterly value across the five years in the data set. That's done in the range G18:J18.

The effect of the trend returned by LINEST() appears in the range G19:J19. The starting value for each year is the observed mean daily hits for the first quarter, so we make no adjustment for the first quarter. One quarter's worth of trend, or 26.5, is subtracted from the second quarter's mean hits, resulting in an adjusted second-quarter value of 329.9 (see cell H21, Figure 5.5). Two quarters' worth of trend, 2 × 26.5 or 53 in cell I19, is subtracted from the third quarter's mean to get an adjusted third-quarter value of 282.6 in cell I21. And similarly for the fourth quarter, subtracting three quarters of trend from 454.4 to get 374.8 in cell J21.

> **NOTE**   Keep in mind that if the trend were down rather than up, as in this example, you would add the periodic trend value to the observed periodic means instead of subtracting it.

Converting the Adjusted Seasonal Means to Seasonal Effects

Per the logic of this method, the values shown in rows 20–21 of Figure 5.5 are the average quarterly results for each of four quarters, with the effect of the general upward trend in the data set removed. (Rows 20 and 21 are merged in columns G through J.) With their trend out of the way, we can convert those figures to estimates of *seasonal effects*: the result of being in the first quarter, in the second quarter, and so on. To get those effects, start by calculating the grand mean of the adjusted quarterly means. That adjusted grand mean appears in cell I23.

The analysis continues in Figure 5.6.

Figure 5.6 repeats the quarterly adjustments and the adjusted grand mean from the bottom of Figure 5.5. They are combined to determine the quarterly indexes (which you can also think of as seasonal effects). For example, the formula in cell D8 is as follows:

```
=D5-$G$5
```

It returns –33.2. That's the effect of being in the second quarter, vis-à-vis the grand mean: With respect to the grand mean, we can expect a result that belongs to the second quarter to fall below the grand mean by 33.2 units.

Figure 5.6
The quarterly effects, or indexes, are used to deseasonalize the observed quarterlies.

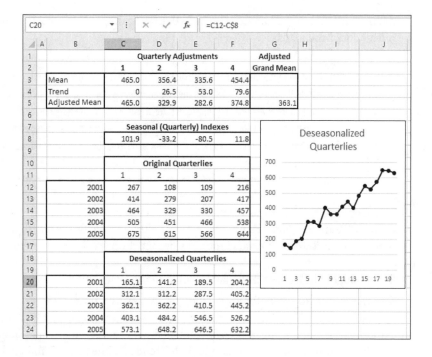

C20		▼	:	✕	✓	f_x	=C12-C$8		

	A	B	C	D	E	F	G	H	I	J
1			Quarterly Adjustments				Adjusted			
2			1	2	3	4	Grand Mean			
3		Mean	465.0	356.4	335.6	454.4				
4		Trend	0	26.5	53.0	79.6				
5		Adjusted Mean	465.0	329.9	282.6	374.8	363.1			
6										
7			Seasonal (Quarterly) Indexes							
8			101.9	-33.2	-80.5	11.8				
9										
10			Original Quarterlies							
11			1	2	3	4				
12		2001	267	108	109	216				
13		2002	414	279	207	417				
14		2003	464	329	330	457				
15		2004	505	451	466	538				
16		2005	675	615	566	644				
17										
18			Deseasonalized Quarterlies							
19			1	2	3	4				
20		2001	165.1	141.2	189.5	204.2				
21		2002	312.1	312.2	287.5	405.2				
22		2003	362.1	362.2	410.5	445.2				
23		2004	403.1	484.2	546.5	526.2				
24		2005	573.1	648.2	646.5	632.2				

Applying the Seasonal Effects to the Observed Quarterlies

To recap: Thus far, we've quantified the annual trend in the data via regression and divided that trend by 4 to prorate it to a quarterly value. Picking up in Figure 5.6, we adjusted the mean for each quarter (in C3:F3) by subtracting the prorated trends in C4:F4. The result is a detrended estimate of the mean for each quarter, regardless of the year in which the quarter takes place, in C5:F5. We subtracted the adjusted grand mean, in cell G5, from the adjusted quarterly means in C5:F5. That converts each quarter's mean to a measure of the effect of each quarter relative to the adjusted grand mean. Those are the seasonal indexes or effects in C8:F8.

Next we remove the seasonal effects from the observed quarterlies. As shown in Figure 5.6, you do so by subtracting the quarterly indexes in C8:F8 from the corresponding values in C12:F16. And the easiest way to do that is to enter this formula in cell C20:

```
=C12-C$8
```

Note the single dollar sign before the 8 in the reference to C$8. That's a mixed reference: partly relative and partly absolute. The dollar sign anchors the reference to the eighth row, but the column portion of the reference is free to vary.

Therefore, after the latter formula is entered in cell C20, you can click on the cell's selection handle (the small square in the lower-right corner of a selected cell) and drag right into cell F20. The addresses adjust as you drag right and you wind up with the values, with the seasonal effects removed, for year 2001 in C20:F20. Select that range of four cells and use the multiple selection's handle, now in F20, to drag down into row 24. So doing fills the remainder of the matrix.

> **NOTE** It's important to bear in mind here that we're adjusting the *original* quarterly values for the seasonal effects. Whatever trend existed in the original values is still there, and—in theory, at least—remains there after we've made the adjustments for seasonal effects. We have removed a trend, yes, but only from the seasonal effects. Thus, when we subtract the (detrended) seasonal effects from the original quarterly observations, the result is the original observations *with* the trend but *without* the seasonal effects.

I have charted those seasonally adjusted values in Figure 5.6. Compare that chart to the chart in Figure 5.4. Notice in Figure 5.6 that although the deseasonalized values do not lie precisely on a straight line, much of the seasonal effect has been removed.

Regressing the Deseasonalized Quarterlies onto the Time Periods

The next step is to create forecasts from the seasonally adjusted, trended data in Figure 5.6, cells C20:F24, and at this point you have several alternatives available. You could use the differencing approach combined with simple exponential smoothing that was discussed in Chapter 3, "Working with Trended Time Series." You could also use Holt's approach to smoothing trended series, discussed in both Chapter 3 and Chapter 4, "Initializing Forecasts." Both methods put you in a position to create a one-step-ahead forecast, to which you would add the corresponding seasonal index.

Another approach, which I'll use here, first puts the trended data through another instance of linear regression and then adds the seasonal index. See Figure 5.7.

Figure 5.7 returns the deseasonalized quarterly means from the tabular arrangement in C20:F24 of Figure 5.6 to the list arrangement in the range C5:C24 of Figure 5.7.

We could use LINEST() in conjunction with the data in B5:C24 in Figure 5.7 to calculate the regression equation's intercept and coefficient; then, we could multiply the coefficient by each value in column B, and add the intercept to each product, to create the forecasts in column D. But although LINEST() returns useful information other than the coefficient and intercept, TREND() is a faster way to get the forecasts, and I use it in Figure 5.7.

The range D5:D24 contains the forecasts that result from regressing the deseasonalized quarterly figures in C5:C24 onto the period numbers in B5:B24. The array formula used in D5:D24 is this:

```
=TREND(C5:C24,B5:B24)
```

That set of results reflects the effect of the general upward trend in the time series. Because the values that TREND() is forecasting from have been deseasonalized, it remains to add the seasonal effects, also known as seasonal indexes, back in to the trended forecast.

Figure 5.7
The first true forecast is
in row 25.

D25			fx	=TREND(C5:C24,B5:B24,B25)		
	B	C	D	E	F
1			Seasonal Indexes		
2		101.93	-33.19	-80.51	11.77
3					
4	**Deseasonalized Quarterlies**	**Linear Regression Forecasts**	**Seasonal Index**	**Forecast**
5	1	165.1	150.9	101.9	252.9
6	2	141.2	177.4	-33.2	144.3
7	3	189.5	204.0	-80.5	123.5
8	4	204.2	230.5	11.8	242.3
9	5	312.1	257.0	101.9	358.9
10	6	312.2	283.5	-33.2	250.3
11	7	287.5	310.0	-80.5	229.5
12	8	405.2	336.6	11.8	348.3
13	9	362.1	363.1	101.9	465.0
14	10	362.2	389.6	-33.2	356.4
15	11	410.5	416.1	-80.5	335.6
16	12	445.2	442.6	11.8	454.4
17	13	403.1	469.1	101.9	571.1
18	14	484.2	495.7	-33.2	462.5
19	15	546.5	522.2	-80.5	441.7
20	16	526.2	548.7	11.8	560.5
21	17	573.1	575.2	101.9	677.2
22	18	648.2	601.7	-33.2	568.6
23	19	646.5	628.3	-80.5	547.8
24	20	632.2	654.8	11.8	666.6
25	21	Forecast	681.3	101.9	783.2

Adding the Seasonal Indexes Back In

The seasonal indexes, calculated in Figure 5.6, are provided in Figure 5.7, first in the range C2:F2 and then repeatedly in the range E5:E8, E9:E12, and so on. The reseasonalized forecasts are placed in F5:F24 by adding the seasonal effects in column E to the trend forecasts in column D.

To get the one-step-ahead forecast in cell F25 of Figure 5.7, the value of t for the next period goes into cell B25. The following formula is entered in cell D25:

```
=TREND(C5:C24,B5:B24,B25)
```

It instructs Excel to calculate the regression equation that forecasts values in the range C5:C24 from those in B5:B24, and apply that equation to the new x-value in cell B25.

The appropriate seasonal index is placed in cell E25, and the sum of D25 and E25 is placed in F25 as the first true forecast of the trended and seasonal time series.

You'll find the entire set of deseasonalized quarterlies and the forecasts charted in Figure 5.8.

Figure 5.8
The seasonal effects are returned to the forecasts.

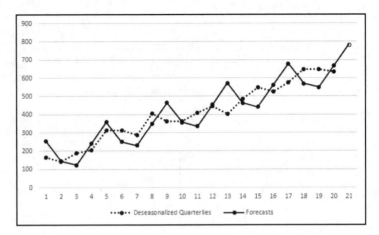

Evaluating Simple Averages

The approach to dealing with a seasonal time series, discussed in several prior sections, has some intuitive appeal. The basic idea seems straightforward:

1. Calculate an annual trend by regressing annual means against a measure of time periods.

2. Divide the annual trend among the periods within the year.

3. Subtract the apportioned trend from the periodic effects to get adjusted effects.

4. Subtract the adjusted effects from the actual measures to deseasonalize the time series.

5. Create forecasts from the deseasonalized series, and add the adjusted seasonal effects back in.

My own view is that several problems weaken the approach, and I would not have included it in this book except that you are likely to encounter it and therefore should be familiar with it. And it provides a useful springboard to discuss some concept and procedures found in other, stronger approaches.

First, there's the issue (about which I complained earlier in this chapter) regarding the very small sample size for the regression of annual means onto consecutive integers that identify each year. Even with only one predictor, as few as 10 observations is really scraping the bottom of the barrel. At the very least you should look at the resulting R^2 adjusted for shrinkage and probably recalculate the standard error of estimate accordingly.

It's true that the stronger the correlation in the population, the smaller the sample you can get away with. But working with quarters within years, you're fortunate to find as many as 10 years' worth of consecutive quarterly observations, each measured in the same way across that span of time.

I'm not persuaded that the answer to the problematic up-and-down pattern you find within a year (see the chart in Figure 5.4) is to average out the peaks and valleys and get a trend estimate from the annual means. Certainly it's *one* answer to that problem, but, as you'll see, there's a much stronger method of segregating the seasonal effects from an underlying trend, accounting for them both, and forecasting accordingly. I'll cover that method later in this chapter, in the "Linear Regression with Coded Vectors" section.

Furthermore, there's no foundation in theory for distributing the annual trend evenly among the periods that compose the year. It's true that linear regression does something similar when it places its forecasts on a straight line. But there's a huge gulf between making a fundamental assumption because the analytic model can't otherwise handle the data, and accepting a flawed outcome whose flaws—errors in the forecasts—can be measured and evaluated.

That said, let's move on to the use of moving averages instead of simple averages as a way of dealing with seasonality.

Moving Averages and Centered Moving Averages

A couple of points about seasonality in a time series bear repeating, even if they seem obvious. One is that the term "season" does not *necessarily* refer to the four seasons of the year that result from the tilting of the Earth's axis. In predictive analytics, "season" often means precisely that, because many of the phenomena that we study do vary along with the progression of spring through winter: sales of winter or summer gear, incidence of certain widespread diseases, weather events caused by the location of the jet stream and changes in the temperature of the water in the eastern Pacific ocean, and so on.

Equally, events that occur regularly can act like meteorological seasons, even though they have only a tenuous connection to the solstices and equinoxes. Eight-hour shifts in hospitals and factories often get expressed in the incidence of intakes and expenditures of energy; there, a season is eight hours long and the seasons cycle every day, not every year. Due dates for taxes signal the beginning of a flood of dollars into municipal, state, and federal treasuries; there, the season might be one year long (personal income taxes), six months (property taxes in many states), quarterly (many corporate taxes), and so on.

> **NOTE** It's a little strange that we have the word "season" to refer generally to the regularly recurring period of time, but no general term for the period of time during which one full turn of the seasons occurs. "Cycle" is possible, but in analytics and forecasting that term is usually taken to mean a period of indeterminate length, such as a business cycle. In the absence of a better term, I've used "encompassing period" in this and subsequent chapters.

This isn't just terminological musing. The ways we identify seasons and the period of time during which the seasons turn have real, if often minor, implications for how we measure their effects. The following sections discuss how some analysts vary the way they calculate moving averages according to whether the number of seasons is odd or even.

Using Moving Averages Instead of Simple Averages

Suppose that a large city is considering the reallocation of its traffic police to better address the incidence of driving while impaired, which the city believes has been increasing. Four weeks ago, new legislation went into effect, legalizing the possession and recreational use of marijuana. Since then, the daily number of traffic arrests for DWI seems to be trending up. Complicating matters is the fact that the number of arrests appears to spike on Fridays and Saturdays. To help plan for manpower requirements into the future, you'd like to forecast any underlying trend that's being established. You'd also like to time the deployment of your resources to take account of any weekend-related seasonality that's taking place.

Figure 5.9 has the relevant data you have to work with.

Figure 5.9
With this data set, each day of the week constitutes a season.

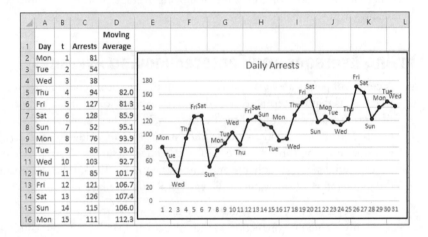

Even by just eyeballing the chart in Figure 5.9, you can tell that the trend of the number of daily arrests is up. You'll have to plan to expand the number of traffic officers, and hope that the trend levels off soon. Further, the data bears out the notion that more arrests occur routinely on Fridays and Saturdays, so your resource allocation needs to address those spikes.

But you need to quantify the underlying trend, to determine how many additional police you'll have to bring on. You also need to quantify the expected size of the weekend spikes, to determine how many additional police you need watching for erratic drivers on those days.

The problem is that as of yet you don't know how much of the daily increase is due to trend and how much is due to that weekend effect. You can start off by detrending the time series. Earlier in this chapter, in "Simple Seasonal Averages," you saw an example of how to detrend a time series in order to isolate the seasonal effects using the method of simple averages. In this section you'll see how to do so using moving averages—very likely, the moving-averages approach is used more often in predictive analytics than is the simple-averages approach.

There are various reasons for the greater popularity of moving averages, among them, that the moving-averages approach does not ask you to collapse your data in the process of quantifying a trend. Recall that the earlier example made it necessary to collapse quarterly averages to annual averages, calculate an annual trend, and then distribute one-fourth of the annual trend across each quarter in the year. That step was needed in order to remove trend from the seasonal effects. In contrast, the moving-averages approach enables you to detrend the time series without resorting to that sort of machination.

Figure 5.10 shows how the moving-averages approach works in the present example.

Figure 5.10
The moving average in the second chart clarifies the underlying trend.

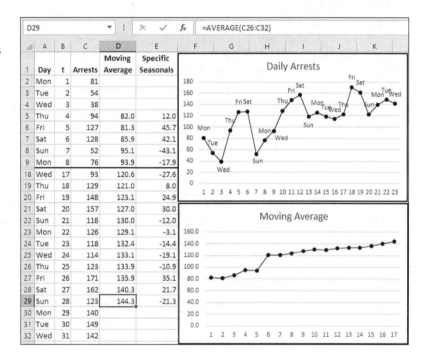

Figure 5.10 adds a moving average column, and a column for *specific seasonals*, to the data set in Figure 5.9. Both additions require some discussion.

The spikes in arrests that take place on weekends gives you reason to believe that you're working with seasons that repeat once each week. Therefore, start by getting the average for the encompassing period—that is, the first seven seasons, Monday through Sunday. The formula for the average in cell D5, the first available moving average, is as follows:

```
=AVERAGE (C2:C8)
```

That formula is copied and pasted down through cell D29, so you have 25 moving averages based on 25 runs of seven consecutive days. Notice that in order to show both the first and the last few observations in the time series, I have hidden rows 10 through 17. You can unhide them, if you want, in this chapter's workbook, available from the publisher's website.

Make a multiple selection of visible rows 9 and 18, right-click one of their row headers, and choose Unhide from the shortcut menu.

> **NOTE**
> When you hide a worksheet's rows, as I've done in Figure 5.10, any charted data in the hidden rows is also hidden on the chart. The x-axis labels identify only the data points that appear on the chart.

Because each moving average in Figure 5.10 encompasses seven days, no moving average is paired with the first three or final three actual observations. Copying and pasting the formula in cell D5 up one day to cell D4 runs you out of observations—there is no observation recorded in cell C1. Similarly, there is no moving average recorded below cell D29. Copying and pasting the formula in D29 into D30 would require an observation in cell C33, and no observation is available for the day that cell would represent.

It would be possible, of course, to shorten the length of the moving average to, say, five instead of seven. So doing would mean that the moving-average formulas in Figure 5.10 could start in cell D4 instead of D5. However, in this sort of analysis, you want the length of the moving average to equal the number of seasons: seven days in a week for events that recur weekly implies a moving average of length seven, and four quarters in a year for events that recur annually implies a moving average of length four.

Along similar lines, we generally quantify seasonal effects in such a way that they total to zero within the encompassing time period. As you saw in this chapter's first section, on simple averages, this is done by calculating the average of (say) the four quarters in a year, and then subtracting the average for the year from each quarterly figure. So doing ensures that the total of the seasonal effects is zero. In turn, that's useful because it puts the seasonal effects on a common footing—a summer effect of +11 is as far from the mean as a winter effect of –11. If you want to average five seasons instead of seven to get your moving average, you're better off finding a phenomenon that repeats every five seasons instead of every seven.

> **NOTE**
> However, when you take the average of the seasonal effects later in the process, those averages are unlikely to sum to zero. It's necessary at that point to recalibrate, or *normalize*, the averages so that their sum is zero. When that's done, the averaged seasonal averages express the effect on a time period of belonging to a particular season. Once normalized, the seasonal averages are termed the *seasonal indexes* that this chapter has already mentioned several times. You'll see how it works later in this chapter, in "Detrending the Series with Moving Averages."

Understanding Specific Seasonals

Figure 5.10 also shows what are called *specific seasonals* in column E. They are what's left after subtracting the moving average from the actual observation. To get a sense of what the specific seasonals represent, consider the moving average in cell D5. It is the average of the observations in C2:C8. The deviations of each observation from the moving average (for example, C2 – D5) are guaranteed to sum to zero—that's a characteristic of an average. Therefore, each deviation expresses the effect of being associated with that particular day in that particular week. It's a specific seasonal, then—specific because the deviation applies to that particular Monday or Tuesday and so on, and seasonal because in this example we're treating each day as though it were a season in the encompassing period of a week.

Because each specific seasonal measures the effect of being in that season vis-à-vis the moving average for that group of (here) seven seasons, you can subsequently average the specific seasonals for a particular season (for example, all the Fridays in your time series) to estimate that season's general, rather than specific, effect. That average is not confounded by an underlying trend in the time series, because each specific seasonal expresses a deviation from its own particular moving average.

Aligning the Moving Averages

There's also the question of aligning the moving averages with the original data set. In Figure 5.10, I have aligned each moving average with the midpoint of the range of observations that it includes. So, for example, the formula in cell D5 averages the observations in C2:C8, and I have aligned it with the fourth observation, the midpoint of the averaged range, by placing it in row 5. This arrangement is termed a *centered moving average*, and many analysts prefer to align each moving average with the midpoint of the observations that it averages.

> **NOTE** Bear in mind that in this context, "midpoint" refers to the middle of a time span: Thursday is the midpoint of Monday through Sunday. It does *not* refer to the median of the observed values, although of course it might work out that way in practice.

Another approach is the *trailing moving average*. In that case, each moving average is aligned with the final observation that it averages—and therefore it trails behind its arguments. This is often the preferred arrangement if you want to use a moving average as a forecast, as is done with exponential smoothing, because your final moving average occurs coincident with the final available observation.

Centered Moving Averages with Even Numbers of Seasons

We usually adopt a special procedure when the number of seasons is even rather than odd. That's the typical state of affairs: There tend to be even numbers of seasons in the encompassing period for typical seasons such as months, quarters, and quadrennial periods (for elections).

The difficulty with an even number of seasons is that there is no midpoint. Two is not the midpoint of a range starting at 1 and ending at 4, and neither is 3; if it can be said to have one, its midpoint is 2.5. Six is not the midpoint of 1 to 12, and neither is 7; its purely theoretical midpoint is 6.5.

To act as though a midpoint exists, you need to add a layer of averaging atop the moving averages. See Figure 5.11.

Figure 5.11
Excel offers several ways to calculate a centered moving average.

	A	B	C	D	E	F	G	H	I
E6						f_x	=AVERAGE(D3:D9)		
1									
2	Year	Season	t	Observation	Moving Average	Centered Moving Average		Weights	Centered Moving Average
3	2011	1	1	13				1	
4			1.5						
5		2	2	15				2	
6			2.5		13.25				
7		3	3	14		13.75		2	13.75
8			3.5		14.25				
9		4	4	11		14.375		2	14.375
10			4.5		14.5				
11	2012	1	5	17		15.125		1	15.125
12			5.5		15.75				
13		2	6	16		16.625			16.625
14			6.5		17.5				
15		3	7	19					
16			7.5						
17		4	8	18					

The idea behind this approach to getting a moving average that's centered on an existing midpoint, when there's an even number of seasons, is to pull that midpoint forward by half a season. You calculate a moving average that would be centered at, say, the third point in time if five seasons instead of four constituted one full turn of the calendar.

That's done by taking two consecutive moving averages and averaging *them*. So in Figure 5.11, there's a moving average in cell E6 that averages the values in D3:D9. Because there are four seasonal values in D3:D9, the moving average in E6 is thought of as centered at the imaginary season 2.5, half a point short of the first available candidate season, 3. (Seasons 1 and 2 are unavailable as midpoints for lack of data to average prior to Season 1.)

Note, though, that the moving average in cell E8 averages the values in D5:D11, the second through the fifth in the time series. That average is centered at (imaginary) point 3.5, a full period ahead of the average centered at 2.5. By averaging the two moving averages, so the thinking goes, you can pull the center point of the first moving average forward by half a point, from 2.5 to 3.

That's what the averages in column F of Figure 5.11 do. Cell F7 provides the average of the moving averages in E6 and E8. And the average in F7 is aligned with the third data point in the original time series, in cell D7, to emphasize that the average is centered on that season.

If you expand the formula in cell F7 as well as the moving averages in cells E6 and E8, you'll see that it turns out to be a weighted average of the first five values in the time series, with the first and fifth value given a weight of 1, and the second through fourth values given a weight of 2. That leads us to a quicker and simpler way to calculate a centered moving average with an even number of seasons.

Still in Figure 5.11, the weights are stored in the range H3:H11. This formula returns the first centered moving average, in cell I7:

```
=SUMPRODUCT(D3:D11,$H$3:$H$11)/8
```

That formula returns 13.75, which is identical to the value calculated by the double-average formula in cell F7. Making the reference to the weights absolute, by means of the dollar signs in $H$3:$H$11, you can copy the formula and paste it down as far as necessary to get the rest of the centered moving averages.

Detrending the Series with Moving Averages

When you have subtracted the moving averages from the original observations to get the specific seasonals, you have removed the underlying trend from the series. What's left in the specific seasonals is normally a stationary, horizontal series with two effects that cause the specific seasonals to depart from an absolutely straight line: the seasonal effects and random error in the original observations. Figure 5.12 shows the results for this example.

Figure 5.12
The specific seasonal effects for Friday and Saturday remain clear in the detrended series.

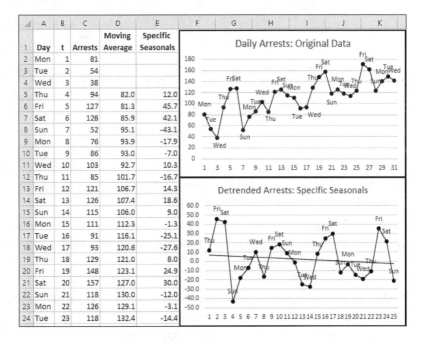

	Day	t	Arrests	Moving Average	Specific Seasonals
1	Day	t	Arrests	Moving Average	Specific Seasonals
2	Mon	1	81		
3	Tue	2	54		
4	Wed	3	38		
5	Thu	4	94	82.0	12.0
6	Fri	5	127	81.3	45.7
7	Sat	6	128	85.9	42.1
8	Sun	7	52	95.1	-43.1
9	Mon	8	76	93.9	-17.9
10	Tue	9	86	93.0	-7.0
11	Wed	10	103	92.7	10.3
12	Thu	11	85	101.7	-16.7
13	Fri	12	121	106.7	14.3
14	Sat	13	126	107.4	18.6
15	Sun	14	115	106.0	9.0
16	Mon	15	111	112.3	-1.3
17	Tue	16	91	116.1	-25.1
18	Wed	17	93	120.6	-27.6
19	Thu	18	129	121.0	8.0
20	Fri	19	148	123.1	24.9
21	Sat	20	157	127.0	30.0
22	Sun	21	118	130.0	-12.0
23	Mon	22	126	129.1	-3.1
24	Tue	23	118	132.4	-14.4

5

The upper chart in Figure 5.12 shows the original daily observations. Both the general upward trend and the weekend seasonal spikes are clear.

The lower chart shows the specific seasonals: the result of detrending the original series with a moving-average filter, as described earlier in "Understanding Specific Seasonals." You can see that the detrended series is now virtually horizontal (a linear trendline for the specific seasonals has a slight downward drift), but the seasonal Friday and Saturday spikes are still in place.

The next step is to move beyond the specific seasonals to the seasonal indexes. See Figure 5.13.

Figure 5.13
The specific seasonals effects are first averaged and then normalized to reach the seasonal indexes.

E5				f_x	=C5-D5

	A	B	C	D	E	F	G	H	I	J	K	L	M	N
1	Day	t	Arrests	Moving Average	Specific Seasonals						Specific Seasonals			
2	Mon	1	81								Day			
3	Tue	2	54				Week	Mon	Tue	Wed	Thu	Fri	Sat	Sun
4	Wed	3	38				1				12.0	45.7	42.1	-43.1
5	Thu	4	94	82.0	12.0		2	-17.9	-7.0	10.3	-16.7	14.3	18.6	9.0
6	Fri	5	127	81.3	45.7		3	-1.3	-25.1	-27.6	8.0	24.9	30.0	-12.0
7	Sat	6	128	85.9	42.1		4	-3.1	-14.4	-19.1	-10.9	35.1	21.7	-21.3
8	Sun	7	52	95.1	-43.1									
9	Mon	8	76	93.9	-17.9				Seasonal Averages					
10	Tue	9	86	93.0	-7.0			Mon	Tue	Wed	Thu	Fri	Sat	Sun
11	Wed	10	103	92.7	10.3			-7.4	-15.5	-12.1	-1.9	30.0	28.1	-16.9
12	Thu	11	85	101.7	-16.7									
13	Fri	12	121	106.7	14.3			Grand Mean Seasonal Average:						0.6
14	Sat	13	126	107.4	18.6									
15	Sun	14	115	106.0	9.0				Seasonal Indexes					
16	Mon	15	111	112.3	-1.3			Mon	Tue	Wed	Thu	Fri	Sat	Sun
17	Tue	16	91	116.1	-25.1			-8.0	-16.1	-12.8	-2.5	29.4	27.5	-17.5
18	Wed	17	93	120.6	-27.6									

In Figure 5.13, the specific seasonals in column E are rearranged in the tabular form shown in the range H4:N7. The purpose is simply to make it easier to calculate the seasonal averages. Those averages are shown in H11:N11.

However, the figures in H11:N11 are averages, not deviations from an average, and therefore we can't expect them to sum to zero. We still need to adjust them so that they express deviations from a grand mean. That grand mean appears in cell N13, and is the average of the seasonal averages.

We can arrive at the seasonal indexes by subtracting the grand mean in N13 from each of the seasonal averages. The result is in the range H17:N17. These seasonal indexes are no longer specific to a particular moving average, as is the case with the specific seasonals in column E. Because they're based on an average of each instance of a given season, they express the average effect of a given season across the four weeks in the time series.

Furthermore, they are measures of a season's—here, a day's—effect on traffic arrests vis-à-vis the average for a seven-day period.

We can now use those seasonal indexes to deseasonalize the series. We'll use the deseasonalized series to get forecasts by way of linear regression or Holt's method of smoothing trended series (discussed in Chapter 4). Then we simply add the seasonal indexes back into the forecasts to reseasonalize them. All this appears in Figure 5.14.

Figure 5.14
After you have the seasonal indexes, the finishing touches as applied here are the same as in the method of simple averages.

K33				▼	:	×	✓	fx	=J33+F33	
◢	A	B	C .	D	E	F	G	H	I	J	K
					Seasonal			Deseasonalized		Linear Regression	Re-seasonalized
1	Day	t	Arrests		Indexes			Series		Forecasts	Series
2	Mon	1	81	Mon	-8.0			89.0		74.6	66.5
3	Tue	2	54	Tue	-16.1			70.1		77.2	61.1
4	Wed	3	38	Wed	-12.8			50.8		79.8	67.1
5	Thu	4	94	Thu	-2.5			96.5		82.5	80.0
6	Fri	5	127	Fri	29.4			97.6		85.1	114.5
7	Sat	6	128	Sat	27.5			100.5		87.8	115.2
8	Sun	7	52	Sun	-17.5			69.5		90.4	72.9
9	Mon	8	76	Mon	-8.0			84.0		93.0	85.0
20	Fri	19	148	Fri	29.4			118.6		122.0	151.4
21	Sat	20	157	Sat	27.5			129.5		124.7	152.2
22	Sun	21	118	Sun	-17.5			135.5		127.3	109.8
23	Mon	22	126	Mon	-8.0			134.0		130.0	121.9
24	Tue	23	118	Tue	-16.1			134.1		132.6	116.5
25	Wed	24	114	Wed	-12.8			126.8		135.2	122.5
26	Thu	25	123	Thu	-2.5			125.5		137.9	135.4
27	Fri	26	171	Fri	29.4			141.6		140.5	169.9
28	Sat	27	162	Sat	27.5			134.5		143.1	170.6
29	Sun	28	123	Sun	-17.5			140.5		145.8	128.3
30	Mon	29	140	Mon	-8.0			148.0		148.4	140.4
31	Tue	30	149	Tue	-16.1			165.1		151.1	134.9
32	Wed	31	142	Wed	-12.8			154.8		153.7	140.9
33	Thu	32		Thu	-2.5					156.3	153.8

The steps illustrated in Figure 5.14 are largely the same as those in Figures 5.6 and 5.7, discussed in the following sections.

Deseasonalizing the Observations

Subtract the seasonal indexes from the original observations to deseasonalize the data. You can do this as shown in Figure 5.14, in which the original observations and the seasonal indexes are arranged as two lists beginning in the same row, columns C and F. This arrangement makes it a little easier to structure the calculations.

You can also do the subtraction as shown in Figure 5.6, in which the original quarterly observations (C12:F16), the quarterly indexes (C8:F8), and the deseasonalized results (C20:F24) are shown in a tabular format. That arrangement makes it a little easier to focus on the seasonal indexes and the deseasoned quarterlies.

5

Forecast from the Deseasonalized Observations

In Figure 5.14, the deseasonalized observations are in column H, and in Figure 5.7 they're in column C. Regardless of whether you want to use a regression approach or a smoothing approach to the forecast, it's best to arrange the deseasonalized observations in a single-column list.

In Figure 5.14, the forecasts are in column J. The following array formula is entered in the range J2:J32.

```
=TREND(H2:H32)
```

Earlier in this chapter, I pointed out that if you omit the x-values argument from the TREND() function's arguments, Excel supplies the default values 1, 2, …, n, where n is the number of y-values. In the formula just given, H2:H32 contains 31 y-values. Because the argument normally containing the x-values is missing, Excel supplies the default values 1, 2, …, 31. Those are the values we would want to use anyway, in column B, so the formula as given is equivalent to =TREND(H2:H32,B2:B32). And that's the structure used in D5:D24 of Figure 5.7:

```
=TREND(C5:C24,B5:B24)
```

Making the One-Step-Ahead Forecast

So far you have arranged for forecasts of the deseasonalized time series from t = 1 through t = 31 in Figure 5.14, and from t = 1 through t = 20 in Figure 5.7. These forecasts constitute useful information for various purposes, including assessing the accuracy of the forecasts by means of an RMSE analysis.

But your main purpose is forecasting at least the next, as yet unobserved time period. To get that, you could first forecast from the TREND() or LINEST() function if you're using regression, or from the exponential smoothing formula if you're using Holt's method. Then you can add the associated seasonal index to the regression or smoothing forecast, to get a forecast that includes both the trend and the seasonal effect.

In Figure 5.14, you get the regression forecast in cell J33 with this formula:

```
=TREND(H2:H32,,B33)
```

In this formula, the y-values in H2:H32 are the same as in the other TREND() formulas in column J. So are the (default) x-values of 1 through 32. Now, though, you supply a new x-value as the function's third argument, which you tell TREND() to look for in cell B33. It's 32, the next value of t. And Excel returns the value 156.3 in cell J33. The TREND() function in cell J33 is telling Excel, in effect, "Calculate the regression equation for the values in H2:H32 regressed on the t values 1 through 31. Apply that regression equation to the new x-value of 32 and return the result."

You'll find the same approach taken in cell D25 of Figure 5.7, where the formula to get the one-step-ahead forecast is this:

```
=TREND(C5:C24,B5:B24,B25)
```

Adding the Seasonal Indexes Back In

The final step is to reseasonalize the forecasts by adding the seasonal indexes to the trend forecasts, reversing what you did four steps back when you subtracted the indexes from the original observations. This is done in column F in Figure 5.7 and column K in Figure 5.14.

Don't forget to add the appropriate seasonal index for the one-step-ahead forecast, with the results shown in cell F25 in Figure 5.7 and in cell K33 in Figure 5.14. (I've shaded the one-step-ahead cells in both Figure 5.7 and Figure 5.14 to highlight the forecasts.)

You can find charts of three representations of the traffic arrest data in Figure 5.15: the deseasonalized series, the linear forecast from the deseasonalized data, and the reseasonalized forecasts. Note that the forecasts incorporate both the general trend of the original data and its Friday/Saturday spikes.

Figure 5.15
Charting the forecasts.

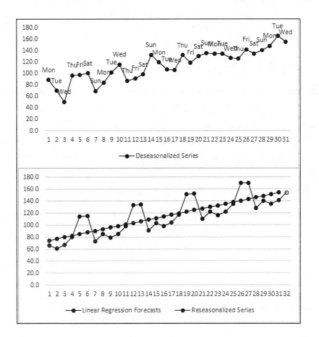

Linear Regression with Coded Vectors

Another method for dealing with seasonal time series, whether trended or not, employs linear regression in combination with effect coding. Effect coding is just a way of representing which season a particular observation belongs to, and Excel makes it particularly easy to set up.

The two broad methods that this chapter has already discussed, those of simple averages and of moving averages, also employ linear regression. Figure 5.5 shows how the simple averages method uses regression to calculate a year-to-year trend and distribute that trend equally across the quarters. Figure 5.7 shows how the same method uses regression to forecast from deseasonalized quarters before adding seasonal effects back in. (It would have been feasible to use Holt's method in Figure 5.7 instead of linear regression.)

Figure 5.14 shows how you can use linear regression just as is done in Figure 5.7, to forecast from deseasonalized observations prior to reseasonalizing them using the seasonal indexes. Again, you could use Holt's method instead of regression.

If you combine effect coding (or, as you'll see, dummy coding) with linear regression, you can get the forecasts of a seasonal time series in one step. It's not necessary to jump through the hoops of calculating averages for each season and for an encompassing period such as a year, deviate them from the grand mean, normalize them, deseasonalize the time series, forecast a trended series, and finally add the seasonal indexes back in. Nor is it necessary to do anything fancy with LINEST() or TREND(). It's all in the way you indicate the season in the time series.

About Effect Coding and Regression

In the 1960s, when computers were becoming more and more accessible in colleges and universities and in business settings, regression analysis began to supplant an older statistical method, the analysis of variance, or *ANOVA*. That method, which first saw light in a 1918 paper by Sir Ronald Fisher, helps the researcher draw inferences about the reliability of an empirical finding. For example: "If I repeat this experiment 100 times, how often can I expect to find differences between groups as large as I just saw, assuming that this time around those differences were due to sampling error?"

ANOVA is one way of expressing something called the General Linear Model, in itself a way of describing contributions to numeric observations. Suppose that you were investigating the distribution of C reactive protein (CRP) in humans. Besides the measured level of that protein for each person in a sample, you might have information about each person's sex, and whether each person has coronary artery disease.

The General Linear Model would tell you that each person's CRP can be expressed by summing the following terms:

- The mean level of CRP in your entire sample
- The elevation or depression from the overall mean in CRP for males, or, if the person is female, for females
- The elevation or depression from the overall mean in CRP for people with coronary disease; otherwise, for those without such disease
- The elevation or depression for males with and without coronary disease, and for females with and without coronary disease
- An error term that measures the difference between a person's actual measured CRP level and the sum of the other effects (grand mean, elevation or depression specific to each sex, elevation or depression due to coronary disease, interaction between sex and coronary disease)

The categories in ANOVA (in this example, sex and the presence or absence of coronary disease) are traditionally handled separately: Various calculations are performed for the males' data, and performed separately from the females' data; and similarly for the presence and absence of coronary disease. In this way, ANOVA can deal with nominal, categorical information.

Regression can't—or, rather, doesn't—work directly with nominal information such as "Male or "Has atherosclerosis." With regression, you use one of several available methods to code those categories numerically. Then, you present those codes along with CRP measures to some function such as Excel's LINEST() or TREND() functions to handle everything at once. Most, perhaps even the overwhelming majority, of analyses that contrast different groups and subgroups since the 1990s have used a regression approach.

This was not true before significant computing power became readily available, before capabilities that once required mainframes became available on the desktop. Or laptop. Or wristwatch.

Researchers had to wait for that computing power because regression analysis requires a lot more in the way of exacting calculations than does ANOVA. It's worth it, though. Regression analysis with coded variables gives you all the results that ANOVA does, plus richer statistics that put you in a position to understand your data much more thoroughly.

I've dragged you through this mini history lesson not because it's intrinsically interesting, but to emphasize that a coding scheme in conjunction with regression analysis has been used successfully and effectively for decades, both in more static research such as medical, agricultural, and financial, and also in research that emphasizes changes over time, such as predictive analytics.

Effect Coding with Seasons

Let's have a look at a full analysis before digging into how it works. Figure 5.16 repeats the time series used with simple averages from Figure 5.5, along with three variables that identify the seasons. Recall that the time series consists of the average number of daily hits on a football-related website, for each quarter in each of five years.

A time period that belongs to the first quarter gets a 1 in column E and a zero in columns F and G. If it belongs to the second quarter, it gets a 1 in column F and a zero in columns E and G. If it belongs to the third quarter, it gets a 1 in column G and zeroes in columns E and F. If it belongs to the fourth quarter, it gets a −1 in all three columns, E, F, and G.

Besides columns C and D, which contain the variable of interest and the time period during which the measurement was taken, there are three new columns: one that represents membership in Quarter 1, one in Quarter 2, and one in Quarter 3. We have four quarters, but three vectors in columns E, F, and G are sufficient to define the quarter for each of the 20 observations. If a record has a −1 in columns E, F, and G, it belongs to Quarter 4.

Figure 5.16
The variables that identify seasons are more frequently termed *vectors*.

	A	B	C	D	E	F	G	H	I	J	K	L	M
	I3						f_x		{=LINEST(C3:C22,D3:G22,,TRUE)}				
1													
2	Year	Quarter	Average Daily Hits	t	Quarter 1	Quarter 2	Quarter 3				LINEST()		
3	2001	1	267	1	1	0	0		-80.51	-33.19	101.93	26.52	124.40
4		2	108	2	0	1	0		14.47	14.47	14.62	1.47	17.59
5		3	109	3	0	0	1		0.96	37.31	#N/A	#N/A	#N/A
6		4	216	4	-1	-1	-1		92.69	15	#N/A	#N/A	#N/A
7	2002	1	414	5	1	0	0		516077.18	20879.38	#N/A	#N/A	#N/A
8		2	279	6	0	1	0						
9		3	207	7	0	0	1						
10		4	417	8	-1	-1	-1				Coefficient	tandard E	t Stat	P-value
11	2003	1	464	9	1	0	0		Intercept	124.403	17.59	7.073	4E-06
12		2	329	10	0	1	0		t	26.5188	1.475	17.98	1E-11
13		3	330	11	0	0	1		Quarter 1	101.928	14.62	6.973	4E-06
14		4	457	12	-1	-1	-1		Quarter 2	-33.1906	14.47	-2.29	0.037
15	2004	1	505	13	1	0	0		Quarter 3	-80.5094	14.47	-5.56	5E-05
16		2	451	14	0	1	0						
17		3	466	15	0	0	1						
18		4	538	16	-1	-1	-1						
19	2005	1	675	17	1	0	0						
20		2	615	18	0	1	0						
21		3	566	19	0	0	1						
22		4	644	20	-1	-1	-1						

> **NOTE**
> Another closely related coding scheme uses zeroes in all three columns for, in this example, the fourth quarter. This chapter provides a brief look at that scheme in a subsequent section, "Dummy Coding."

In Figure 5.16, notice that the LINEST() function results in the range I3:M7. The values in I3:K3 correspond exactly to the seasonal indexes shown for the same data set in Figure 5.7, cells C2:E2. The values are in reverse order in Figure 5.16 due to a peculiarity in LINEST(), which has been around since the 1990s and which I criticized in a Note toward the end of Chapter 4.

Furthermore, if you used the LINEST() function on Figure 5.7 to regress the values in column C on those in column B, you'd find that the intercept and coefficient correspond exactly to those reported in cells L3:M3 in Figure 5.16. The regression of the deseasonalized quarterlies on the time periods corresponds precisely to the intercept and coefficient in the omnibus analysis in Figure 5.16.

In other words, by coding quarterly membership in the input range for LINEST() by means of effect codes, you can get precisely the same results as you do by going through all the computations in the simple-averages method. I included the simple-averages method earlier in this chapter because if you understand its flow of overt events, you're better placed to understand what's going on inside the black box when you submit effect codes to LINEST() along with the actual observations and their time periods.

Given that LINEST() returns the intercept, the trend coefficient and the seasonal indexes that the simple-averages method returns, it shouldn't be surprising to see that you can easily get the same forecasts from the TREND() function. See Figure 5.17.

Figure 5.17
The forecasts are identical to those shown in Figure 5.7.

I3					f_x	=$M$7+$L$7*D3+$K$7*E3+$J$7*F3+$I$7*G3					

	C	D	E	F	G	H	I	J	K	L	M
1											
2	Average Daily Hits	t	Quarter 1	Quarter 2	Quarter 3	TREND()	LINEST() COEFFICIENTS				
3	267	1	1	0	0	252.9	252.9				
4	108	2	0	1	0	144.3					
5	109	3	0	0	1	123.5					
6	216	4	-1	-1	-1	242.3		LINEST()			
7	414	5	1	0	0	358.9	-80.51	-33.19	101.93	26.52	124.40
8	279	6	0	1	0	250.3	14.47	14.47	14.62	1.47	17.59
9	207	7	0	0	1	229.5	0.96	37.31	#N/A	#N/A	#N/A
10	417	8	-1	-1	-1	348.3	92.69	15.00	#N/A	#N/A	#N/A
11	464	9	1	0	0	465.0	516077.18	20879.38	#N/A	#N/A	#N/A
12	329	10	0	1	0	356.4					
13	330	11	0	0	1	335.6					
14	457	12	-1	-1	-1	454.4					
15	505	13	1	0	0	571.1					
16	451	14	0	1	0	462.5					
17	466	15	0	0	1	441.7					
18	538	16	-1	-1	-1	560.5					
19	675	17	1	0	0	677.2					
20	615	18	0	1	0	568.6					
21	566	19	0	0	1	547.8					
22	644	20	-1	-1	-1	666.6					
23		21	1	0	0	783.2	One-step-ahead forecast				

The LINEST() analysis from Figure 5.16 is repeated in Figure 5.17, and the intercept and coefficients in its first row are used in cell I3 to calculate the forecast for the first observation. It's identical to the value returned by TREND() in cell H3. No surprise there, of course: That's exactly what TREND() is supposed to do.

One useful aspect of effect coding is that the regression coefficient associated with a particular coded vector equals the difference between the grand mean of the outcome variable and the mean of the group associated with that vector. Because that's a confusing concept when it's presented in words, let's look at it more closely in Figure 5.18.

There's a lot going on in Figure 5.18. First, the original observations in column C are regressed onto the time periods in column D. The results of that regression are shown in the range E3:E22, where the array formula is as shown here:

```
=TREND(C3:C22,D3:D22)
```

So the values in column E are the forecasts of average daily hits based on the relationship between the observations in column C and the time periods in column D.

Figure 5.18
The reason it's termed *effect* coding.

M10 =AVERAGE(F6,F10,F14,F18,F22)

	C	D	E	F	G	H	I	J
2	Hits	t	TREND() on *t*	Resid-uals	Qtr 1	Qtr 2	Qtr 3	Residual TREND() on Qtrs
3	267	1	162.27	104.73	1	0	0	100.14
4	108	2	187.60	-79.60	0	1	0	-33.79
5	109	3	212.92	-103.92	0	0	1	-79.91
6	216	4	238.24	-22.24	-1	-1	-1	13.56
7	414	5	263.57	150.43	1	0	0	100.14
8	279	6	288.89	-9.89	0	1	0	-33.79
9	207	7	314.22	-107.22	0	0	1	-79.91
10	417	8	339.54	77.46	-1	-1	-1	13.56
11	464	9	364.86	99.14	1	0	0	100.14
12	329	10	390.19	-61.19	0	1	0	-33.79
13	330	11	415.51	-85.51	0	0	1	-79.91
14	457	12	440.84	16.16	-1	-1	-1	13.56
15	505	13	466.16	38.84	1	0	0	100.14
16	451	14	491.48	-40.48	0	1	0	-33.79
17	466	15	516.81	-50.81	0	0	1	-79.91
18	538	16	542.13	-4.13	-1	-1	-1	13.56
19	675	17	567.46	107.54	1	0	0	100.14
20	615	18	592.78	22.22	0	1	0	-33.79
21	566	19	618.10	-52.10	0	0	1	-79.91
22	644	20	643.43	0.57	-1	-1	-1	13.56

	L	M	N	O	P	Q
2				LINEST()		
3		13.56	-79.91	-33.79	100.14	0.00
4			14.29	14.29	14.29	8.25
5			0.80	36.91	#N/A	#N/A
6			21.71	16	#N/A	#N/A
7			88693.88	21792.84	#N/A	#N/A
9	Quarter	4	3	2	1	
10	Average	13.56	-79.91	-33.79	100.14	

Column F subtracts the forecast hits in column E from the actual figures in column C. The results of the subtractions are termed *residuals*—what's left over of the original observations after the effect of their relationship to the time periods has been removed.

5

NOTE You seldom see residuals called out like this in published research. They appear mainly in papers written by careful authors who look for patterns in the residuals, which might point to poor modeling, lack of independence between observations, and other problems. So I'll take this opportunity to mention that the Excel function `DEVSQ()`, pointed at the forecasts in column E of Figure 5.18, returns the regression sum of squares from the final row of the `LINEST()` results, and, pointed at the residuals in column F, returns the residual sum of squares, also from `LINEST()`'s final row. The `DEVSQ()` function subtracts each of the observations from their mean, squares the differences, and totals the squares.

Finally, the residuals in column F are analyzed with another instance of `LINEST()`, regressing the residuals on the effect codes in columns G, H, and I. There are a couple of points of interest about the `LINEST()` results, in N3:Q7:

- The intercept in cell Q3 is zero. With effect coding, the intercept equals the grand mean of the outcome variable. We're analyzing residuals here, and residuals always sum to zero in effect coding. Therefore, the intercept also equals zero.
- The regression coefficients appear in N3:P3. With effect coding, the coefficients equal the difference between the mean of the associated group and the grand mean. Because

the grand mean of the residuals is zero, each coefficient equals the mean of the residuals in the associated group.

Figure 5.18 also shows in the range M10:P10 the residual number of hits in each quarter, calculated as a mean for each quarter from the values in column F. So, the formula in cell P10 is as follows:

```
=AVERAGE(F3,F7,F11,F15,F19)
```

Notice that the result, 100.14, is equal to the regression coefficient for the first coded vector in cell P3. And the calculated means for the second and third quarters, in O10 and N10, equal the regression coefficients in cells O3 and N3. Again, this is characteristic of pure effect coding. The regression coefficients quantify the effect of being in a given group when all you have as predictors are effect codes. If, as in analysis of covariance, you include one or more covariates—and here the time period is analogous to a covariate—the regression coefficients do not precisely equal the group means.

Also notice that because the design of the analysis includes three coded vectors, not four, you get only three coefficients. (Adding a fourth vector to identify quarterly membership explicitly makes it impossible for linear regression to analyze the problem correctly.) The way to get the fourth seasonal index is to add the other indexes together and multiply by –1. So in Figure 5.18, the formula for cell M3 is this:

```
=-SUM(N3:P3)
```

Note that the result in cell M3 is identical to the average of the Quarter 4 residuals calculated in cell M10.

Setting Up the Coded Vectors

If you have just a few observations in your time series—say, on the order of 20 or fewer—it's probably quicker and easier to enter the 1s, 0s and –1s by hand. You can speed things up a little by selecting the range that the codes will occupy, typing a 0, and then entering it with Ctrl+Enter. That will populate most of the cells with their correct code. There are always more 0s than 1s or –1s when you have at least three vectors. Then, replace the 0s with 1s and –1s where needed.

With so many observations and vectors that you can't bring yourself to enter the codes by hand, you can speed things up appreciably by using Excel's VLOOKUP() function. See Figure 5.19 for an example.

Excel uses the term *lookup range* to refer to a range that's used as A2:D5 is used in this example. The first column in your lookup range should contain the characters or numbers you use to identify your seasons. Those identifiers could be the numbers 1 through 4 if your seasons are quarters; or 1 through 12 if they are months; or Monday, Tuesday, and so on if they are days. The characters or numbers in the first column of the lookup range must correspond to the characters in the time-period portion of your time series. (So if your seasons are days and are represented as Mon, Tue, Wed, Thu, Fri, Sat, and Sun, you should use the same abbreviations in the first column of the lookup table.)

Figure 5.19

The range A2:D5 serves as a sort of template for the actual code vectors.

| E8 | | | | : | × | ✓ | fx | =VLOOKUP($B8,$A$2:$D$5,2) |

▲	A	B	C	D	E	F	G	H	I	J
1	Quarter	Vector 1	Vector 2	Vector 3				LINEST()		
2	1	1	0	0		-80.51	-33.19	101.93	26.52	124.40
3	2	0	1	0		14.47	14.47	14.62	1.47	17.59
4	3	0	0	1		0.96	37.31	#N/A	#N/A	#N/A
5	4	-1	-1	-1		92.69	15	#N/A	#N/A	#N/A
6						516077.18	20879.38	#N/A	#N/A	#N/A
7	Year	Quarter	Average Daily Hits	t	Vector 1	Vector 2	Vector 3			TREND()
8	2001	1	267	1	1	0	0			252.85
9		2	108	2	0	1	0			144.25
10		3	109	3	0	0	1			123.45
11		4	216	4	-1	-1	-1			242.25
12	2002	1	414	5	1	0	0			358.93
13		2	279	6	0	1	0			250.33
14		3	207	7	0	0	1			229.53
15		4	417	8	-1	-1	-1			348.33
16	2003	1	464	9	1	0	0			465.00
17		2	329	10	0	1	0			356.40
18		3	330	11	0	0	1			335.60
19		4	457	12	-1	-1	-1			454.40
20	2004	1	505	13	1	0	0			571.08
21		2	451	14	0	1	0			462.48
22		3	466	15	0	0	1			441.68
23		4	538	16	-1	-1	-1			560.48

You'll also need as many vector columns in the lookup range as you have seasons, minus 1. In Figure 5.19, for example, there are four quarters, so the lookup range has three columns—one for each vector.

Enter the 1s, 0s, and –1s as shown. Using the codes in this way results in a set of regression coefficients which quantify the *effect* of being in a given group.

The basic rules are these:

- Enter a 1 in the column that represents the season identified in the lookup range's first column, and 0s in the remaining columns of that row.
- For the final season, enter –1s throughout the vectors on its row.

Then, enter this formula in the first row, first code vector (in Figure 5.19, that's cell E8):

```
=VLOOKUP($B8,$A$2:$D$5,2)
```

The first argument, which here is $B8, should be a reference to the season identifier for the first record. It anchors the reference to column B so that you can drag it to the right without column B adjusting to columns C and D. Note that cell B8 contains a 1. The fact that the value 1 is in column B means that the record on row 8 belongs to Quarter 1.

The second argument, in this case $A$2:$D$5, should refer to the lookup range (without the column headers that Figure 5.19 shows in row 1). The third argument should identify the column with the codes for the first vector; here, that's column B, the second column in the lookup range.

Use cell E8's selection handle to drag the formula into columns F and G. You'll need to edit the final argument from 2 to 3 in column F, and from 2 to 4 in column G. The formulas in F8 and G8 should now be, respectively,

```
=VLOOKUP($B8,$A$2:$D$5,3)
```

and

```
=VLOOKUP($B8,$A$2:$D$5,4)
```

Finally, make a multiple selection of E8:G8 and drag it down as far as your time series goes—in the layout shown in Figure 5.19, that's through row 27, although only the first 23 rows are visible in the figure. If the column immediately to the left of the coded vectors has data all the way to the end of the time series, just double-click cell G8's selection handle to copy and paste the formulas all the way down, and no farther.

At this point, you're in a position to use LINEST() to get the regression equation and associated statistics to evaluate it, and TREND() to get the seasonal forecasts. Figure 5.19 uses this array formula in F2:J6:

```
=LINEST(C8:C27,D8:G27,,TRUE)
```

And this one in J8:J27:

```
=TREND(C8:C27,D8:G27)
```

You can get the one-step-ahead forecast for the first quarter of 2006 using the same approach as shown at the bottom of Figure 5.17.

Dummy Coding

Effect coding has a close relative called *dummy coding*. It uses the same data setup as effect coding, with one crucial difference: The records that get –1s in each vector with effect coding get 0s instead in dummy coding. Figure 5.20 shows the data in Figure 5.19 set up for dummy coding.

Using dummy coding instead of effect coding changes no regression statistics other than the regression coefficients and intercept for the coded vectors, and their standard errors (found in LINEST()'s second row). With dummy coding, the coefficient for each coded variable expresses the difference between the mean of the group associated with that variable, and the mean of the group that gets 0s on all vectors.

This characteristic makes dummy coding helpful in experiments in which two or more treatment groups are contrasted with a control group. Dummy coding can also prove useful in logistic regression because it can make interpretation of the results more straightforward.

Figure 5.20
Notice that the overall regression statistics such as R^2 are unaffected by the choice of coding method.

| J8 | | | ▼ | : | × | ✓ | f_x | {=TREND(C8:C27,D8:G27)} |

	A	B	C	D	E	F	G	H	I	J
1	Quarter	Vector 1	Vector 2	Vector 3		LINEST()				
2	1	1	0	0		-92.28	-44.96	90.16	26.52	136.18
3	2	0	1	0		23.64	23.78	24.01	1.47	24.32
4	3	0	0	1		0.96	37.31	#N/A	#N/A	#N/A
5	4	0	0	0		92.69	15	#N/A	#N/A	#N/A
6						516077.18	20879.38	#N/A	#N/A	#N/A
7	Year	Quarter	Average Daily Hits	t	Vector 1	Vector 2	Vector 3			TREND()
8	2001	1	267	1	1	0	0			252.85
9		2	108	2	0	1	0			144.25
10		3	109	3	0	0	1			123.45
11		4	216	4	0	0	0			242.25
12	2002	1	414	5	1	0	0			358.93
13		2	279	6	0	1	0			250.33
14		3	207	7	0	0	1			229.53
15		4	417	8	0	0	0			348.33
16	2003	1	464	9	1	0	0			465.00
17		2	329	10	0	1	0			356.40
18		3	330	11	0	0	1			335.60
19		4	457	12	0	0	0			454.40
20	2004	1	505	13	1	0	0			571.08
21		2	451	14	0	1	0			462.48
22		3	466	15	0	0	1			441.68

Simple Seasonal Exponential Smoothing

The remaining sections of this chapter omit the use of regression-based solutions to seasonal time series and focus on smoothing solutions. The Holt method for dealing with trended, but not seasonal, time series employs two smoothing constants, one for the series' level and one for its trend or slope. The constant for the series level is usually termed *Alpha*, and I referred to the constant for the series trend as *Gamma* in Chapter 4.

In this chapter, you'll see that we need yet another constant for the series' seasonality, and I'll term that *Delta*. As I have mentioned in prior chapters, authors on these matters are just not consistent in their naming conventions. It's my sense that the usage of Alpha, Gamma, and Delta for level, trend, and season conforms to more authors' usage than do other names for smoothing constants.

For the moment, though, we can set Gamma aside. This section discusses horizontal, stationary time series that therefore are not trended but that display regular seasonal fluctuations. We can wait until a later section, "Holt-Winters Models," on series with both trend and seasonality to start worrying about Gamma again.

Start with Figure 5.21, which shows a horizontal, stationary time series with six two-month seasons per year.

Figure 5.21
No trend appears in this time series, but some seasonality is present.

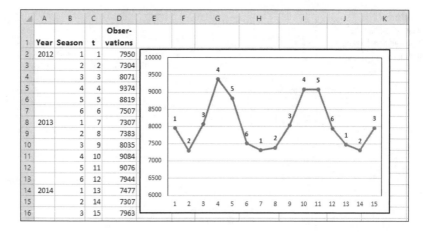

	A	B	C	D
1	Year	Season	t	Obser-vations
2	2012	1	1	7950
3		2	2	7304
4		3	3	8071
5		4	4	9374
6		5	5	8819
7		6	6	7507
8	2013	1	7	7307
9		2	8	7383
10		3	9	8035
11		4	10	9084
12		5	11	9076
13		6	12	7944
14	2014	1	13	7477
15		2	14	7307
16		3	15	7963

Suppose that the numbers in column D in Figure 5.21, the values that are shown in the chart, represent new or renewing subscriptions to a magazine that is published once every two months. Over the two-and-a-half-year period shown, the number of subscriptions appears to be holding steady, but if you're willing to take two years as a reasonable time slice, there's some evidence of a seasonal effect. The number of new or renewing subscriptions appears to peak in the fourth season, and perhaps the fifth, falling back during the remaining four or five seasons.

There's reason enough, at least, to try to model the series and see what turns up. The first step is to initialize some forecasts. See Figure 5.22.

To keep the focus on how the seasons are handled, I have initialized the seasonal indexes by defining them as simple deviations from the mean of the first year. The steps are straight-forward:

1. Put the average of the observations from the first six seasons—the first year—in cell L3 with the formula =AVERAGE(D2:D7).

2. Give cell L3 a name such as Year_1_Mean. The main idea behind doing so (apart from its convenience) is to ensure that references to that value are fixed, and will not adjust when you copy and paste formulas that make use of it.

3. Enter the formula =D2-Year_1_Mean in cell H2. This seasonal index expresses the distance between the first year's average and the first season's value.

4. Copy cell H2 and paste it into the range H3:H7. You now have initial seasonal index values for the six seasons in H2:H7.

Figure 5.22
Seasonal indexes are initialized here by simple deviations from the Year 1 mean.

	G7	▼	:	× ✓	f_x	=Year_1_Mean					
	A	B	C	D	E	F	G	H	I	J	K	L
1	Year	Season	t	Obser-vations	Forecast for this period		Estimated Level	Estimated Seasonal Index	Forecast for next period			
2	2012	1	1	7950				-220.8				
3		2	2	7304				-866.8			Year 1 Mean	8170.8
4		3	3	8071				-99.8				
5		4	4	9374				1203.2				
6		5	5	8819				648.2				
7		6	6	7507			8170.8	-663.8	7950.0			
8	2013	1	7	7307	7950.0							
9		2	8	7383								
10		3	9	8035								
11		4	10	9084								
12		5	11	9076								
13		6	12	7944								
14	2014	1	13	7477								
15		2	14	7307								
16		3	15	7963								
17		4	16									
18		5	17									
19		6	18									
20	2015	1	19									
21		2	20									
22		3	21									

While you're at it, you might as well get the forecasts going. These three formulas form the basis:

- Cell G7: =Year_1_Mean. Simplistically, the mean of the first year of observations gives you the estimate of the level of the first season of the second year.

- Cell I7: =G7+H2. The forecast for the next period, season 1 year 2, is the sum of the estimated level in G7 and the seasonal index in H2. Notice that the seasonal index in H2 is the index for the first season, which is the season we're forecasting.

- Cell E8: =I7. The purpose of the formulas in column E is simply to display the forecast in another cell. The forecast that's computed in cell I7 shows that you can make the forecast in the season prior to the one that you're forecasting. The forecast that's displayed in E8 shows the same value as part of the data for the season that you're forecasting.

Now you're ready to complete the forecasts. See Figure 5.23 for the remaining entries.

Add the labels Alpha and Delta in cells K1 and K2, and add the values 0.1 and 0.3 in L1 and L2. It's not strictly necessary, but I suggest that you use Define Name on the Ribbon's Formula tab to name cell L1 as Alpha and L2 as Delta. That will help keep the contents of your smoothing formulas clearer. If you don't name those cells, you'll want to make references to them fixed—for example, $L$1 instead of L1.

Figure 5.23
The named smoothing constants make it easy to experiment with different smoothing values.

	A	B	C	D	E	F	G	H	I	J	K	L
	Year	Season	t	Observations	Forecast for this period	Error	Estimated Level (Error Correction)	Seasonal Index (Error Correction)	Forecast for next period			
1											Alpha	0.1
2	2012	1	1	7950				-220.8			Delta	0.3
3		2	2	7304				-866.8			Year 1 Mean	8170.8
4		3	3	8071				-99.8				
5		4	4	9374				1203.2			RMSE	321.59
6		5	5	8819				648.2				
7		6	6	7507			8170.8	-663.8	7950.0			
8	2013	1	7	7307	7950.0	-643.0	8106.5	-394.4	7239.7			
9		2	8	7383	7239.7	143.3	8120.9	-828.1	8021.0			
10		3	9	8035	8021.0	14.0	8122.3	-96.1	9325.4			
11		4	10	9084	9325.4	-241.4	8098.1	1138.0	8746.3			
12		5	11	9076	8746.3	329.7	8131.1	737.2	7467.3			
13		6	12	7944	7467.3	476.7	8178.8	-535.1	7784.3			
14	2014	1	13	7477	7784.3	-307.3	8148.0	-477.4	7319.9			
15		2	14	7307	7319.9	-12.9	8146.7	-831.6	8050.7			
16		3	15	7963	8050.7	-87.7	8138.0	-119.7	9276.0			
17		4	16		9276.0		8138.0		8875.2			
18		5	17		8875.2		8138.0		7602.9			
19		6	18		7602.9		8138.0		7660.6			
20	2015	1	19		7660.6		8138.0		7306.4			
21		2	20		7306.4		8138.0		8018.2			
22		3	21		8018.2		8138.0					

L5 = =SQRT(SUMXMY2(D8:D16,E8:E16)/9)

Establish the smoothing process with the following four steps, which you can take in any order:

- Calculate the error involved in your first forecast. Enter =D8-E8 in cell F8.
- Start smoothing the series level. Enter =G7+Alpha*F8 in cell G8.
- Start smoothing the seasonal indexes. Enter =H2+Delta*(1-Alpha)*F8 in cell H8.
- Get your forecast for year 2, season 2. Enter =G8+H3 in cell I8.
- Prepare to evaluate your forecast accuracy via root mean square error. Enter =SQRT(SUMXMY2(D8:D16,E8:E16)/9) in cell L5.

Finally, extend your forecasts through the third season of the fourth year. Copy and paste, or autofill:

- Cell I8 through I21
- Cell H8 through H16
- Cell G8 through G22
- Cell F8 through F16
- Cell E8 through E22

Notice that with seasonal smoothing, you're not limited to one-step-ahead forecasts, as you are with simple exponential smoothing limits. You do run out of actual observations at Period 15, the third season in the third year. Without additional observations, you can't smooth the level—this is the reason that continuing to forecast past the end of the time series with simple exponential smoothing turns into a series of constant forecasts.

However, your forecasts lag one year behind your seasonals: To get a forecast for season 1 in year 2, you look to the seasonal index for season 1 in year 1. So by the time you reach the end of your actual observations, you still have some seasonal indexes to come.

You've assumed that you have a stationary series. Therefore, one good assumption is that the most recent estimated level of the series is the best available estimate of its level for subsequent periods. That assumption grows legs in the form of the constant level estimates returned in the range G16:G22 of Figure 5.23.

The forecasts from E17:E22, then, are based on the sum of the constant estimate of the series level, 8138.0, and the seasonal indexes in H11:H16. You can get a different view of how this works out in Figure 5.24.

Figure 5.24
Forecasts from Period 16 and forward are based on a constant level estimate plus varying seasonal indexes.

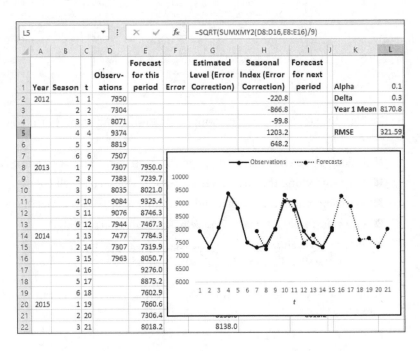

So simple seasonal smoothing enables you to get varying forecasts beyond the one-step-ahead available from simple smoothing. But it doesn't follow that the seasonal forecasts necessarily have any more validity or accuracy than you find in a pile of wet tea leaves. You can drag a regression forecast as far as you want in either direction, and beyond some point it loses meaning. Your regression equation might tell you that if you reduce a person's LDL cholesterol level to 0.5, his life expectancy increases to 254, but you don't have to believe it.

Nevertheless, you're likely to find that your forecasts come close to the actuals they're meant to estimate much more often than not. Just maintain a healthy skepticism. If the results are used to help make important decisions, revisit your analysis and its underlying assumptions frequently.

About the Level Smoothing Formulas

The smoothing formulas that I've used in Figures 5.23 and 5.24 use the *error correction* form. Smoothing formulas, whether for levels, trends, or seasonal indexes, can use either the error correction or the *smoothing* form. I used the smoothing forms in examples in Chapter 4. I use the error correction form in this chapter, mainly so that you'll have a chance to see both forms.

The forms are arithmetically equivalent. The error correction form was perhaps more popular than the smoothing form through the 1980s because it was harder then to get access to computing power, and applications like VisiCalc and Lotus 1-2-3 were, by today's standards, crude. The error correction forms were easier to calculate if you were using a TRS-80 or the back of an envelope.

The virtue of the smoothing form is that it emphasizes the fact that you use a smoothing constant—again, for the level, trend, or seasonality in a time series—to create a weighted average of a current observation and a prior forecast. So the smoothing form of the formula for a series' level is

$$\hat{L}_t = \alpha\left(y_t - \hat{S}_{t-m}\right) + \left(1-\alpha\right)\hat{L}_{t-1}$$

where

- $\hat{L}_t$ is the series level at time t.
- y_t is the observed value at time t.
- $\hat{S}_{t-m}$ is the seasonal effect for season $t - m$, where m is the number of seasons in the encompassing period.

> **NOTE**
> For example, if each month is a season, $m = 12$ and the seasonal effect to use for the second instance of January would be $t - m$ or $13 - 12 = 1$.

- $\hat{L}_{t-1}$ is the level forecast for time t made at time $t - 1$.

So this formula is an example of the smoothing form, Alpha times the current actual plus (1 – Alpha) times the prior forecast—a weighted average in which the weights can be thought of as percentages, such that if Alpha is .3 or 30%, then (1 – Alpha) is .7 or 70%.

Notice that the actual value used in the formula is the *seasonally adjusted* observation, $\left(y_t - \hat{S}_{t-m}\right)$.

We can get to the error correction form of the equation in just a few steps:

$$\hat{L}_t = \alpha\left(y_t - \hat{S}_{t-m}\right) + (1-\alpha)\hat{L}_{t-1}$$

$$\hat{L}_t = \alpha\left(y_t - \hat{S}_{t-m}\right) + \hat{L}_{t-1} - \alpha\hat{L}_{t-1}$$

$$\hat{L}_t = \hat{L}_{t-1} + \alpha\left(y_t - \hat{S}_{t-m}\right) - \alpha\hat{L}_{t-1}$$

$$\hat{L}_t = \hat{L}_{t-1} + \alpha\left(y_t - [\hat{S}_{t-m} + \hat{L}_{t-1}]\right)$$

Now, $\hat{S}_{t-m} + \hat{L}_{t-1}$ is the forecast for the level at time t made at time $t-1$. If you subtract that forecast from the actual value observed at time t, you get the error in the forecast at time t, or e_t. That leads to the error correction form for the series level:

$$\hat{L}_t = \hat{L}_{t-1} + \alpha\,e_t$$

About the Season Smoothing Formulas

Similarly, here's the smoothing form of the equation for the seasonal indexes:

$$\hat{S}_t = \delta\left(y_t - \hat{L}_t\right) + (1-\delta)\hat{S}_{t-m}$$

We're assuming a horizontal, stationary series, so we assign any difference between the currently observed value y_t and the current level estimate, $\hat{L}_t$, to the seasonal effect. Notice also that (1 – Delta) is multiplied by the most recent estimate of the seasonal index. If t is 10, so that we're in season 4, we use the forecast seasonal index from $(t - m) = (10 - 6) = 4$, or 1203.2 in cell H5 (shown in both Figure 5.23 and Figure 5.24).

And here's the error correction form for the seasonal indexes:

$$\hat{S}_t = \hat{S}_{t-m} + \delta\left(1 - \alpha\right)\varepsilon_t$$

I have used the error correction form for the levels and the seasonal indexes in Figures 5.23 and 5.24. Figure 5.25 uses the smoothing forms so that you can verify their equivalence.

Figure 5.25
The level formulas for periods 16 through 21 need special handling.

				G17		▾	⋮	✕	✓	*fx*	=G16	

	A	B	C	D	E	F	G	H	I	J	K	L
1	Year	Season	t	Observ-ations	Forecast for this period	Error	Estimated Level (Smoothing)	Seasonal Index (Smoothing)	Forecast for next period		Alpha	0.1
2	2012	1	1	7950				-220.8			Delta	0.3
3		2	2	7304				-866.8			Year 1 Mean	8170.8
4		3	3	8071				-99.8				
5		4	4	9374				1203.2			RMSE	321.6
6		5	5	8819				648.2				
7		6	6	7507			8170.8	-663.8	7950.0			
8	2013	1	7	7307	7950.0	-643.0	8106.5	-394.4	7239.7			
9		2	8	7383	7239.7	143.3	8120.9	-828.1	8021.0			
10		3	9	8035	8021.0	14.0	8122.3	-96.1	9325.4			
11		4	10	9084	9325.4	-241.4	8098.1	1138.0	8746.3			
12		5	11	9076	8746.3	329.7	8131.1	737.2	7467.3			
13		6	12	7944	7467.3	476.7	8178.8	-535.1	7784.3			
14	2014	1	13	7477	7784.3	-307.3	8148.0	-477.4	7319.9			
15		2	14	7307	7319.9	-12.9	8146.7	-831.6	8050.7			
16		3	15	7963	8050.7	-87.7	8138.0					
17		4	16		9276.0		8138.0					
18		5	17		8875.2		8138.0					
19		6	18		7602.9		8138.0					
20	2015	1	19		7660.6		8138.0		7306.4			
21		2	20		7306.4		8138.0		8018.2			
22		3	21		8018.2		8138.0					

Note that the formula must change here, whereas the error correction version need not.

Dealing with the End of the Time Series

Comparing Figures 5.23 and 5.25 reveals another, relatively minor, reason to prefer the error correction form of the level equations, at least as you'd design them in Excel. I've altered the formula in cell G17 (for the level estimate at *t* = 16) from

```
=Alpha*(D17-H11)+(1-Alpha)*G16
```

to

```
=G16
```

and copied that alteration down though G22 (the range G17:G22 is shaded in Figure 5.25). The reason is that when you run out of new observations, as you do at *t* = 16, you're no longer able to estimate the current level by subtracting the existing seasonal index from the current observation. The current observation, from *t* = 16 through the end of the time series, is missing and treated as zero. So you're no longer smoothing the level with Alpha times the current season estimate of D17 – H11; you're smoothing it with Alpha times 0 minus the prior estimate in H11.

In contrast, the error correction form uses this formula for the level estimate at *t* = 16 (see cell G17 in Figure 5.23):

```
=G16+Alpha*F17
```

But F17 through F22 are empty because you can no longer calculate error values when you run out of actual observations, so the formula reduces to

```
=G16+Alpha*0
```

5

in cell G17, and similarly in later time periods. The result is that the level formula returns a constant after the final actual observation. This happens automatically using the error correction form of the seasonal index estimate, but you have to make special provision with the smoothing form.

Apart from that, and for time periods when actual observations are available, the smoothing form and the error correction form are functionally equivalent. You can base your choice on whether you prefer to think of a smoothing formula as a weighted average of an actual observation and a prior forecast or as the prior forecast plus a percentage of the forecast error.

> **NOTE**   Yes, you could insert a test in the smoothing form of the seasonal index formula, to check whether you've reached the end of the actual observations. But that test would have to be included in all the formulas found in column G of Figure 5.25. That's a needless complication when a simple fix at the end of the series accomplishes the same end.

Holt-Winters Models

When you add a trend to a seasonal time series, you enter the bailiwick of what's usually known as the Holt-Winters model. At first glance it might seem as though all you need to do is add a smoothing constant for the trend, as discussed in "Using Holt's Linear Exponential Smoothing" in Chapter 3. And that first glance is largely correct—it's only a little more complicated than that.

The smoothing form (and therefore the error correction form) of the equation to update each season is the same as is given earlier in this chapter, in "About the Season Smoothing Formulas." Here it is again:

$$\hat{S}_t = \delta \left(y_t - \hat{L}_t \right) + (1 - \delta) \hat{S}_{t-m}$$

In words, the seasonal index for time t starts with Delta times the difference between the current observation and the current level of the series. To that is added (1 – Delta) times the index for the season associated with the current period, or the index that's m seasons back.

No difference with the untrended seasonal series so far, but here's the smoothing formula for the trend:

$$b_t = \gamma \left(L_t - L_{t-1} \right) + (1 - \gamma) b_{t-1}$$

The difference between the current level, L_t, and the prior level, L_{t-1}, is taken to be the value of the current trend. That difference is multiplied by Gamma. Then we obtain the value of the immediately previous trend, b_{t-1}, and multiply by (1 – Gamma). The sum of the two terms gets us a measure of the current trend.

Finally, the formula for the level is nearly the same as in the untrended seasonal model. Here's the formula for a trended, seasonal model:

$$L_t = \alpha\left(y_t - \hat{S}_{t-m}\right) + (1-\alpha)\left(L_{t-1} + b_{t-1}\right)$$

For the untrended, seasonal model the formula is this:

$$L_t = \alpha\left(y_t - \hat{S}_{t-m}\right) + (1-\alpha)L_{t-1}$$

The difference between the two formulas is of course due to the presence of the b_{t-1} term in the former formula. The value of the trend as of time $t - 1$ is included because we're now dealing with a trended series. In an untrended series we assume that there is no trend, that any difference between observations not caused by season or level is part of the error in the model.

But in a trended series the trend term is explicitly acknowledged. Let's see how it works out in practice. Figure 5.26 has the first few observations from the well-known Series G, found in Box and Jenkins's seminal book on ARIMA analysis. Series G is a count of airline passengers during each month of a 12-year period. Because the number of airline passengers is seasonal and, at the time (1949 through 1960), was trending strongly up, a Holt-Winters model is apt.

Figure 5.26
This time series clearly demonstrates both trend and seasonality.

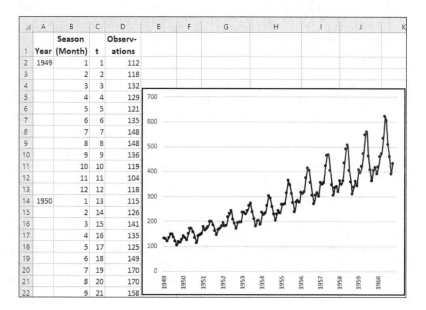

The degree of seasonality appears to vary with the level of the series—that is, the higher the level of the series, the greater the swings between a year's high month and its low month.

This is a characteristic that suggests using a multiplicative model, which sounds a lot more forbidding than it really is, and which I discuss in Chapter 7, "Multiplicative and Damped Trend Models." But for the time being, this chapter builds an additive Holt-Winters model that's directly analogous to the one discussed in the preceding section, "Simple Seasonal Exponential Smoothing."

Initializing the Forecasts

As Chapter 4 shows, there are many ways to go about initializing forecasts, and the more complicated the model the more choices you have. For example, in various sources, I've seen the Box-Jenkins Series G initialized using these approaches, among others, for a Holt-Winters analysis:

- By treating the mean of the first 12 months as the level of Period 0.

- By treating the difference between the result of Period 1 and each monthly observation during the first year as initial values of the seasonal indexes.

- By dividing the difference between the series' 12th and 1st observations by 11; more generally, subtract the first observation from the mth observation and divide by $(m - 1)$. Treat the result as the initial value of the monthly trend.

That's a kind of rough-and-ready way to initialize the estimates of level, season, and trend; it might be a little crude compared to the more sophisticated approaches such as optimization, backcasting, and regression. But it's quick, reasonable, and unlikely to steer you far wrong, particularly if you're fortunate enough to have a lengthy baseline.

> **NOTE** More precisely: The Series G data set has 144 observations. If you have so lengthy a baseline, your choice of initialization methods is likely to have a vanishingly small effect on the one-step-ahead forecast of the 145th time period. But two different initialization methods can easily result in meaningful differences in the early forecasts. Those forecast differences will bring about differences, possibly meaningful ones, in measures of forecast accuracy such as RMSE and MAD—even though they are averages.

There's also the issue of when you start your forecasts. Figure 5.27 shows the first 14 periods of the Box-Jenkins Series G data, with the actual observations in column D. (The full set of 144 observations is included in the workbook for this chapter, which you can download from the publisher's website.) In Figure 5.27, the forecasts begin after the first year.

Figure 5.27
The forecasts, and therefore the forecast errors, start one year later in Figure 5.28 than they do in this figure.

	J13		▼	:	×	✓	*fₓ*	=G13+H13+I2				

	C	D	E	F	G	H	I	J	K	L	M
1	t	Observ-ations	Forecast for this period	Error	Estimated Level	Estimated Trend	Estimated Seasonal Index	Forecast for next period		Alpha	0.1
2	1	112					-14.7			Gamma	0.1
3	2	118					-8.7			Delta	0.2
4	3	132					5.3			Year 1 Mean	126.67
5	4	129					2.3			Year 1 Trend	0.55
6	5	121					-5.7			RMSE	24.51
7	6	135					8.3				
8	7	148					21.3				
9	8	148					21.3				
10	9	136					9.3				
11	10	119					-7.7				
12	11	104					-22.7				
13	12	118			126.7	0.5	-8.7	112.5			
14	13	115	112.5	2.5	127.5	0.6	-14.2	119.4			
15	14	126	119.4	6.6	128.7	0.6	-7.5	134.7			

Here's how the formulas are set up in Figure 5.27:

- The mean of the observations for the first encompassing period—in this case, that's 1949—is entered with this formula in cell M4:

    =AVERAGE(D2:D13)

    The cell is named Year_1_Mean.

- An estimate of the monthly trend during the first year is entered with this formula in cell M5:

    =(D13-D2)/11

    The cell is named Year_1_Trend. Bear in mind that it estimates the *monthly* trend during the first year.

- The seasonal indexes for the first year are initiated with this formula in cell I2:

    =D2-Year_1_Mean

    The formula is simply the difference between the observation for the first month, less the mean observation for the first year. That formula is copied and pasted down through I13, to initialize each of the 12 seasonal estimates.

- Cell G13 carries the first year's mean into the column for level estimates with this formula:

    =Year_1_Mean

- Cell H13 carries the first year's monthly trend into the column for trend estimates with this formula:

    =Year_1_Trend

- Cell J13 calculates the first smoothing forecast, this one for the 13th period, the first month of the second year. As with all the remaining forecasts, the one in cell J13 totals the level, the trend, and the seasonal index. This is the formula in cell J13:

    =G13+H13+I2

5

Notice that the formula uses the seasonal value from the first month of the first year in cell I2.

■ The forecast for Period 13 is repeated from cell J13 to cell E14 with this formula in E14:

```
=J13
```

And the forecast error, the difference between the current observation and the forecast for the 13th period, is entered in cell F14 with this formula:

```
=D14-E14
```

■ The smoothing forecasts begin with the level estimate in cell G14, with this formula:

```
=Alpha*(D14-I2)+(1-Alpha)*(G13+H13)
```

You remove the seasonal effect from the observed value for the current period by subtracting the seasonal index (cell I2) from the observed value (cell D4); the result is multiplied by Alpha. The projected level (cell G13) and the projected trend (cell H13) as of the prior period are summed and the result is multiplied by (1 – Alpha). The two terms are summed to return the estimated series level as of Period 13.

■ The trend as of Period 13 is forecast in cell H14 with this formula:

```
=Gamma*(G14-G13)+(1-Gamma)*H13
```

The difference between the prior level and the current level (cells G13 and G14) is taken to be the current trend observation, and is multiplied by Gamma. The value in cell H13 is the forecast trend as of the prior period, and is multiplied by (1 – Gamma). The two terms are summed to return the estimated series trend as of Period 13.

■ The seasonal index as of Period 13 is forecast in cell I14 with this formula:

```
=Delta*(D14-G14)+(1-Delta)*I2
```

The difference between the current observation in cell D14 and the current level in cell G14 is taken to be the current seasonal effect; it is multiplied by Delta. The prior seasonal effect in cell I2 is multiplied by (1 – Delta). The two terms are summed to reach a smoothed seasonal index for Period 13.

■ The forecast for the next period is placed in cell J13 with the formula

```
=G14+H14+I3
```

totaling the current level, trend, and seasonal index. Notice that although we have just calculated the value of the seasonal index for Period 13 in cell I14, for the purpose of making the current forecast we use the seasonal index from one year back in cell I3.

■ The remainder of the time series can now be forecast by selecting cells E14:J14, copying them, and pasting them from E15 to J145. You can get the one-step-ahead forecast by copying G145:J145 into G146:J146. And you can push the final forecast a little further out by following the procedures I suggest in an earlier section of this chapter, "Dealing with the End of the Time Series."

Starting the Forecasts Earlier

Notice in Figure 5.27 that the forecasting process does not begin until the 13th period. There's no particular reason that this should be so. Compare Figure 5.27 with Figure 5.28.

Figure 5.28
The forecasts start at $t = 1$.

| J14 | | | × | ✓ | f_x | =G14+H14+I3 | | | | |

	C	D	E	F	G	H	I	J	K	L	M
	t	Observ-ations	Forecast for this period	Error	Estimated Level	Estimated Trend	Estimated Seasonal Index	Forecast for next period			
1										Alpha	0.253
2	-11						-14.7			Gamma	0.044
3	-10						-8.7			Delta	1
4	-9						5.3			Year 1 Mean	126.7
5	-8						2.3			Year 1 Trend	0.5
6	-7						-5.7			RMSE	13.02
7	-6						8.3				
8	-5						21.3				
9	-4						21.3				
10	-3						9.3				
11	-2						-7.7				
12	-1						-22.7				
13	0				126.7	0.5	-8.7	112.5			
14	1	112	112.5	-0.5	127.1	0.5	-15.1	118.9			
15	2	118	118.9	-0.9	127.4	0.5	-9.4	133.2			
16	3	132	133.2	-1.2	127.6	0.5	4.4	130.4			

In Figure 5.28, I have inserted extra rows for periods –11 through 0. This provides a place to store the seasonal estimates based on the differences between the first year's mean and its monthly observations. Notice that in Figure 5.28, the first forecast is for $t = 1$, whereas the first forecast is for $t = 13$ in Figure 5.27.

With a good, long baseline such as is available in Box-Jenkins Series G, this difference isn't cause for much concern. Notice, for example, that the values for the root mean square error are very close to one another in Figures 5.27 and 5.28. And see Figure 5.29 for another sort of comparison.

In Figure 5.29, I show the individual errors based on the actual versus forecast differences for time periods 13 through 144; column A shows the errors when the forecasts begin at $t = 13$, and column B shows the errors when the forecasts begin at $t = 1$. When the forecasts begin at $t = 13$, the forecast error for that period is different than when they begin at $t = 1$. Therefore the level forecast for $t = 14$, and for subsequent periods, is different for the two sets of forecasts.

5

Figure 5.29

The errors are indistinguishable in the chart, but the swings are greater later in both series.

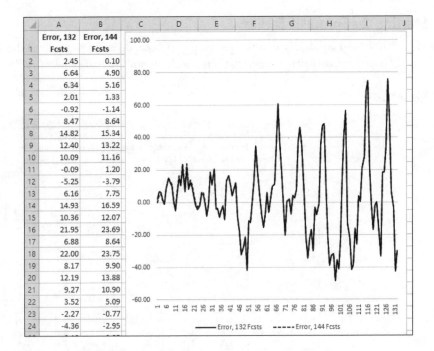

	A	B
1	Error, 132 Fcsts	Error, 144 Fcsts
2	2.45	0.10
3	6.64	4.90
4	6.34	5.16
5	2.01	1.33
6	-0.92	-1.14
7	8.47	8.64
8	14.82	15.34
9	12.40	13.22
10	10.09	11.16
11	-0.09	1.20
12	-5.25	-3.79
13	6.16	7.75
14	14.93	16.59
15	10.36	12.07
16	21.95	23.69
17	6.88	8.64
18	22.00	23.75
19	8.17	9.90
20	12.19	13.88
21	9.27	10.90
22	3.52	5.09
23	-2.27	-0.77
24	-4.36	-2.95

In this case the differences between the forecast errors in columns A and B are very small relative to the overall series mean. Nevertheless, the differences are greater during the first 40 to 50 time periods than during the final 40 or 50. You can't tell that from the chart because the charted values are so close to one another that one charted series obscures the other. But you could easily get a very different result with another set of observations, perhaps one that isn't so well behaved.

Also, note in the chart that the swings are greater as the level of the series increases. This is an argument for using a multiplicative model rather than an additive model. I discuss the differences between the models in Chapter 7.

First, though, Chapter 6, "Names, Addresses, and Formulas," discusses some techniques in Excel that can make it much more straightforward to design and interpret the more complex smoothing models.

Names, Addresses, and Formulas

6

When you first start learning about and using exponential smoothing, things are pretty straightforward. Yes, it might take a little study before the *exponential* part of exponential smoothing starts to become clear. And it's not immediately obvious what the consequences of using an Alpha smoothing constant of zero, or of 1.0, might be.

But the basic notion of a weighted average of a forecast and an observation is not terribly involved. Neither is the companion notion of building a forecast by combining the prior forecast with a correction of the prior forecast.

Things begin to get more involved when you start working with more complex models. Add a trend to a series, as occurs when a new virus starts to stress the health-care system, and you need to deploy a method such as Holt's to account for change in the trend as well as the level.

Or take note of seasons in a series, as when a new product hits the market with revenues that rise and fall with regularity. Now you need to account for that seasonality with methods such as those originated by Winters and Holt. And of course it's often useful to bring Holt-Winters methods to bear on series that evidence both trend and seasonality.

That's three fundamental models—trended, seasonal, and trended-seasonal—each with a different wrinkle vis-à-vis simple smoothing, and we still have damped models to account for.

Furthermore, we have both additive and multiplicative methods of dealing with seasonality. What begins as a fairly clear means of forecasting a horizontal series without seasonality becomes a matrix of models by methods: a matrix that has prompted some writers—quite reasonably in my view—to propose an entire taxonomy of smoothing methods.

Fortunately, Microsoft Excel provides such an intuitive interface for these sorts of analyses that the complexities I've just mentioned turn out to be much less of a problem. Automatic recalculation of formulas, to say nothing of the power inherent in copying and pasting formulas, removes many of the difficulties that characterized smoothing before VisiCalc, before 1-2-3, and before Excel.

One aspect of using any really interactive application such as Excel to perform smoothing analyses is that, by default, you find yourself pointing at and clicking on cells. Those cells are identified precisely by means of their column letter and row number, but by themselves their locations carry no conceptual meaning.

It's precise but unhelpful to see an expression such as (C10 – F9) in a formula. To interpret that expression, you have to determine the meaning of the contents of cell C10, do the same for cell F9, and decide on the meaning of the difference between the two values.

But what if instead of looking at (C10 – F9), you were looking at an expression such as (CurrentObservation – PriorForecast)? Now you immediately know what's supposed to be subtracted from what. Furthermore, if you've studied exponential smoothing at all, you know both that the difference between the current observation and the prior forecast represents the error in the forecast, and the role that the forecast error plays in calculating the next forecast.

You can arrange for those clarifications in Excel by means of *range names*. It requires a little care to make sure that the names you assign refer to precisely the ranges you want them to. But if you take that care at the outset, you'll find that you can refer to the worksheet cells and ranges as precisely as if you use standard column-and-row addressing. In fact, you'll probably find that your formulas are more accurate when you use range names, because accidental errors are much more likely to jump out at you.

I've used range names in earlier chapters of this book, primarily to clarify the use of the smoothing constants for level, trend, and season. Because the values of those constants don't change during the course of a given analysis (they're called *constants*, after all), there's no need to arrange for their values to change as you move from the start to the end of the time series.

The same is not true for the current estimate of a series' level or its trend or its seasonal effect. Those are variables, not constants, and they vary as the time periods move forward. If we're to refer to them by meaningful name instead of by conceptually meaningless column and row, we have to use special procedures to define the names and to use them effectively. As you've inferred by now, if you didn't know it already, Excel offers those special procedures.

In this chapter, you'll see how to use the implicit intersection and the relative range name to save time during setup, and to avoid errors when you're examining or tweaking your analysis down the road a ways. (As you'll see, in this context *mixed* range names crop up more frequently than *relative* range names.)

6

Okay, if defined names are so useful in smoothing, why haven't I started using names before this point?

Certainly I could have introduced these concepts in the context of smoothing earlier, but I wanted to keep the focus in earlier chapters on the mechanics of the more basic models: stationary versus trended, seasonal versus nonseasonal, even the smoothing forms versus the error correction forms of the equations.

At this point, though, before I take up the topic of additive and multiplicative formulas, the models become somewhat less intuitive, if not markedly more complex. Early on, most people need to spend more time studying the multiplicative formulas before their meanings become clear. Any tools that make the meanings of the formulas less remote are useful.

Different models—defined by no-trend versus trended series, by series with seasons versus those without, and by series that have both trend and seasonality—need different smoothing formulas. It's important to understand how those formulas differ both in concept and in execution.

Further, as you read more about the smoothing approach to predictive analytics—or as you read reports of how others have applied the techniques—you still encounter the use of a given formula's smoothing form as well as its error correction form. There remains a good argument for understanding both forms, even though one rationale for preferring the error correction form, computational ease, has all but disappeared as personal computer applications such as Excel and R have become dominant.

I believe that it's important to understand how it is that apparently unrelated forms of a given formula come to return exactly the same result. That belief is based on the different perspectives that the different forms offer: weighted averages versus error correction.

Therefore, I spend a fair amount of space in this chapter showing how to derive one form from another. Some of these demonstrations are carried out in traditional ways, using symbols to represent the concepts. I also carry them out in the context of the worksheet so that you can see how the result of a given form remains constant as one form is derived from the other. And I carry them out using the tools I mentioned earlier, implicit intersections and mixed range names, so that the formulas carry actual meaning by way of their components.

We Interrupt This Program...

So it's at this point in discussing the smoothing approach to predictive analytics that it becomes useful to introduce, or review, a couple of Excel tools that can make your life a lot easier. I learned about them early in my Excel education, and for some reason I haven't seen them discussed much, in books or articles, since then. Perhaps I just need to read more.

You find opportunities to use these tools only occasionally, but when you do they're indispensable. One is the *implicit intersection*. The other is the *mixed range name*. I use both of them throughout this chapter's examples of smoothing formulas, so let's first take a look at how intersections and mixed references work.

Implicit Intersections

Suppose you're working with the financials table in Figure 6.1.

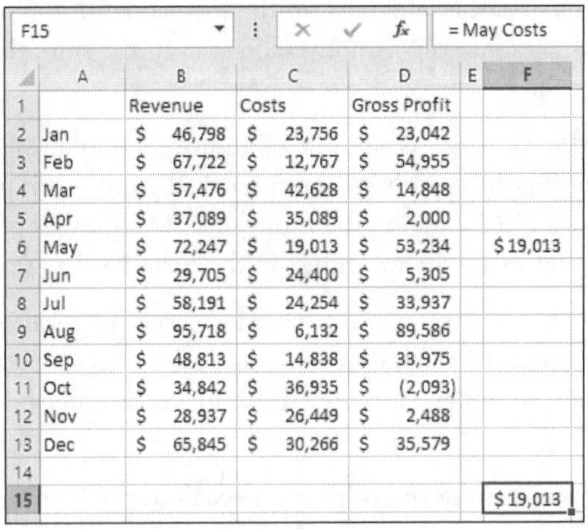
F15 = May Costs

	A	B	C	D	E	F
1		Revenue	Costs	Gross Profit		
2	Jan	$ 46,798	$ 23,756	$ 23,042		
3	Feb	$ 67,722	$ 12,767	$ 54,955		
4	Mar	$ 57,476	$ 42,628	$ 14,848		
5	Apr	$ 37,089	$ 35,089	$ 2,000		
6	May	$ 72,247	$ 19,013	$ 53,234		$ 19,013
7	Jun	$ 29,705	$ 24,400	$ 5,305		
8	Jul	$ 58,191	$ 24,254	$ 33,937		
9	Aug	$ 95,718	$ 6,132	$ 89,586		
10	Sep	$ 48,813	$ 14,838	$ 33,975		
11	Oct	$ 34,842	$ 36,935	$ (2,093)		
12	Nov	$ 28,937	$ 26,449	$ 2,488		
13	Dec	$ 65,845	$ 30,266	$ 35,579		
14						
15						$ 19,013

Figure 6.1
Intersecting named ranges can result in *explicit* intersections.

Each populated row, and each populated column, contains a defined range name. So, for example, the range B3:D3 is named Feb, and B11:D11 is named Oct; similarly, B2:B13 is named Revenue and D2:D13 is named Gross_Profit.

TIP

A quick way to establish names for these ranges is to select, say, A1:D13, click the Ribbon's Formulas tab, and click Create from Selection in the Defined Names group. Choose both Left Column and Top Row as the location of the names' labels, and click OK. This method of defining range names automatically replaces embedded blanks in row and column labels with underscores. So, Gross Profit becomes Gross_Profit.

The possible drawbacks to this quick method are that the names automatically refer to fixed ranges (e.g., $B$2:$D$2), and that the names' scopes are automatically workbook-level instead of restricted to the worksheet where their ranges exist. The notion of a name's *scope* is an important one; if you're not familiar with it, I urge you to look in a book that focuses specifically on Excel's tools.

With this setup—a series of named horizontal ranges that intersect with a series of named vertical ranges—you can use Excel's intersection operator, the blank space, to call for the value of a cell that represents the intersection of two ranges. So the formula

```
=May Costs
```

calls for the value in the cell where the May range intersects the Costs range. So does this:

```
=Costs May
```

In Figure 6.1, the formula is entered in cell F15 and returns the value $19,013, precisely the same as exists in cell C6 where May intersects Costs. It's an explicit intersection because it specifies both of the intersecting ranges you're interested in. You can use it anywhere in the worksheet or, if the names' scopes are both workbook-level, anywhere in the workbook.

In contrast, the formula in cell F6 of Figure 6.1 is

```
=Costs
```

and represents an implicit intersection. It refers to the column where the name Costs is found, but the row is *implied* by the location of the formula itself. Because the formula is located in row 6, the implicit intersection refers to the cell where row 6 intersects the range named Costs.

You can use the implicit intersection only where the cell that contains it intersects the range that it names. For example, still in Figure 6.1, cell F6 is in the sixth worksheet row, which does in fact intersect the Costs range (found in C2:C13); therefore, the intersection exists and Excel can find it.

But if you were to enter that implicit intersection formula in, say, cell F14, it would return the error value #VALUE! (using both capital letters and an exclamation point, which has always struck me as over the top). Row 14 does not intersect the Costs range, and Excel can't return a value found in an intersection that doesn't exist.

The forecast error, the difference between the forecast for a period and the actual observation for that period, plays as central a role in the models discussed in this chapter as it does in simple exponential smoothing, or in the Holt-Winters method, or anything in between. You'll see how the use of a range name such as Error in implicit intersections makes it much easier to see what's going on in a smoothing formula than the use of a cell address such as F8.

The Relative Range Name

When you define a range name in Excel, it is by default a fixed reference. Suppose you use the Name box, or the Ribbon's Define Name control, or its Create from Selection control, to give the name Season1 to cell H8. Unless you take special steps, the name Season1 will refer to cell $H$8—a fixed reference. Therefore, wherever you use the name Season1 on that worksheet, it returns the value found in cell H8. If a formula uses the name Season1, you can copy and paste or autofill it up or down, left or right, and the resulting formulas will all refer to cell H8 via the name Season1, because it was defined as referring to a fixed address, $H$8. The first dollar sign fixes the name Season1 to column H, and the second dollar sign fixes it to row 8.

Much of the time this is exactly what you want. If you're taking the time and effort to define a name that refers to a cell or range, there's reason to believe that the contents of that cell or range are important enough to warrant taking even a few seconds to name it. And if it's that important, most of the time you don't want the meaning of the reference to change as a function of where you use it, be that in row 18 or in row 36.

6

So the Name box and the Create from Selection control assume that you want a fixed reference for the name you're defining. If you want to change it afterward to a relative reference, you can use the Name Manager in the Formula tab's Defined Names group to edit the reference and get rid of its dollar signs.

If you use the Define Name control, you can make it a relative reference on the fly. See Figure 6.2.

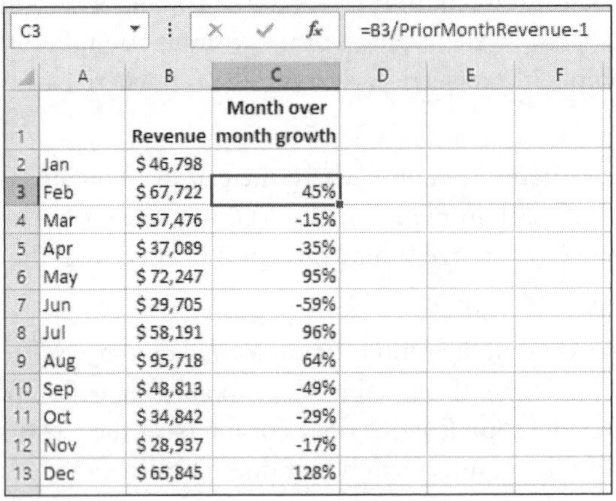

C3 =B3/PriorMonthRevenue-1

	A	B	C	D	E	F
1		Revenue	Month over month growth			
2	Jan	$ 46,798				
3	Feb	$ 67,722	45%			
4	Mar	$ 57,476	-15%			
5	Apr	$ 37,089	-35%			
6	May	$ 72,247	95%			
7	Jun	$ 29,705	-59%			
8	Jul	$ 58,191	96%			
9	Aug	$ 95,718	64%			
10	Sep	$ 48,813	-49%			
11	Oct	$ 34,842	-29%			
12	Nov	$ 28,937	-17%			
13	Dec	$ 65,845	128%			

Figure 6.2
The target of the relative reference depends on the location where you use it.

In Figure 6.2, the values shown in column B are the revenues for February through December, divided by the prior month's revenue, minus 1. This gives a running month-to-month growth rate. The easiest way to arrange that is to enter the formula

```
=B3/B2-1
```

in cell C3 and copy and paste it into C4:C13. Nine times out of ten that's what I'd do. But what if you're working with a formula that's very much more complicated? Then, to help keep things straight, you might consider mapping the concept of "prior month's result" into the syntax of the formula itself, using terminology in place of an address that consists of a row and a column. Here's one way to do that, in the context of an oversimplified example.

Begin with a worksheet with a layout like the one in Figure 6.2. Then take these steps:

1. Select cell C3.
2. Click Define Name in the Defined Names group on the Ribbon's Formulas tab.
3. In the New Name dialog box, enter a name such as `PriorMonthRevenue` in the Name box.
4. You can leave the scope at the Workbook level if you prefer. (But changing the name's scope to the worksheet where the name is defined usually works out better for me.)
5. Clear the contents of the Refers To box. While that box is still active, click in cell B2 to establish its address in the Refers To box.

6. Excel responds by putting the worksheet name and the fixed cell address $B$2 in the Refers To box. Edit that address to remove the dollar signs, leaving just the worksheet name and relative cell address, e.g.,

```
='Fig 6.2'!B2
```

To recapitulate, here's what you've done. *With cell C3 active*, you have designated the name PriorMonthRevenue to refer to cell B2. Because you made a relative reference out of what was initially a fixed reference, the name PriorMonthRevenue now refers to the cell one row above and one column to the left of any cell where you use it. This is the same effect that you arranged when, with C3 active, you pointed the name PriorMonthRevenue at cell B2, one row above and one column left of cell C3.

If you use the name PriorMonthRevenue in some other cell, its target is *relative* to the location of the cell where you use it. If you enter such a formula in cell Z26, PriorMonthRevenue refers to the value in cell Y25.

I've described how to define a relative range name in this section. There are times when you'll want to create what's termed a *mixed* range name: a name with a mixed reference such as B$2 or $B2, in which either the row or the column, but not both, is fixed. You'll see some examples of that usage later in this chapter.

The rationale is that you might want to use the same name in different columns—for example, the same seasonal effect in the calculation of both the forecast level in column G and the forecast seasonal effect in column H. In that case, you don't want the name's target cell to depend on the column where you enter the reference. You want to fix the name's target to, say, column F so that it will stay there whether you use the name in column G or column H.

That's simple enough to arrange. In the context of the example from Figure 6.2, just edit the initial cell reference (in the New Name dialog box) from $B$2 to $B2 instead of to B2. Then, wherever you make reference to the name, it will point to the value in column B, one row above the cell where you use it. Because it's fixed to column B but relative to any row, it's termed a *mixed reference* or a *mixed range name*.

In the context of smoothing, this groundwork puts you in a position to use a multiplicative model's formula that might look like

```
=PriorLevel+(Alpha*Error)/SameSeasonLastYear
```

where SameSeasonLastYear could—and, given its name, probably should—refer to the seasonal effect for the current period's season, calculated one year earlier. Now, when you examine your formula, you immediately see that you're adjusting (Alpha*Error) by the seasonal effect from one year back, when you last had an opportunity to calculate it.

Suppose that instead you were looking at this:

```
=PriorLevel+(Alpha*Error)/H4
```

In that case you'd have to recognize that column H contains seasonal effects, *and* that row 4 contains the seasonal effect from a year earlier. For my money, the increment in clarity is well worth the slight added effort to define the name at the outset.

Establishing Names for Forecasting Formulas

We can take a look at how this approach—that is, substituting concepts for cell addresses—works out in practice by comparing two versions of a model that's just moderately complex. Figure 6.3 repeats the analysis shown in Figure 5.23, the application of an additive model to a time series without trend but with seasonality.

Figure 6.3
The results of seasonal, no-trend modeling from Figure 5.23.

G8 ▼ : ✕ ✓ fx =PriorLevel+Alpha*Error

	A	B	C	D	E	F	G	H	I	J	K	L
1	Year	Season	t	Observ-ations	Forecast for this period	Error	Estimated Level (Error Correction)	Seasonal Index (Error Correction)	Forecast for next period		Alpha	0.1
2	2012	1	1	7950				-220.8			Delta	0.3
3		2	2	7304				-866.8			Year 1 Mean	8170.8
4		3	3	8071				-99.8				
5		4	4	9374				1203.2			RMSE	321.59
6		5	5	8819				648.2				
7		6	6	7507			8170.8	-663.8	7950.0			
8	2013	1	7	7307	7950.0	-643.0	8106.5	-394.4	7239.7			
9		2	8	7383	7239.7	143.3	8120.9	-828.1	8021.0			
10		3	9	8035	8021.0	14.0	8122.3	-96.1	9325.4			
11		4	10	9084	9325.4	-241.4	8098.1	1138.0	8746.3			
12		5	11	9076	8746.3	329.7	8131.1	737.2	7467.3			
13		6	12	7944	7467.3	476.7	8178.8	-535.1	7784.3			
14	2014	1	13	7477	7784.3	-307.3	8148.0	-477.4	7319.9			
15		2	14	7307	7319.9	-12.9	8146.7	-831.6	8050.7			
16		3	15	7963	8050.7	-87.7	8138.0	-119.7	9276.0			
17		4	16		9276.0		8138.0		8875.2			
18		5	17		8875.2		8138.0		7602.9			
19		6	18		7602.9		8138.0		7660.6			
20	2015	1	19		7660.6		8138.0		7306.4			
21		2	20		7306.4		8138.0		8018.2			
22		3	21		8018.2		8138.0					

In Figures 5.23 and 6.3, the smoothing starts in row 8; the calculations through row 7 are solely to initialize the forecasts. In Figure 6.3 I have used range names and implicit intersections to write the formulas. For example, the formula in cell G8 (actually, every cell in the range G8:G22) refers to the defined names PriorLevel, Alpha, and Error.

Figure 6.4 shows how the formulas are written using cell addressing (but the smoothing constants Alpha and Delta are named cells with fixed references $L$1 and $L$2, just as shown in prior chapters).

It's far from impossible to understand what the formulas in Figure 6.4 are up to. Consider the formula in cell H8, for example:

```
=H2+Delta*(1-Alpha)*F8
```

Figure 6.4
To save space I have omitted columns J through L, which contain Alpha, Delta, and Year_1_Mean.

	A	B	C	D	E	F	G	H	I
1	Year	Season	t	Observ-ations	Forecast for this period	Error	Estimated Level (Error Correction)	Seasonal Index (Error Correction)	Forecast for next period
2	2012	1	1	7950				=D2-Year_1_Mean	
3		2	2	7304				=D3-Year_1_Mean	
4		3	3	8071				=D4-Year_1_Mean	
5		4	4	9374				=D5-Year_1_Mean	
6		5	5	8819				=D6-Year_1_Mean	
7		6	6	7507			=Year_1_Mean	=D7-Year_1_Mean	=G7+H2
8	2013	1	7	7307	=I7	=D8-E8	=G7+Alpha*F8	=H2+Delta*(1-Alpha)*F8	=G8+H3
9		2	8	7383	=I8	=D9-E9	=G8+Alpha*F9	=H3+Delta*(1-Alpha)*F9	=G9+H4
10		3	9	8035	=I9	=D10-E10	=G9+Alpha*F10	=H4+Delta*(1-Alpha)*F10	=G10+H5
11		4	10	9084	=I10	=D11-E11	=G10+Alpha*F11	=H5+Delta*(1-Alpha)*F11	=G11+H6
12		5	11	9076	=I11	=D12-E12	=G11+Alpha*F12	=H6+Delta*(1-Alpha)*F12	=G12+H7
13		6	12	7944	=I12	=D13-E13	=G12+Alpha*F13	=H7+Delta*(1-Alpha)*F13	=G13+H8
14	2014	1	13	7477	=I13	=D14-E14	=G13+Alpha*F14	=H8+Delta*(1-Alpha)*F14	=G14+H9
15		2	14	7307	=I14	=D15-E15	=G14+Alpha*F15	=H9+Delta*(1-Alpha)*F15	=G15+H10
16		3	15	7963	=I15	=D16-E16	=G15+Alpha*F16	=H10+Delta*(1-Alpha)*F16	=G16+H11
17		4	16		=I16		=G16+Alpha*F17		=G17+H12
18		5	17		=I17		=G17+Alpha*F18		=G18+H13
19		6	18		=I18		=G18+Alpha*F19		=G19+H14
20	2015	1	19		=I19		=G19+Alpha*F20		=G20+H15
21		2	20		=I20		=G20+Alpha*F21		=G21+H16
22		3	21		=I21		=G21+Alpha*F22		

This is the error correction form of the formula for forecasting the seasonal index. Tracing the cell references in the formula, you can see that

- H2 contains the initial estimate of the seasonal effect for the first season. (Notice from cell B2 that cell H2 belongs to season 1.)
- F8 contains the current forecast error: the current observation less the immediately prior forecast of that current observation.

So the formula, translated, says to take the effect of the most recent instance of the first season, and add to it the product of Delta, 1 – Alpha, and the forecast error. It hangs together conceptually if you remember that you're working with last year's estimate of the effect of the current season, and how cell F8 comes by its value.

Now, in Figure 6.5, have a look at the same formulas as appear in Figure 6.4, but with meaningful names instead of column letters and row numbers:

I hope that you'll find helpful the use of the implicit intersection and mixed range names in Figure 6.5. To continue the previous example, the formula in cell H8 does precisely the same thing as in Figure 6.4:

```
=SameSeasonLastYear+Delta*(1-Alpha)*Error
```

Here you can focus on what the formula is doing. You don't need to keep track of the meanings of cell addresses; those meanings are part of the formula. You use the most recent estimate of the current season's effect, plus a portion of the current forecast error, determined by the product of the two smoothing constants.

6

Figure 6.5
In this figure I have omitted columns A through E and J through L, but the use of names means you don't need those columns to understand the formulas.

	F	G	H	I
1	Error	Estimated Level (Error Correction)	Seasonal Index (Error Correction)	Forecast for next period
2			=D2-Year_1_Mean	
3			=D3-Year_1_Mean	
4			=D4-Year_1_Mean	
5			=D5-Year_1_Mean	
6			=D6-Year_1_Mean	
7		=Year_1_Mean	=D7-Year_1_Mean	=ForecastLevel+ForecastSeason
8	=D8-E8	=PriorLevel+Alpha*Error	=SameSeasonLastYear+Delta*(1-Alpha)*Error	=ForecastLevel+ForecastSeason
9	=D9-E9	=PriorLevel+Alpha*Error	=SameSeasonLastYear+Delta*(1-Alpha)*Error	=ForecastLevel+ForecastSeason
10	=D10-E10	=PriorLevel+Alpha*Error	=SameSeasonLastYear+Delta*(1-Alpha)*Error	=ForecastLevel+ForecastSeason
11	=D11-E11	=PriorLevel+Alpha*Error	=SameSeasonLastYear+Delta*(1-Alpha)*Error	=ForecastLevel+ForecastSeason
12	=D12-E12	=PriorLevel+Alpha*Error	=SameSeasonLastYear+Delta*(1-Alpha)*Error	=ForecastLevel+ForecastSeason
13	=D13-E13	=PriorLevel+Alpha*Error	=SameSeasonLastYear+Delta*(1-Alpha)*Error	=ForecastLevel+ForecastSeason
14	=D14-E14	=PriorLevel+Alpha*Error	=SameSeasonLastYear+Delta*(1-Alpha)*Error	=ForecastLevel+ForecastSeason
15	=D15-E15	=PriorLevel+Alpha*Error	=SameSeasonLastYear+Delta*(1-Alpha)*Error	=ForecastLevel+ForecastSeason
16	=D16-E16	=PriorLevel+Alpha*Error	=SameSeasonLastYear+Delta*(1-Alpha)*Error	=ForecastLevel+ForecastSeason
17		=PriorLevel+Alpha*Error		=ForecastLevel+ForecastSeason
18		=PriorLevel+Alpha*Error		=ForecastLevel+ForecastSeason
19		=PriorLevel+Alpha*Error		=ForecastLevel+ForecastSeason
20		=PriorLevel+Alpha*Error		=ForecastLevel+ForecastSeason
21		=PriorLevel+Alpha*Error		=ForecastLevel+ForecastSeason
22		=PriorLevel+Alpha*Error		

Establishing the Fixed Range Names

Figure 6.6 shows the pertinent formulas for a series with seasons but no trend, using range names instead of cell addresses. Figures 6.3 through 6.5 show the error correction form of the formulas, but Figures 6.6 through 6.8 show their smoothing form.

Figure 6.6
The worksheet is in Formula View. You can toggle back and forth between Formulas and Results with the Formula tab's Show Formulas control.

	G	H
1	Estimated Level (Smoothing)	Seasonal Index (Smoothing)
2		=CurrentObs-Year_1_Mean
3		=CurrentObs-Year_1_Mean
4		=CurrentObs-Year_1_Mean
5		=CurrentObs-Year_1_Mean
6		=CurrentObs-Year_1_Mean
7	=Year_1_Mean	=CurrentObs-Year_1_Mean
8	=Alpha*(CurrentObs-SameSeasonLastYear)+(1-Alpha)*PriorLevel	=Delta*(CurrentObs-CurrentLevel)+(1-Delta)*SameSeasonLastYear
9	=Alpha*(CurrentObs-SameSeasonLastYear)+(1-Alpha)*PriorLevel	=Delta*(CurrentObs-CurrentLevel)+(1-Delta)*SameSeasonLastYear
10	=Alpha*(CurrentObs-SameSeasonLastYear)+(1-Alpha)*PriorLevel	=Delta*(CurrentObs-CurrentLevel)+(1-Delta)*SameSeasonLastYear
11	=Alpha*(CurrentObs-SameSeasonLastYear)+(1-Alpha)*PriorLevel	=Delta*(CurrentObs-CurrentLevel)+(1-Delta)*SameSeasonLastYear
12	=Alpha*(CurrentObs-SameSeasonLastYear)+(1-Alpha)*PriorLevel	=Delta*(CurrentObs-CurrentLevel)+(1-Delta)*SameSeasonLastYear
13	=Alpha*(CurrentObs-SameSeasonLastYear)+(1-Alpha)*PriorLevel	=Delta*(CurrentObs-CurrentLevel)+(1-Delta)*SameSeasonLastYear
14	=Alpha*(CurrentObs-SameSeasonLastYear)+(1-Alpha)*PriorLevel	=Delta*(CurrentObs-CurrentLevel)+(1-Delta)*SameSeasonLastYear
15	=Alpha*(CurrentObs-SameSeasonLastYear)+(1-Alpha)*PriorLevel	=Delta*(CurrentObs-CurrentLevel)+(1-Delta)*SameSeasonLastYear
16	=Alpha*(CurrentObs-SameSeasonLastYear)+(1-Alpha)*PriorLevel	=Delta*(CurrentObs-CurrentLevel)+(1-Delta)*SameSeasonLastYear
17	=PriorLevel	
18	=PriorLevel	
19	=PriorLevel	
20	=PriorLevel	
21	=PriorLevel	
22	=PriorLevel	

Figure 6.6 uses the fixed range names described in the following sections.

Alpha, Delta, and Year_1_Mean

These names refer to single cells via fixed references and are not involved in any implicit intersections. You can find plenty of other examples of their use in Chapters 5 and 6.

CurrentObs

Figure 6.6 uses the names *CurrentObs* and *CurrentLevel* in implicit intersections. The names refer to fixed ranges, so the ranges' addresses do not depend on the location where the name is used (as is the case with mixed or relative references). To define the range names CurrentObs and CurrentLevel, you could simply select the appropriate range of cells, type the range name in the Formula Bar's Name box, and press Enter. That's quick and easy, but you wind up with a workbook-level name. If you anticipate keeping more than one smoothing analysis in one workbook, you should consider limiting the scope of all range names to the worksheet where they're defined.

To set the scope of a range name to a particular worksheet, use the Define Name control as described in the prior section "The Relative Range Name." Then supply the range name and address, and override the default scope, Workbook, by specifying a particular worksheet for the name's scope.

Figure 6.7 has the same named ranges and formulas as Figure 6.6, but it shows the results instead of the formulas.

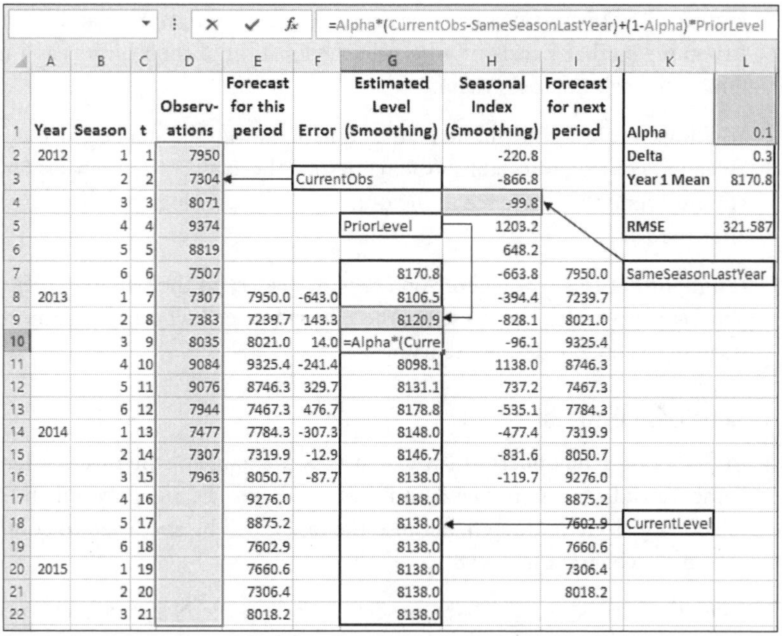
=Alpha*(CurrentObs-SameSeasonLastYear)+(1-Alpha)*PriorLevel

	A	B	C	D	E	F	G	H	I	J	K	L
1	Year	Season	t	Observ-ations	Forecast for this period	Error	Estimated Level (Smoothing)	Seasonal Index (Smoothing)	Forecast for next period		Alpha	0.1
2	2012	1	1	7950				-220.8			Delta	0.3
3		2	2	7304		CurrentObs		-866.8			Year 1 Mean	8170.8
4		3	3	8071				-99.8				
5		4	4	9374			PriorLevel	1203.2			RMSE	321.587
6		5	5	8819				648.2				
7		6	6	7507			8170.8	-663.8	7950.0		SameSeasonLastYear	
8	2013	1	7	7307	7950.0	-643.0	8106.5	-394.4	7239.7			
9		2	8	7383	7239.7	143.3	8120.9	-828.1	8021.0			
10		3	9	8035	8021.0	14.0	=Alpha*(Curre	-96.1	9325.4			
11		4	10	9084	9325.4	-241.4	8098.1	1138.0	8746.3			
12		5	11	9076	8746.3	329.7	8131.1	737.2	7467.3			
13		6	12	7944	7467.3	476.7	8178.8	-535.1	7784.3			
14	2014	1	13	7477	7784.3	-307.3	8148.0	-477.4	7319.9			
15		2	14	7307	7319.9	-12.9	8146.7	-831.6	8050.7			
16		3	15	7963	8050.7	-87.7	8138.0	-119.7	9276.0			
17		4	16		9276.0		8138.0		8875.2			
18		5	17		8875.2		8138.0		7602.9		CurrentLevel	
19		6	18		7602.9		8138.0		7660.6			
20	2015	1	19		7660.6		8138.0		7306.4			
21		2	20		7306.4		8138.0		8018.2			
22		3	21		8018.2		8138.0					

Figure 6.7
The range names are as shown by the callouts.

The range named CurrentObs contains the current observations. I established CurrentObs in the range D2:D22. It *could* end at D16 instead of D22, but extending it to the 22nd row allows the name to pick up subsequent observations. In fact, the range could extend from row 1 to row 1,048,576 because the implicit intersection depends on where the row and the column intersect. So long as they do so, it makes no difference where the range's row and column start and stop.

The name CurrentObs is used by both the estimate of the series' level in column G and the estimate of seasonal effects in column H.

CurrentLevel

The range named CurrentLevel contains the current estimates of the level of the series and is established in the range G7:G22. Again, as a technical matter it could start in the second row, but for clarity it makes sense to start the range where its first value appears. Because Figure 6.7 uses the first year of observations to initialize the seasonal effects, actual estimation doesn't start until row 7 (in columns G, H, and I), so that's a sensible row to start the named range.

The name CurrentLevel is used in the estimate of seasonal effects in column H and in the calculation of the forecast of the next period in column I.

Establishing the Mixed Range Names

Figure 6.7 uses two mixed range names: SameSeasonLastYear and PriorLevel. They are structured so that Excel will interpret the location of their targets as a function of the location of the cell that uses them.

You'll need to use the Define Name control, not the Name box or the Create from Selection control, to establish the names for these mixed references. Only in that way can you fine-tune the reference at the outset, without having to go in using the Name Manager after the fact.

It's important to know where you are with respect to the name's target when you start the naming process. It's best to select the uppermost cell where the name will be used before starting to actually define the name.

SameSeasonLastYear

In Figure 6.7, the uppermost row that uses the name of the mixed reference, SameSeasonLastYear, is row 8 (in columns G and H). So I recommend that you begin by selecting cell H8 (although, because the range will be anchored to column H, you could start in any column in row 8).

Click Define Name, type `SameSeasonNextYear` in the Name box, choose the active worksheet for the name's scope, and then delete the contents of the Refers To box. With that box still active, click in cell H2. That's the cell that contains the seasonal effect for the first season, one year back.

Recall that in this example, a season is two months long and therefore each year contains six seasons. Therefore, as of Period 7, one year back is Period 1, found in row 2.

Make the name's reference a mixed one by deleting the dollar sign before "2" that Excel automatically provided when you clicked in cell H2. In the Refers To box, just click immediately to the right of that dollar sign and press Backspace. In this particular case, you're turning

```
='Fig 6.7'!$H$2
```

into this:

```
='Fig 6.7'!$H2
```

Click OK to dismiss the New Name dialog box. You now have a name that refers to a cell in column H, and that refers to a row that's six rows above the active cell.

Figure 6.7 uses that name, SameSeasonLastYear, in both columns G and H. Therefore, we want to leave it anchored to column H, and so we leave the dollar sign before the H in place. Now no matter where we use that name, it refers to the value in column H, six rows above the cell where it's used.

PriorLevel

Still in Figure 6.7, the name PriorLevel refers to the model's estimate of the level of the series as of one *period* earlier. (Be sure to distinguish this from the name SameSeasonLastYear, which refers to the seasonal effect one *year* earlier.)

The procedure for defining the name PriorLevel is generally the same as that used to define SameSeasonLastYear:

1. Begin by selecting the cell in column H that's immediately below the first instance of the series' level; in Figure 6.7, that's cell G8.
2. Click the Define Name control and enter `PriorLevel` in the Name box.
3. Set the name's scope to the active worksheet.
4. Identify the name's target. Clear the Refers To box and click in cell G7.
5. To make the reference mixed, delete the dollar sign between the "G" and the "7."
6. Lastly, click OK to establish the name and return to the worksheet.

The name PriorLevel is used only in formulas in column G. Therefore, you could make the reference completely relative and delete both dollar signs from the target address. You needn't worry about the column adjusting if you use the name in a different column because you don't intend to do that. Nevertheless, for safety and consistency, you might as well leave the name's reference anchored to column G.

6

TIP

You're less likely to need this tip if you think through the purposes of your range names before you establish them. But we all need to pick up after ourselves at some point.

The F4 function key on a Windows machine allows you to toggle a reference in a worksheet cell through the different addressing modes: $A$1, A$1, $A1, and A1. Just select the cell that contains the reference, click immediately to the right of the reference in the formula box, and press F4 (repeatedly if necessary).

What's not quite so well known is that you can do exactly the same thing with the Name Manager, if you need to revise the reference of a range name that you've already defined. Click the Name Manager control in the Defined Names group, select an existing name, click in the Refers To box at the bottom of the Name Manager window, and press F4 repeatedly until you have the reference type you want.

Using the Names in Forecasting Formulas

With the names, both fixed and mixed, defined as I've described in this section, it's easy to use them in formulas, and to copy and paste or autofill the formulas. For example, you could begin by entering this formula in cell G8 of Figure 6.7:

```
=Alpha*(CurrentObs-SameSeasonLastYear)+(1-Alpha)*PriorLevel
```

Then, copy and paste or autofill down to cell G16. At that point you have run out of fresh observations and the formulas in cell G17:G22 would have to be changed to =PriorLevel. (I discuss the reason that this change is needed in Chapter 5, "Working with Seasonal Time Series," in the section titled "Dealing with the End of the Time Series.")

Notice that when you autofill or paste the formulas using the names, the names don't change. What changes are the names' *targets*, and the addresses of the targets aren't visible to you in the Formula box. Unless you're trying to trace an error in the worksheet, you're a lot less interested in what specific cells a formula depends on, and a lot more interested in how the formula accomplishes what it's intended to.

Interpreting the Formula for Series Level

In Chapter 3, "Working with Trended Time Series," in the section titled "The Equation's Smoothing Form," I noted that the smoothing form of the formula for the series' level is useful because it expresses more clearly than does the error correction form that each forecast is a mix of the current actual and the prior forecast for the current period. You multiply Alpha times the current actual observation, and (1 – Alpha) times the prior period's forecast of the current actual.

That's nice and clean when you're working with the simplest version of exponential smoothing: a horizontal series without seasons. Then the formula, using symbols and in its smoothing form, is this:

$$\hat{y}_{t+1} = \alpha y_t + (1 - \alpha)\hat{y}_t$$

Bear in mind the notation:

- α is Alpha, the smoothing constant.
- y_t is the actual observation at period t.
- $\hat{y}_t$ is the forecast of the series value at period t.
- $\hat{y}_{t+1}$ is the forecast of the series value at period $t + 1$.

As things get more complex, the simple concept of a weighted average of an actual and the associated forecast also gets more complex.

For example, if you were using names instead of cell addresses in a situation that called for simple exponential smoothing, you might use something like this worksheet formula:

```
=Alpha * CurrentObs + (1 - Alpha) * PriorForecast
```

And that's all you'd need, because in a simple exponential smoothing situation all you have to forecast is the series' level. There's no trend or slope, and no seasonal effect, to estimate and build into the next forecast.

But step the complexity up a tick so that the series has seasonality but no trend, and you need to estimate the current level of the series, plus the current effect of the associated season, and total the two estimates to get your forecast. Again using symbols and the smoothing form of the equation, your estimate of the level might look like this:

$$L_t = \alpha\left(y_t - S_{t-m}\right) + \left(1 - \alpha\right)L_{t-1}$$

More notation:

- L_t is the level of the series at period t.
- L_{t-1} is the level of the series at period $t - 1$.
- S_{t-m} is the seasonal effect associated with period $t - m$.
- m is the number of seasons in the encompassing period.

Here, we're estimating the series level. We can't observe that directly in a time series that's seasonal, or trended, or both, because the value of the actual observation is a combination of the level and the seasonal effect (or the trend, or both). We've left behind the simple formulation of multiplying Alpha times an actual empiric observation. The best we can do in a seasonal, untrended situation is to estimate the actual level by subtracting the most recent estimate of a seasonal effect from the current observation at period t—that is,

$$y_t - \hat{S}_{t-m}$$

So, in an untrended but seasonal series, each observation is taken to be the combination of the current level of the series and the effect of the season—and, therefore, the current level can be estimated by subtracting the season's effect from the current observation. And it's that quantity, which is as close as we can come to observing the current level directly, that is multiplied by Alpha in the forecasting model.

NOTE I hate to belabor this point, but it's important. Suppose seasons are quarters of the year. Then the encompassing period, the year, has four quarterly seasons and $m = 4$. Also suppose we're dealing with the sixth period in our time series, Quarter 2 of Year 2, so $t = 6$. Then the seasonal estimate to use is the estimate made at the end of the second quarter in the first year. It's the most recent available estimate of the effect of the second season on the time series. And the quickest and clearest way of identifying that particular estimate is via $t - m$, or 6 – 4, which points us to the second period in the time series.

On the other hand, we do have a forecast to multiply by (1 – Alpha) on our way to a new level estimate; it's the level that was forecast at the end of the prior period. And the full, smoothing form of the estimated level in an untrended but seasonal equation, given earlier as

$$L_t = \alpha(y_t - S_{t-m}) + (1 - \alpha)L_{t-1}$$

works out to the following in Excel syntax using names in place of cell addresses:

```
=Alpha*(CurrentObs-SameSeasonLastYear)+(1-Alpha)*PriorLevel
```

Let's see what that looks like in the worksheet shown in Figure 6.8.

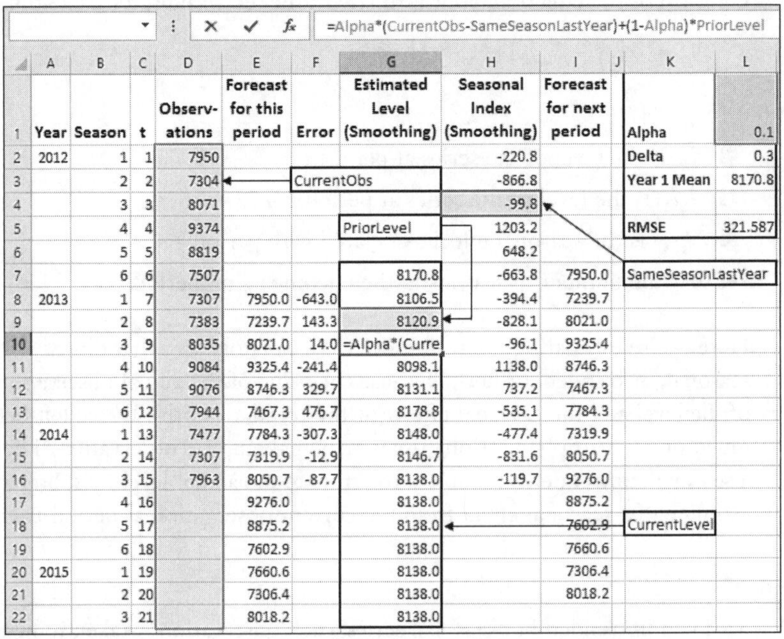

=Alpha*(CurrentObs-SameSeasonLastYear)+(1-Alpha)*PriorLevel

	A	B	C	D	E	F	G	H	I	J	K	L
1	Year	Season	t	Observ-ations	Forecast for this period	Error	Estimated Level (Smoothing)	Seasonal Index (Smoothing)	Forecast for next period		Alpha	0.1
2	2012	1	1	7950				-220.8			Delta	0.3
3		2	2	7304		CurrentObs		-866.8			Year 1 Mean	8170.8
4		3	3	8071				-99.8				
5		4	4	9374			PriorLevel	1203.2			RMSE	321.587
6		5	5	8819				648.2				
7		6	6	7507			8170.8	-663.8	7950.0		SameSeasonLastYear	
8	2013	1	7	7307	7950.0	-643.0	8106.5	-394.4	7239.7			
9		2	8	7383	7239.7	143.3	8120.9	-828.1	8021.0			
10		3	9	8035	8021.0	14.0	=Alpha*(Curre	-96.1	9325.4			
11		4	10	9084	9325.4	-241.4	8098.1	1138.0	8746.3			
12		5	11	9076	8746.3	329.7	8131.1	737.2	7467.3			
13		6	12	7944	7467.3	476.7	8178.8	-535.1	7784.3			
14	2014	1	13	7477	7784.3	-307.3	8148.0	-477.4	7319.9			
15		2	14	7307	7319.9	-12.9	8146.7	-831.6	8050.7			
16		3	15	7963	8050.7	-87.7	8138.0	-119.7	9276.0			
17		4	16		9276.0		8138.0		8875.2			
18		5	17		8875.2		8138.0		7602.9		CurrentLevel	
19		6	18		7602.9		8138.0		7660.6			
20	2015	1	19		7660.6		8138.0		7306.4			
21		2	20		7306.4		8138.0		8018.2			
22		3	21		8018.2		8138.0					

Figure 6.8
The worksheet is the same as in Figure 6.7; it is repeated here for convenience.

You very likely know that when you edit a formula, the formula itself appears in the Formula box and the formula's precedent cells appear highlighted on the worksheet. That's the case in Figure 6.8, which I'm showing so that you can compare the formula's arguments—the named ranges—with the contents of the worksheet.

The formula, which appears in full in the Formula box, uses these named ranges:

- *Alpha.* A fixed reference, in cell L1. The smoothing constant for the series level.
- *CurrentObs.* A fixed reference, occupying the range D2:D22. In Figure 6.8, the active cell is G10. The worksheet's tenth row intersects the CurrentObs range in cell D10, so the formula in G10 uses 8035 for the value of CurrentObs.
- *SameSeasonLastYear.* A mixed reference whose target depends on the location of the cell where the reference is used. In Figure 6.8, with cell G10 active, SameSeasonLastYear points to cell H4, where the value is –99.8. The reference is anchored to column H, but it points six rows up from the cell using the reference. Because cell G10 is in the tenth row, the reference points to the fourth row in column H. Cell H4 contains the most recent estimate of the index for the third season. That's the same season to which CurrentObs belongs—compare cells B4 and B10.
- *PriorLevel.* Another mixed reference, this one pointing one row up from the cell where it's used, in column G. With cell G10 active, the reference points to cell G9, which contains 8120.9, the forecast level for the time series in Period 9, made at the end of Period 8.

So, as advertised, the formula does the following:

1. It subtracts the most recent estimate of the time period's seasonal effect from the current observation. The result estimates the current level.
2. It multiplies the result by Alpha.
3. It gets the prior forecast of the level.
4. It multiplies the prior forecast by (1 – Alpha).
5. It sums the two results of steps 2 and 4 to get the level component of the next forecast.

Interpreting the Formula for the Seasonal Effect

Figure 6.9 provides a similar analysis of the seasonal portion of the forecast.

The formula in cell H10 uses these range names:

- *Delta.* A fixed reference, pointing to cell L2. The smoothing constant for the seasonal effects.
- *CurrentObs.* A fixed reference to the range D2:D22. (Figure 6.8 shows the locations for CurrentObs, CurrentLevel, and SameSeasonLastYear.) In cell H10, the implicit intersection of row 10 with the CurrentObs range returns the value 8035, just as it does for the level calculation in cell G10.
- *CurrentLevel.* A fixed reference to the range G7:G22. Using the implicit intersection in cell H10 returns the value in the tenth row of column G, or 8122.3, shown in Figure 6.10.

6

■ *SameSeasonLastYear.*   Just as with the level calculation in cell G10, the name SameSeasonLastYear is a mixed reference, fixed to column H, relative to the row that's six rows up from the cell where the name is used. So in cell H10, the name returns the value in H4, or –99.8.

Figure 6.9
The worksheet is the same as in Figure 6.8, but its focus is on the seasonal estimate.

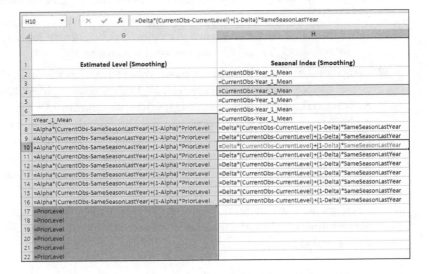

Figure 6.10 shows how the implicit intersection and mixed range names come together as precedents to the formula in cell H10.

The formula in cell H10 (more generally, in each cell in the range H8:H16, at which point we run out of actual observations in column D) is this:

```
=Delta*(CurrentObs-CurrentLevel)+(1-Delta)*SameSeasonLastYear
```

At this point we're in the business of estimating the seasonal effect that, along with an estimate of the series level, will be used to forecast the series value for a subsequent period. In this smoothing form of the equation, the formula multiplies the seasonal smoothing constant, Delta, times the current seasonal effect.

Again, we can't observe the seasonal effect directly so we infer it. Just as we estimated the current series level by subtracting the seasonal effect from the current observation, we can infer the current seasonal effect by subtracting the current level from the current observation. That is, in symbols,

$$y_t = L_t + S_{t-m}$$

in a seasonal but untrended series, simple rearrangement gives us this:

$$S_{t-m} = y_t - L_t$$

Or, using Excel formula syntax with named ranges:

```
CurrentObs-CurrentLevel
```

Figure 6.10
The formula's precedent cells are highlighted.

| | | | fx | =Delta*(CurrentObs-CurrentLevel)+(1-Delta)*SameSeasonLastYear |

	A	B	C	D	E	F	G	H	I	J	K	L
				Observ-	Forecast for this		Estimated Level	Seasonal Index	Forecast for next			
1	Year	Season	t	ations	period	Error	(Smoothing)	(Smoothing)	period	Alpha		0.1
2	2012	1	1	7950				-220.8		Delta		0.3
3		2	2	7304		CurrentObs		-866.8		Year 1 Mean		8170.8
4		3	3	8071				-99.8				
5		4	4	9374				1203.2		RMSE		321.587
6		5	5	8819				648.2				
7		6	6	7507			8170.8	-663.8	7950.0	SameSeasonLastYear		
8	2013	1	7	7307	7950.0	-643.0	8106.5	-394.4	7239.7			
9		2	8	7383	7239.7	143.3	8120.9	-828.1	8021.0			
10		3	9	8035	8021.0	14.0	8122.3	=Delta*(Curre	9325.4			
11		4	10	9084	9325.4	-241.4	8098.1	1138.0	8746.3			
12		5	11	9076	8746.3	329.7	8131.1	737.2	7467.3			
13		6	12	7944	7467.3	476.7	8178.8	-535.1	7784.3			
14	2014	1	13	7477	7784.3	-307.3	8148.0	-477.4	7319.9			
15		2	14	7307	7319.9	-12.9	8146.7	-831.6	8050.7			
16		3	15	7963	8050.7	-87.7	8138.0	-119.7	9276.0			
17		4	16		9276.0		8138.0		8875.2			
18		5	17		8875.2		8138.0		7602.9	CurrentLevel		
19		6	18		7602.9		8138.0		7660.6			
20	2015	1	19		7660.6		8138.0		7306.4			
21		2	20		7306.4		8138.0		8018.2			
22		3	21		8018.2		8138.0					

We pick up those values by way of the implicit intersection of cell H10 with the fixed range names CurrentObs and CurrentLevel, shown highlighted in Figure 6.10 in the ranges D2:D22 and G7:G22, to return the current observation value of 8035 and the current series level of 8122.3. The difference, our best estimate of the current seasonal effect, is multiplied by Delta.

Then we multiply (1 – Delta) times the most recent forecast of the seasonal effect, found by means of the mixed range name SameSeasonLastYear. When used in cell H10, that name points six rows (that is, six seasons) back, in column H, to cell H4, returning the seasonal effect forecast of –99.8, the most recent for the third season.

Finally, the two terms are added in cell H10 to return the forecast seasonal effect of –96.1.

Interpreting the Forecast Formula

In Figure 6.11, we're in a position to calculate the forecast for Period 10, in row 11. Cell I10 accomplishes that with this formula:

```
=CurrentLevel+ForecastSeason
```

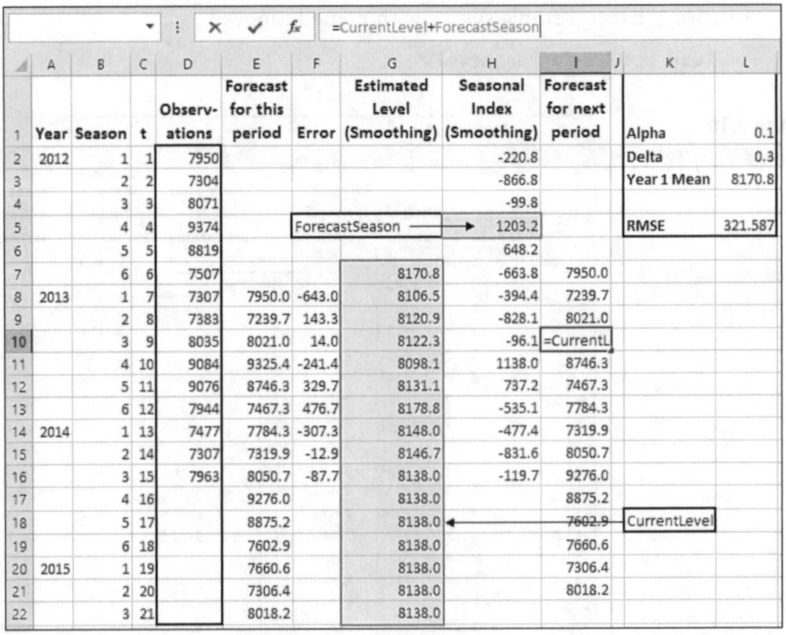

Figure 6.11
The Level and Season forecasts combine to create the forecast of the next observation.

										fx	=CurrentLevel+ForecastSeason	

	A	B	C	D	E	F	G	H	I	J	K	L
1	Year	Season	t	Observations	Forecast for this period	Error	Estimated Level (Smoothing)	Seasonal Index (Smoothing)	Forecast for next period		Alpha	0.1
2	2012	1	1	7950				-220.8			Delta	0.3
3		2	2	7304				-866.8			Year 1 Mean	8170.8
4		3	3	8071				-99.8				
5		4	4	9374			ForecastSeason ⟶	1203.2			RMSE	321.587
6		5	5	8819				648.2				
7		6	6	7507			8170.8	-663.8	7950.0			
8	2013	1	7	7307	7950.0	-643.0	8106.5	-394.4	7239.7			
9		2	8	7383	7239.7	143.3	8120.9	-828.1	8021.0			
10		3	9	8035	8021.0	14.0	8122.3	-96.1	=CurrentL			
11		4	10	9084	9325.4	-241.4	8098.1	1138.0	8746.3			
12		5	11	9076	8746.3	329.7	8131.1	737.2	7467.3			
13		6	12	7944	7467.3	476.7	8178.8	-535.1	7784.3			
14	2014	1	13	7477	7784.3	-307.3	8148.0	-477.4	7319.9			
15		2	14	7307	7319.9	-12.9	8146.7	-831.6	8050.7			
16		3	15	7963	8050.7	-87.7	8138.0	-119.7	9276.0			
17		4	16		9276.0		8138.0		8875.2			
18		5	17		8875.2		8138.0 ◀		7602.9	CurrentLevel		
19		6	18		7602.9		8138.0		7660.6			
20	2015	1	19		7660.6		8138.0		7306.4			
21		2	20		7306.4		8138.0		8018.2			
22		3	21		8018.2		8138.0					

We pick up the current level by implicit intersection with the CurrentLevel range, fixed at G6:G22. You've seen the CurrentLevel range before, in a prior section, in the calculation of the forecast of the seasonal effect in Period 9.

The seasonal forecast, referenced in cell I10 by ForecastSeason, is a different matter. In row 10 we're creating the series forecast for row 11. Note that the forecast for the Period 10, in cell I10, is identical to the forecast for Period 10 in cell E11 (just as is the case for the remainder of columns I and E). Because we're forecasting into Period 10, we're forecasting into season 4; see cell B11. To get the most recent seasonal effect for season 4 in column I of row 10, we need to go back five seasons instead of six, from row 10 to row 5.

Therefore, we need to use a different mixed range name than SameSeasonLastYear, which goes back six rows. Instead we use the mixed range name ForecastSeason, which goes back only five rows in column H. On the sheet named Fig 6.11, if we define ForecastSeason when cell I7 is active, its Refers To address in the New Name dialog box would be this:

```
='Fig 6.11'!$H2
```

We wind up with the values 8122.3 (cell G10) for the estimated level and 1203.2 (cell H5) for the estimated seasonal effect, giving us a forecast of 9325.4 for Period 10.

Deriving the Error Correction Formulas

As I've noted in several places, both in earlier chapters and in this one, the formulas for level, trend, and season have what's termed a smoothing form and an error correction form. The two forms are equivalent in the sense that, correctly used, each returns the same result.

You can check that if you want: I use the error correction forms for level and season in Figures 6.3, 6.4, and 6.5, and the smoothing forms in Figures 6.6 through 6.11. The formulas return the same results regardless of which form is used.

> **NOTE** An exception is the range G17:G22 in Figures 6.6 through 6.11, which requires special handling of the smoothing formula after you've run out of new observations.

Both forms are useful in a conceptual sense; each emphasizes a different and important aspect of the smoothing process. The smoothing form makes it clear how each component—level, trend, and season—constitutes a weighted average of new information and old information. The error correction form shows how each new estimate—again, of level, trend, and season—adjusts the prior estimate by adding a term that partly corrects the error in that prior estimate.

Fifty and sixty years ago, when these methods were still quite new, access to computing equipment was more difficult to come by, and many practitioners opted for the error correction form because they found it less cumbersome for pencil-and-paper calculations, even with the aid of a hand calculator.

Today the ease of use is no longer an issue and the choice of method is a matter of personal preference. Therefore, you're as likely to encounter one form as another in papers and books that employ the smoothing techniques. You'll find it helpful to know that both forms exist, that they are equivalent to one another, and how to get back and forth between the two forms.

Before moving on to using defined names with series that are seasonal *and* trended, then, let's have a look at how the error correction forms are derived from the smoothing forms for different types of series. You'll then be able to work out for yourself how to go the other direction.

The Level Equation

Using Excel syntax and range names as defined in Figures 6.8, 6.10, and 6.11, you can calculate the current level of a seasonal series with this formula:

```
=Alpha*(CurrentObs-SameSeasonLastYear)+(1-Alpha)*PriorLevel
```

Using symbols, here's the smoothing form of the same equation for the series level:

$$L_t = \alpha\left(y_t - S_{t-m}\right) + \left(1 - \alpha\right)L_{t-1}$$

Here's how to convert that equation to the error correction form. First, distribute Alpha and (1 – Alpha):

$$L_t = \alpha y_t - \alpha S_{t-m} + L_{t-1} - \alpha L_{t-1}$$

Rearrange the terms:

$$L_t = L_{t-1} + \alpha y_t - \alpha L_{t-1} - \alpha S_{t-m}$$

Regroup:

$$L_t = L_{t-1} + \alpha y_t - \alpha \left(L_{t-1} + S_{t-m} \right)$$

$$L_t = L_{t-1} + \alpha y_t - \alpha \hat{y}_t$$

$$L_t = L_{t-1} + \alpha (y_t - \hat{y}_t)$$

Which gets us to the error correction form:

$$L_t = L_{t-1} + \alpha \varepsilon$$

Here, ε is the forecast error, the difference between the forecast value of the series at period t and the actual observation at period t.

Or, again using Excel syntax and range names:

```
PriorLevel+Alpha*Error
```

The Trend Equation

Here's how to get from the smoothing form of the trend equation in a trended series without seasonality to the error correction form. Starting with the smoothing form of the trend equation, we multiply Gamma times the difference in consecutive levels of the series, and add (1 – Gamma) times the slope estimate at the prior period,

$$b_t = \gamma \left(L_t - L_{t-1} \right) + \left(1 - \gamma \right) b_{t-1}$$

where

- b_t is the value of the trend (or if you prefer, the slope) at period t.
- γ is Gamma, the smoothing constant for trend.

In Excel syntax, that works out to

```
=Gamma*(CurrentLevel-PriorLevel)+(1-Gamma)*PriorTrend
```

Rearrange the terms,

$$b_t = \left(1 - \gamma \right) b_{t-1} + \gamma \left(L_t - L_{t-1} \right)$$

and multiply $\left(1 - \gamma \right)$ by b_{t-1}:

$$b_t = b_{t-1} - \gamma b_{t-1} + \gamma \left(L_t - L_{t-1} \right)$$

Combine γb_{t-1} with $\gamma \left(L_t - L_{t-1} \right)$

$$b_t = b_{t-1} + \gamma \left(L_t - L_{t-1} - b_{t-1} \right)$$

Notice that the expression $L_t - L_{t-1}$ is the difference between the levels of the series at period t and at period $t–1$: that is, the estimate of the slope as of period t. Also notice that the expression b_{t-1} is the slope as of period $t–1$. Therefore, the quantity in parentheses in the last equation above is the difference between the measured slope and the forecast slope—that is, the error in the forecast slope. And that gets us to one possible version of the error correction form of the trend equation:

$$b_t = b_{t-1} + \gamma\ \varepsilon_{Slope}$$

Another version of the trend equation looks a little strange at first and is close to pointless now that we've all turned in our pencils, erasers, and hand calculators. But you're likely to encounter it and you should understand where it comes from. To get there we have to start with one formula, the smoothing version for the series level and the derivation of its error correction form:

$$L_t = \alpha y_t + (1- \alpha)\hat{y}_t$$

$$L_t = \hat{y}_t - \alpha(y_t - \hat{y}_t)$$

$$L_t = \hat{y}_t - \alpha\varepsilon_t$$

If we now turn to the forecast equation for a trended series,

$$\hat{y}_t = L_{t-1} + b_{t-1}$$

we can replace $\hat{y}_t$, the forecast for period t in the smoothing equation, with its components,

$$L_t = L_{t-1} + b_{t-1} - \alpha\varepsilon_t$$

and rearrange:

$$L_t - L_{t-1} = b_{t-1} - \alpha\varepsilon_t$$

Finally, return to the former equation for the slope,

$$b_t = b_{t-1} + \gamma(L_t - L_{t-1} - b_{t-1})$$

and substitute for the difference in levels,

$$b_t = b_{t-1} + \gamma(b_{t-1} - \alpha\varepsilon_t - b_{t-1})$$

to reach this mildly surprising form of the trend equation:

$$b_t = b_{t-1} + \gamma\ \alpha\ \varepsilon_t$$

The latter form is useful if you're doing the arithmetic by hand because you can multiply Gamma by Alpha at the outset and use that product in each subsequent slope estimate.

It has been a while since that shortcut was truly helpful in a practical sense; it's virtually devoid of the sort of meaning that leads to insight, but you still run into its use. Now you know where it comes from.

The Season Equation

Back for the moment to assuming a seasonal but horizontal (that is, untrended) model, we start with the smoothing form of the equation for the seasonal effect. The actual current seasonal effect is estimated by taking the difference between the current actual observation and the estimate of the current level. That estimate of the seasonal effect is multiplied by the seasonal smoothing constant Delta. Added to that is the prior seasonal estimate multiplied by (1 – Delta), as shown here:

$$S_t = \delta\left(y_t - L_t\right) + \left(1 - \delta\right)S_{t-m}$$

We can lay some groundwork by rearranging,

> **NOTE** See the earlier section of this chapter "Interpreting the Formula for Series Level" for an explanation of the $t-m$ notation, but briefly it refers to the period identified by the current value of t, minus m, the number of seasons in the encompassing period. So if we have quarterly data and we're working with the third period of the second year, then $t = 7$ and $m = 4$, so S_{t-m} refers to the seasonal effect calculated for the third season of the first year.
>
> There are other popular ways to represent the same sort of notion. For example, some sources index S with the letter i and use the notation $S_i(t-1)$ where $(t-1)$ means "as of period $t-1$." Other sources use the pipe symbol "|" to represent "as of." For example, $S_{i|t-1}$ would mean the seasonal effect for Season i as of period $t-1$. There's nothing at all wrong with these symbols if you understand and feel comfortable with them. My own view is that new and unfamiliar methods of notation tend to delay understanding, whatever their long-term advantages.

$$S_t = \left(1 - \delta\right)S_{t-m} + \delta\left(y_t - L_t\right)$$

and then by expanding the expression:

$$S_t = S_{t-m} + \delta\left(y_t - L_t - S_{t-m}\right)$$

Taking one error correction form of the equation for the series level in an untrended, seasonal model,

$$L_t = L_{t-1} + \alpha\varepsilon$$

then,

$$L_t = y_{t-1} - S_{t-m} + \alpha\varepsilon$$

because

$$L_{t-1} = y_{t-1} - S_{t-m}$$

and substituting that expression into the equation for the season,

$$\hat{S}_t = \hat{S}_{t-m} + \delta\left(y_t - (\hat{y}_{t-1} - S_{t-m} + \alpha\varepsilon) - \hat{S}_{t-m}\right)$$

gets us to

$$\hat{S}_t = \hat{S}_{t-m} + \delta\left(y_t - \hat{y}_{t-1} - \alpha\varepsilon + S_{t-m}\right) - \hat{S}_{t-m}$$

and, simplifying, to

$$\hat{S}_t = \hat{S}_{t-m} + \delta\left((y_t - \hat{y}_{t-1}) - \alpha\varepsilon\right)$$

Now, because the difference between the current observation and the forecast for the current period constitutes the forecast error, we can write the previous expression as

$$\hat{S}_t = \hat{S}_{t-m} + \delta(\varepsilon - \alpha\varepsilon)$$

and finally

$$\hat{S}_t = \hat{S}_{t-m} + \delta(1-\alpha)\varepsilon$$

Demonstrating the Formulas on the Worksheet

As an exercise to convince yourself that the smoothing and the error correction forms of the smoothing equations are in fact arithmetically equivalent, you might try the following suggestion. Figure 6.12 has the same data, formulas, and names as Figure 6.11.

On the worksheet for Figure 6.12, perhaps in K8:N8, enter these four different formulas for the seasonal effect:

- Smoothing form using standard Excel row-and-column addressing
- Smoothing form using implicit intersections and mixed range names
- Error correction form with row-and-column addressing
- Error correction form using implicit intersections and mixed range names

If you enter the formulas and range names correctly, you'll see that all four return exactly the same result.

Entering the formulas yourself helps to lock these concepts in place. It also helps to compare the formulas on the Excel worksheet with the symbolic formulas such as the following for the seasonal effect, error correction form.

6

Figure 6.12
The range K8:N8 is a handy location to enter the four formulas.

Formula bar: K8 | =Delta*(CurrentObs-CurrentLevel)+(1-Delta)*SameSeasonLastYear

	D Observations	E Forecast for this period	F Error	G Estimated Level (Smoothing)	H Seasonal Index (Smoothing)	I Forecast for next period	J	K	L	M	N
2	7950				-220.8			Alpha	0.1		
3	7304				-866.8			Delta	0.3		
4	8071				-99.8			Year 1 Mean	8170.8		
5	9374				1203.2			RMSE	321.59		
6	8819				648.2						
7	7507			8170.8	-663.8	7950.0					
8	7307	7950.0	-643.0	8106.5	-394.4	7239.7		-394.44	-394.44	-394.44	-394.44
9	7383	7239.7	143.3	8120.9	-828.1	8021.0					
10	8035	8021.0	14.0	8122.3	-96.1	9325.4					
11	9084	9325.4	-241.4	8098.1	1138.0	8746.3					
12	9076	8746.3	329.7	8131.1	737.2	7467.3					
13	7944	7467.3	476.7	8178.8	-535.1	7784.3					
14	7477	7784.3	-307.3	8148.0	-477.4	7319.9					
15	7307	7319.9	-12.9	8146.7	-831.6	8050.7					
16	7963	8050.7	-87.7	8138.0	-119.7	9276.0					
17		9276.0		8138.0		8875.2					
18		8875.2		8138.0		7602.9					
19		7602.9		8138.0		7660.6					
20		7660.6		8138.0		7306.4					
21		7306.4		8138.0		8018.2					
22		8018.2		8138.0							

Start with the smoothing version of the formula for the seasonal effect given at the start of this section:

$$S_t = \delta\left(y_t - L_t\right) + (1-\delta)S_{t-m}$$

If that formula were entered in some empty cell on, say, row 8 of the worksheet shown in Figure 6.12, here's what it would look like using conventional Excel row and column addressing (and the fixed range name Delta):

```
=Delta*(D8-G8)+(1-Delta)*H2
```

Here's that same formula using the implicit intersection and mixed range names:

```
=Delta*(CurrentObs-CurrentLevel)+(1-Delta)*SameSeasonLastYear
```

Both versions of the season smoothing formula, one using conventional addressing and the other using implicit intersections and mixed range names, return the same value; entered in row 8, that value is −394.443.

Here again is the error correction version of the season formula as derived earlier in this section:

$$\hat{S}_t = \hat{S}_{t-m} + \delta(1-\alpha)\varepsilon$$

Using row and column addressing in combination with the named ranges Alpha and Delta, the error correction formula is as follows:

```
=H2+Delta*(1-Alpha)*F8
```

6

Entered in some empty cell in row 8 of Figure 6.12's worksheet, it also returns the value
−394.443.

And using range names, the error correction formula is this:

```
=SameSeasonLastYear+Delta*(1-Alpha)*Error
```

Entered in some empty cell on row 8 (so that it picks up the proper values from the named
ranges), it also returns −394.443.

Similar demonstrations (*not* proofs) of the equivalence of the smoothing and error correction versions for the series level and its trend follow.

The smoothing version of the formula for the series level, in an untrended seasonal series, is

$$L_t = \alpha\left(y_t - s_{t-m}\right) + \left(1 - \alpha\right)L_{t-1}$$

The error correction form of the equation, derived in the earlier section "The Level Equation," is

$$L_t = L_{t-1} + \alpha\varepsilon$$

It often helps to see these 10 formulas in one place: the smoothing and error correction forms, and the level, season, and trend components. See Figure 6.13.

Figure 6.13
These formulas have certain consistencies.

	A	B	C
1		Season, no trend: Simple seasonal exponential smoothing	
2		*Level*	*Season*
3	Smoothing	$L_t = \alpha(y_t - S_{t-m}) + (1 - \alpha) L_{t-1}$	$S_t = \delta(y_t - L_t) + (1 - \delta) S_{t-m}$
4			
5	Error correction	$L_t = L_{t-1} + \alpha e_t$	$S_t = S_{t-m} + \delta(1 - \alpha) e_t$
6			
7			
8		Trend, no season: Holt's method	
9		*Level*	*Trend*
10	Smoothing	$L_t = \alpha y_t + (1 - \alpha) (L_{t-1} + T_{t-1})$	$T_t = \gamma(L_t - L_{t-1}) + (1 - \gamma)T_{t-1}$
11			
12	Error correction	$L_t = L_{t-1} + T_{t-1} + \alpha e_t$	$T_t = T_{t-1} + \alpha\gamma e_t$
13			
14			
15		Neither trend nor season: Simple exponential smoothing	
16		*Level only*	
17	Smoothing	$L_t = \alpha y_t + (1 - \alpha)L_{t-1}$	
18		or $L_t = \alpha y_t + (1 - \alpha)\hat{y}_{t-1}$	
19			
20	Error correction	$L_t = L_{t-1} + \alpha e_t$	

Notice first the differences between cells B3 and B5 in Figure 6.13. The final factor in the smoothing equation is the level of the series at period $t-1$, L_{t-1}. That quantity remains in the error correction form of the equation, as its first term. The second term in the error correction form is Alpha times the forecast error, e_t. The forecast error of course includes a reference to the forecast of period t made at period $t-1$; the error is the difference between the forecast of period t and the actual observation at period t.

Also notice that because the formulas in cells B3 and B5 of Figure 6.13 are concerned with simple seasonal smoothing, a reference to the seasonal effect, S_{t-m}, appears in the smoothing formula for the level. (The seasonal effect is subtracted from the actual observation y_t to leave an estimate of the series level at period t.) What happens to S_{t-m} in the error correction version of the formula?

If you follow the individual steps of the derivation of the error correction form for the level from the smoothing form given in an earlier section, "The Level Equation," you'll see that the associated seasonal effect disappears when the prior forecast, $\hat{y}_t$, replaces $L_{t-1}+S_{t-m}$ on its way to calculating the current forecast error, e_t. The seasonal effect is still in there pitching, but it's hidden inside the expression e_t.

Similar comments apply to the season equations in cells C3 and C5. Again, the final factor in the smoothing form, S_{t-m}, is retained in the error correction form. In the error correction form the forecast error e_t is again multiplied by smoothing constants, but this time both Delta and (1 – Alpha) come into play. Alpha gets into the picture along with Delta due to the substitution of $(Y_{t-1} - S_{t-m} + \alpha\varepsilon)$ for L_t. See "The Season Equation," earlier in this chapter, for the specifics.

And again a component of the smoothing form—this time the series level L_t—seems to disappear from the error correction form. The disappearance is again due to the calculation of the forecast error, but this time the reason is that the level gets reexpressed as the difference between the actual observation y_t and the seasonal effect S_{t-1}.

You'll find that the same sort of thing is going on with the equations for level and trend as they apply to Holt's method, appropriate for a series that includes a trend but not a seasonal effect. See rows 10 and 12 in Figure 6.13. The basic pattern for building the error correction form applies: Add the prior calculation of the level (or the trend) to a measure of the forecast error, multiplied by one or more smoothing constants.

It's important to see here that the way you calculate the forecast error is critical to correct calculation of the next value of the level, trend, or seasonal component. The forecast error for the series, which is always the difference between the forecast value of the series made at period $t-1$ and the actual observation at period t, depends on how the forecast value is calculated at period $t-1$.

In simple exponential smoothing, with no trend or seasonality involved, the forecast for period t at period $t-1$ is simply L_{t-1}. But in a seasonal model, the forecast is the total of the estimated level *and* the estimated seasonal effect. In a trended model with no seasonal effect, the forecast is the total of the estimated level *and* the current trend estimate. In Holt-Winters models, the forecast is the sum of the level, the trend, and the seasonal effect.

So you can see that the seasonal effects do not really disappear from the level equation as it applies to a seasonal model when you use the error correction form. Nor does the trend disappear from the level equation in a trended model's error correction form. Nor the level from either the seasonal or the trend calculations. They're merely buried in the computation of the forecast error.

That means you must be careful, if you're using the error correction form, to use the correct method of calculating the forecast for period t that's made at period t–1. Otherwise, you're liable to lose track of what's going on, and backtracking to find an error of this sort is a huge pain in the backside.

Deriving the Formulas on the Worksheet

One further viewpoint is often helpful for conceptualizing what's going on inside the smoothing and the error correction versions of the smoothing formulas. That viewpoint comes about from deriving the formulas directly on the worksheet. In this section you'll step through the derivation of the formulas for the level and the season with simple seasonal exponential smoothing. You'll also see an analogous derivation that uses Holt's method for a series that has trend but is without seasonal effects.

Deriving Error Correction of Level and Season Effects

Figures 6.14 and 6.15 repeat much of Figure 5.25: the analysis of a seasonal but untrended model that's appropriate for simple seasonal exponential smoothing. As such, we need one smoothing formula for the level of the series and one for the seasonal effects.

Figure 6.14
The range L8:L12 contains, as *text*, the formulas in K8:K12 for the series level.

			D	E	F	G	H	I	J	K	L	M
K8			f_x	=Alpha*(D8-H2)+(1-Alpha)*G7								
	A	B	C	D	E	F	G	H	I	J	K	L	M
					Forecast				Forecast				
				Observ-	for this		Estimated	Seasonal	for next				
1	Year	Season	t	ations	period	Error	Level	Index	period	Alpha	0.1	
2	2012	1	1	7950				-220.8		Delta	0.3	
3		2	2	7304				-866.8		Year 1 Mean	8170.8	
4		3	3	8071				-99.8				
5		4	4	9374				1203.2		RMSE	643.00	
6		5	5	8819				648.2				
7		6	6	7507			8170.8	-663.8	7950.0	Level	Formula as Text
8	2013	1	7	7307	7950.0	-643.0	8106.5	-394.4	7239.7	8106.5	=Alpha*(D8-H2)+(1-Alpha)*G7
9										8106.5	=Alpha*(D8-H2)+G7-Alpha*G7
10										8106.5	=G7+Alpha*(D8-(H2+G7))
11										8106.5	=G7+Alpha*(D8-I7)
12										8106.5	=G7+Alpha*F8

Nearly all the information in Figure 6.14 is as it is in Figure 5.25, including the use of row-and-column addressing instead of implicit intersections and mixed range names. However, I have added formulas in two ranges:

- K8:K12 contains the steps to derive the error correction form from the smoothing form for the level formula. Each step is in the form of a formula derived from the prior step, and therefore each cell returns the same value.
- L8:L12 shows the formulas from K8:K12 as text.

My intent here is to show the derivation of the error correction form from the smoothing form. All that's needed to demonstrate the derivation is one time period, so for clarity I have deleted all time periods after the first period of the second year.

Cell K8. The smoothing form of the equation:

```
=Alpha*(D8-H2)+(1-Alpha)*G7
```

Cell K9. Multiply G7 through (1 – Alpha):

```
=Alpha*(D8-H2)+G7-Alpha*G7
```

Cell K10. Group G7 together with D8 and H2:

```
=G7+Alpha*(D8-(H2+G7))
```

Cell K11. The quantity (H2 + G7) constitutes the series forecast for the seventh period. The sum is found in cell I7, which replaces (H2 + G7) here:

```
=G7+Alpha*(D8-I7)
```

Cell K12. The quantity (D8-I7) is the forecast error found in cell F8:

```
=G7+Alpha*F8
```

And the formula in cell K12 is the error correction form of the level equation.

Figure 6.15 shows the derivation of the error correction form of the formula for the seasonal effects.

Figure 6.15
The range L8:L16 contains, as *text*, the formulas in K8:K16 for the seasonal effects.

Cell K8. The smoothing form of the formula for the seasonal effect:

```
=Delta*(D8-G8)+(1-Delta)*H2
```

Cell K9. Reverse the order of the terms:

```
=(1-Delta)*H2+Delta*(D8-G8)
```

Cell K10. Multiply H2 through (1 – Delta):

```
=H2-Delta*H2+Delta*(D8-G8)
```

Cell K11. Group H2 with D8 and G8:

```
=H2+Delta*(D8-G8-H2)
```

Cell K12. Replace the reference to G8, the estimated level for the current period, with I7-H2+Alpha*F8. This expression is the *seasonally adjusted* error correction formula for the current series level:

```
=H2+Delta*(D8-(I7-H2+Alpha*F8)-H2)
```

Cell K13. Rearrange the order of the terms:

```
=H2+Delta*(D8-I7-Alpha*F8+H2-H2)
```

Cell K14. Simplify:

```
=H2+Delta*(D8-I7-Alpha*F8)
```

Cell K15. Replace D8-I7 with F8, the current forecast error:

```
=H2+Delta*(F8-Alpha*F8)
```

Cell K16. Break F8 out of the parentheses:

```
=H2+Delta*(1-Alpha)*F8
```

And cell K16 contains the error correction form of the equation for the current seasonal effect.

Deriving Error Correction of Level and Trend

The worksheets shown in Figures 6.16 and 6.17 appear in Chapter 3 as Figure 3.10, where they are used to illustrate the use of Holt's method. To keep the figures in this chapter a little more crisp, I have deleted the observations and forecasts subsequent to Period 5. In both Figures 6.16 and 6.17, the derivation of the error correction formulas in columns H and I are based on Period 5.

Figure 6.16 shows how to get from the smoothing form of the level equation to the error correction form, for a series with trend but without seasonality.

Figure 6.16
The range I6:I9 contains, as *text*, the formulas in H6:H9 for the series level.

	A	B	C	D	E	F	G	H	I	J
	Period	Observed, Trended Series	Forecast of Current Period	Forecast Level	Forecast Trend	Forecast of Next Period		Alpha:	0.1	
2	1	9,174		9,174.0	0	9,174.0		Gamma:	0.1	
3	2	9,408	9,174.0	9,197.4	2.3	9,199.7		RMSE:	746.92	
4	3	8,540	9,199.7	9,133.8	-4.3	9,129.5				
5	4	8,314	9,129.5	9,048.0	-12.4	9,035.5		Level	Formula as Text	
6	5	7,998	9,035.5	8,931.8	-22.8	8,909.0		8931.8	=Alpha*B6+(1-Alpha)*F5	
7								8931.8	=(1-Alpha)*F5+Alpha*B6	
8								8931.8	=F5-Alpha*F5+Alpha*B6	
9								8931.8	=F5+Alpha*(B6-F5)	

H6 ▾ : ✕ ✓ *fx* =Alpha*B6+(1-Alpha)*F5

Cell H6. The smoothing form of the formula for the level:

```
=Alpha*B6+(1-Alpha)*F5
```

Cell H7. Reverse the order of the terms:

```
=(1-Alpha)*F5+Alpha*B6
```

Cell H8. Multiply F5 through (1 – Alpha):

```
=F5-Alpha*F5+Alpha*B6
```

Cell H9. Combine B6 with F5:

```
=F5+Alpha*(B6-F5)
```

The difference between B6 and F5 is the forecast error for time Period 5. Therefore, cell H9 contains the error correction form of the equation for the level in a trended but nonseasonal series.

Figure 6.17 derives the error correction form from the smoothing form, for the trend equation in a nonseasonal series.

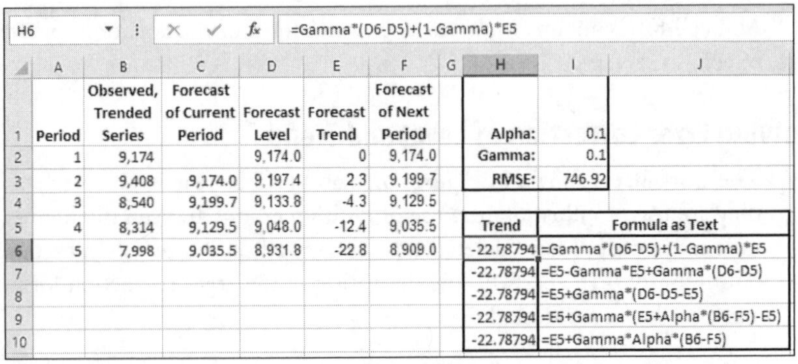

Figure 6.17
The range I6:I10 contains, as *text*, the formulas in H6:H10 for the series trend.

Cell H6. Begin with the smoothing form of the equation for trend. The quantity (D6-D5) uses the difference between consecutive level estimates as the best estimate of the current trend, and E5 is the most recent trend forecast:

```
=Gamma*(D6-D5)+(1-Gamma)*E5
```

Cell H7. Multiply (1-Gamma) by E5, and reverse the order of the terms in the equation:

```
=E5-Gamma*E5+Gamma*(D6-D5)
```

Cell H8. Combine E5 with D6 and D5:

```
=E5+Gamma*(D6-D5-E5)
```

Cell H9. Here you replace (D6-D5) with E5+Alpha*(B6-F5):

```
=E5+Gamma*(E5+Alpha*(B6-F5)-E5)
```

The rationale for getting from H8 to H9 is a little involved. Start with the equation to fore-cast the series level at Period 5, in error correction form:

```
=F5+Alpha*(B6-C6)
```

You can replace F5, the series forecast at Period 4, with its constituents, the forecast level and the forecast trend:

```
=(D5+E5)+Alpha*(B6-C6)
```

That equation returns the value 8931.8, found in cell D6. So:

```
D6 =(D5+E5)+Alpha*(B6-C6)
```

Therefore:

```
D6 - D5 = E5+Alpha*(B6-C6)
```

And that's the replacement that's made to get from cell H8 to cell H9, which is repeated here:

```
=E5+Gamma*(E5+Alpha*(B6-F5)-E5)
```

Cell H10. Finally, simplify cell H9 to get rid of the references to cell E5 and reach the error correction form of the trend equation:

```
=E5+Gamma*Alpha*(B6-F5)
```

Named Ranges for Holt-Winters Models

Adding a trend component to the simple seasonal smoothing model discussed in earlier sections of this chapter does not make it more difficult to understand what's going on. Admittedly, the model is more complex because you're smoothing through three compo-nents rather than two; and to get the forecast you add the trend to the level and the sea-sonal effect.

But as discussed in Chapter 5, the concepts—particularly the notion of a weighted average of old and new information, and that of error correction—remain unchanged. Let's review an example of trended, seasonal smoothing presented in the section "Holt-Winters Models" of Chapter 5. Figure 6.18 repeats the analysis of the Box-Jenkins Series G in Figure 5.28.

In this analysis, the initialization procedures are simplistic, using the mean of the first year's observations as the initial value of the series' level. The initial values of the seasonal effects are simply the difference between each month's observation and the first year's mean. The initial value for the series trend is taken to be the difference between the 1st and 12th months' observations divided by 11, to scale it down to a monthly trend. Although cal-culated simply, these initial values are probably sufficient with a series as long as this one (144 observations). Inaccurate initial values are likely to wash out by the time we're ready to forecast the 145th time period: remember that one effect of exponential smoothing is to make the influence of an early value vanishingly small by the end of a lengthy time series.

6

Figure 6.18
You'll recognize some of these range names from prior examples.

	G16		▾	:	×	✓	fx		=Alpha*(CurrentObs-SameSeasonLastYear)+(1-Alpha)*(PriorLevel+PriorTrend)			

⊿	A	B	C	D	E	F	G	H	I	J	K	L	M
				Observ-	Forecast for this		Estimated	Estimated	Estimated Seasonal	Forecast for next			
1	Year	Season	t	ations	period	Error	Level	Trend	Index	period		Alpha	0.1
2	1949	1	1	112						-14.7		Gamma	0.1
3		2	2	118						-8.7		Delta	0.2
4		3	3	132						5.3		Year 1 Mean	126.67
5		4	4	129						2.3		Year 1 Trend	0.55
6		5	5	121						-5.7		RMSE	24.51
7		6	6	135						8.3			
8		7	7	148						21.3			
9		8	8	148						21.3			
10		9	9	136						9.3			
11		10	10	119						-7.7			
12		11	11	104						-22.7			
13		12	12	118			126.7	0.5		-8.7	112.5		
14	1950	1	13	115	112.5455	2.5	127.5	0.6		-14.2	119.4		
15		2	14	126	119.3609	6.6	128.7	0.6		-7.5	134.7		
16		3	15	141	134.6612	6.3	130.0	0.7		6.5	133.0		
17		4	16	135	132.9949	2.0	130.9	0.7		2.7	125.9		
18		5	17	125	125.9152	-0.9	131.5	0.7		-5.8	140.5		
19		6	18	149	140.5344	8.5	133.0	0.8		9.9	155.2		
20		7	19	170	155.1763	14.8	135.3	0.9		24.0	157.6		
21		8	20	170	157.6022	12.4	137.5	1.1		23.6	147.9		
22		9	21	158	147.9095	10.1	139.6	1.2		11.1	133.1		
23		10	22	133	133.0870	-0.1	140.7	1.2		-7.7	119.2		

Estimating the Series Level in Holt-Winters Models

At any rate, the focus here is on writing formulas that foster understanding. Let's start with the formula for the series' level, shown in column G of Figure 6.18.

Just as in simple seasonal exponential smoothing, the level is estimated by subtracting the current seasonal estimate from the current actual observation to get the unseasonalized level. I've named the fixed range of current observations as CurrentObs, so we can get to the current actual by means of the implicit intersection.

Here's the formula used in cell G16:

```
=Alpha*(CurrentObs-SameSeasonLastYear)+(1-Alpha) *(PriorLevel+PriorTrend)
```

The implicit intersection returns the value 141 from cell D16.

Then the value of SameSeasonLastYear is subtracted from the current observation of 141 to deseasonalize it, leaving only the best estimate of the current level of the series. In row 16, we're in the third season (see cell B16), and the SameSeasonLastYear mixed reference points 12 rows up in column I, to cell I4, which represents the most recent estimate of the effect of season 3.

Still in cell G16, we now multiply (1–Alpha) times the total of PriorLevel and PriorTrend, found, via mixed references, in G15 and H15. Their total is the forecast of the current level of the series. Once again, the smoothing form of the formula multiplies Alpha times our best estimate of the level of the series, plus (1–Alpha) times the forecast of the current level.

Estimating the Current Trend

The current trend is estimated in cell H16 by this formula:

```
=Gamma*(CurrentLevel-PriorLevel)+(1-Gamma)*PriorTrend
```

In this smoothing form of the trend equation, we get the current estimate of the trend by subtracting the series' prior level, retrieved by mixed reference, from the series' current level. *CurrentLevel* is a fixed reference to the range G13:G145, and its implicit intersection with row 16 returns the value 130.0 to the equation for the current trend. The equation multiplies Gamma by the current trend estimate—the difference between the current and the prior levels.

> **NOTE** Notice that the trend equation estimates the current trend by subtracting the prior level estimate from the current *level estimate*. In contrast, the level equation given in the immediately preceding section subtracts the prior seasonal estimate from the current *actual observation*.

Then (1–Gamma) is multiplied by the PriorTrend, retrieved via mixed reference just as is done in the level equation. The result of summing the two terms is the estimate of the current trend of the series.

Estimating the Current Seasonal Effect

It won't be used until we get another 12 seasons into the time series, but it's convenient to calculate the current value of the seasonal effect while we're estimating the level and the trend components for the current season. The smoothing formula for the seasonal effect for cell I16 is this:

```
=Delta*(CurrentObs-CurrentLevel)+(1-Delta)*SameSeasonLastYear
```

Just as you subtract the seasonal effect from the current observation to help estimate the current level of the series, you subtract the current level of the series from the current observation to estimate the current seasonal effect. And you multiply the result by Delta.

Then, multiply (1–Delta) by the most recent forecast of the effect of the current season, which is returned by the mixed reference SameSeasonLastYear. Total the two terms to get the current estimate of the seasonal effect.

> **NOTE** Bear in mind that the defined name SameSeasonLastYear is just a convenience to help remind you, and me for that matter, that the seasonal effect we're interested in is as far back as the number of seasons in the encompassing period. That number is often 4, when you're working with quarterly data. It's 12 in this example, when we're working with monthly data. But if you were treating, say, daily shifts in a hospital as three distinct seasons, then the applicable season would be three periods back. Furthermore, the mnemonic you choose as a defined name might well be something more apt such as SameShiftYesterday.

6

Error Correction Formulas for Holt-Winters Models

If you prefer to use the error correction forms of the smoothing equations in a series that's trended and has seasonality, it's fairly straightforward to do so—particularly if you're using named ranges. See Figure 6.19.

Figure 6.19
The range names are
nearly the same as in
Figure 6.18.

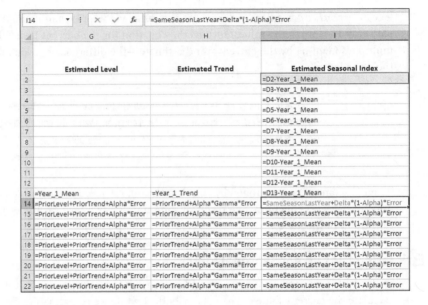

The range names used by the smoothing forms in Figure 6.18 are as follows:

- Alpha
- Gamma
- Delta
- CurrentObs
- Level
- SameSeasonLastYear
- PriorLevel
- PriorTrend

The error correction forms in Figure 6.19 are as follows:

- Alpha
- Gamma
- Delta

- SameSeasonLastYear
- PriorLevel
- PriorTrend
- Error

The error correction forms of the equations, as used in Figure 6.19, are as follows:

Level, in column G starting in row 14:

```
=PriorLevel+PriorTrend+Alpha*Error
```

Trend, in column H starting in row 14:

```
=PriorTrend+Alpha*Gamma*Error
```

Season, in column I starting in row 14:

```
=SameSeasonLastYear+Delta*(1-Alpha)*Error
```

Toward the end of Chapter 5, Holt-Winters models were discussed but not illustrated graphically. Figure 6.20 shows the observations and forecasts from Figure 6.19.

Figure 6.20
The seasonal swings in the forecasts are narrower than the swings in the actual observations.

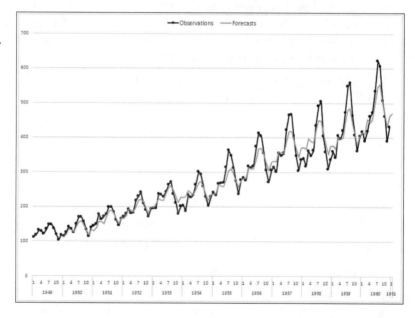

Notice in Figure 6.20 that the forecast seasonal highs fall farther and farther below the observed seasonal highs as time moves forward. Similarly, the forecast seasonal lows fall higher above the observed seasonal lows.

The reason for this phenomenon is that this chapter—indeed, all this book's chapters thus far—has used an *additive* model for the forecasts. Particularly with trended series, the additive model can underestimate the size of the seasonal swings.

With an additive model, we forecast by adding to the estimated level an estimate of the seasonal effect. The estimated seasonal effect is expressed in the same units of measurement as is the estimated level—say, dollars spent each fiscal quarter.

With a multiplicative model, we forecast by multiplying the estimated level by an estimate of the seasonal effect. The estimated seasonal effect is *not* expressed in the same units of measurement as the estimated level. The estimated level might be measured in, say, dollars, but the seasonal effect is expressed as a fraction or a percent. So the third-quarter level estimate of $200,000 might be multiplied by a seasonal effect of 110% rather than by adding $20,000.

The example in the preceding paragraph comes to the same thing whether you add $20,000 or multiply by 1.1. But when the long-term effect of a trend shows up in the current level of the series, you might well want to multiply instead of add.

If the current level has grown from $200,000 to $2,000,000, it could be and probably is more realistic to estimate a multiplicative seasonal effect of 1.1 than to estimate an additive seasonal effect of $20,000. So doing keeps your model from underrepresenting the size of the forecast swings, as occurs in Figure 6.20.

The next chapter, "Multiplicative and Damped Trend Models," takes up this issue in greater detail.

6

Multiplicative and Damped Trend Models

7

Throughout this book the approaches to smoothing have become twice as complicated with each new concept. We start out with simple exponential smoothing. Then we note that the smoothing formulas can take two equivalent forms: smoothing and error correction. When we add the notion of trend to the series, we have both stationary and trended series to deal with, and each has smoothing and error correction forms, which provide different perspectives on what's going on in the smoothing process.

The same sort of complication occurs when we add the notion of seasonality to both untrended and trended time series. And in this chapter we deal with the distinction between additive and multiplicative models, necessitated by seasonal effects that vary in proportion to the current level of the time series.

About Multiplicative Models

Suppose that 10 years ago you invested $1,000 in a new venture that was paying a 5% dividend per year. You opt to have the annual earnings reinvested in fractional account shares.

The first year that you have that investment, it distributes a $50 dividend. On your Excel worksheet, you enter =A2 + 50 in cell A3 to get a current value.

Over the years you keep making similar entries, adding $50 to the prior year's ending balance, without reference to the annual account statements that the company sends you. This year, though, you open the statement and find that the balance is $1,628.89, not the $1,500.00 that your Excel workbook told you. See Figure 7.1.

Figure 7.1
An additive and a multiplicative model, both oversimplified.

C3 =B3*$C$13

	A	B	C	D	E	F	G	H	I
1	Year	Balance	Interest	Ending Balance		Year	Balance	Interest	Ending Balance
2	2005	$1,000.00	$ 50.00	$ 1,050.00		2005	$1,000.00	$ 50.00	$ 1,050.00
3	2006	$1,050.00	$ 52.50	$ 1,102.50		2006	$1,050.00	$ 50.00	$ 1,100.00
4	2007	$1,102.50	$ 55.13	$ 1,157.63		2007	$1,100.00	$ 50.00	$ 1,150.00
5	2008	$1,157.63	$ 57.88	$ 1,215.51		2008	$1,150.00	$ 50.00	$ 1,200.00
6	2009	$1,215.51	$ 60.78	$ 1,276.28		2009	$1,200.00	$ 50.00	$ 1,250.00
7	2010	$1,276.28	$ 63.81	$ 1,340.10		2010	$1,250.00	$ 50.00	$ 1,300.00
8	2011	$1,340.10	$ 67.00	$ 1,407.10		2011	$1,300.00	$ 50.00	$ 1,350.00
9	2012	$1,407.10	$ 70.36	$ 1,477.46		2012	$1,350.00	$ 50.00	$ 1,400.00
10	2013	$1,477.46	$ 73.87	$ 1,551.33		2013	$1,400.00	$ 50.00	$ 1,450.00
11	2014	$1,551.33	$ 77.57	$ 1,628.89		2014	$1,450.00	$ 50.00	$ 1,500.00
12									
13	Annual interest:		5%			Annual interest:		$ 50.00	

Maybe, you think, all those people who complain on various websites about Excel's numeric accuracy are right. Then you reflect on the fact that those people never sound like the brightest glowworms on the dung heap, and you take another look at the annual statement. It turns out that reinvesting the dividend year after year raises the basis for the dividend calculations. Instead of adding $50 per year in the original dollar metric, you should have been multiplying by 105%, using a percentage factor that takes its metric from the context of the calculation.

The point of this homely little tale is that different situations call for different calculations, and sometimes there's no ironclad rule you can use to choose your formula. In smoothing you have *additive* models and *multiplicative* models, which correspond, not too roughly, to the alternatives in the example just given. When it's called for, you can arrange for your smoothing calculations to add some more-or-less constant number of dollars to the last period's balance, to account for a trend or for a new season. Doing so is conceptually similar to adding $5 each year to an account balance.

Most of the examples in prior chapters of this book have used additive models. This chapter looks at how you can use multiplicative models when the circumstances warrant—for example, when your account balance increases by 5% per year instead of by $5 per year.

Additive Models and Multiplicative Models

Formally, a multiplicative trend model could be used when the trend is proportional to the level of the series. In that case, it's typical to find that the higher the level, the greater the trend. For example, from 1975 to 1979, the Dow Jones Industrial Average's opening level each year was between 600 and 800. It gained an average of 44 points during each of those years.

But from 2010 to 2014, the Dow opened each year at an average level of 12,780 and posted an average annual gain of 1,480. The higher the level, the steeper the trend.

That's usually termed an *exponential trend model*. You might find that situation either by itself or in combination with a seasonal effect in a Holt-Winters context. In practice, though, you often find that analysts have converted an exponentially trended series to a linear trend by taking logarithms of the original observations. They then forecast the logs and convert the forecasts back to the original scale of measurement by means of antilogs. Excel offers several functions that return logs and the EXP() function to convert a natural log back to its original scale.

Holt's linear smoothing method uses an additive model. The Holt-Winters method uses an additive model for the trend component and either an additive or a multiplicative model for the level and seasonal components. The multiplicative version of Holt-Winters is discussed later in this chapter.

Of course, you want to consider additive and multiplicative models as alternatives when you have a series that displays seasonal behavior and, perhaps, a trend over time. If you're looking at a stationary series, the question doesn't arise. Consider Figure 7.2.

Figure 7.2
A stationary time series has neither an additive nor a multiplicative component.

C4			×	✓	*fx*	=$F$1*B3+(1-$F$1)*C3	

▲	A	B	C	D	E	F
1	Period	Observed Series	Forecast of Current Period		Alpha:	0.35387
2	1	147	#N/A			
3	2	137	147.0		RMSE:	50.8066
4	3	170	143.5			
5	4	139	152.9			
6	5	143	148.0			
7	6	183	146.2			
8	7	205	159.2			
9	8	56	175.4			
10	9	145	133.2			
11	10	114	137.4			
12	11	104	129.1			
13	12	38	120.2			
14	13	68	91.1			
15	14	15	82.9			
16	15	19	58.9			
17	16	117	44.8			
18	17	165	70.3			
19	18	103	103.8			
20	19	72	103.5			
21	20	55	92.4			
22	21	118	79.2			

Figure 7.2 displays a horizontal, stationary time series. Standard, simple exponential smoothing results in the forecasts shown in column C. As discussed in earlier chapters, Excel's Solver was used to minimize the root mean square forecast error in cell F3.

Compare the contents of Figure 7.2 with those of Figure 7.3.

7

Figure 7.3

The optimized Alpha and RMSE are identical to those in Figure 7.2.

	A	B	C	D	E	F	G	H	I
			F3 ▾ : × ✓ *fx* =D3+E3						
1	Period	Observed Series	Forecast of Current Period	Forecast Level	Forecast Trend	Forecast of Next Period		Alpha:	0.35387
2	1	49		49.0	0	49.0		Gamma:	0.00000
3	2	39	49.0	45.5	0.0	45.5		RMSE:	50.8066
4	3	72	45.5	54.9	0.0	54.9			
5	4	41	54.9	50.0	0.0	50.0			
6	5	45	50.0	48.2	0.0	48.2			
7	6	85	48.2	61.2	0.0	61.2			
8	7	107	61.2	77.4	0.0	77.4			
9	8	-42	77.4	35.2	0.0	35.2			
10	9	47	35.2	39.4	0.0	39.4			
11	10	16	39.4	31.1	0.0	31.1			
12	11	6	31.1	22.2	0.0	22.2			
13	12	-60	22.2	-6.9	0.0	-6.9			
14	13	-30	-6.9	-15.1	0.0	-15.1			
15	14	-83	-15.1	-39.1	0.0	-39.1			
16	15	-79	-39.1	-53.2	0.0	-53.2			
17	16	19	-53.2	-27.7	0.0	-27.7			
18	17	67	-27.7	5.8	0.0	5.8			
19	18	5	5.8	5.5	0.0	5.5			
20	19	-26	5.5	-5.6	0.0	-5.6			
21	20	-43	-5.6	-18.8	0.0	-18.8			
22	21	20	-18.8	-5.1	0.0	-5.1			

Figure 7.3 analyzes the same time series as is used in Figure 7.2, but Holt's method is used instead of simple exponential smoothing. When Solver was used to try different values for Alpha and Gamma so as to minimize RMSE, Solver returned precisely the same value for Alpha as it did using simple exponential smoothing. Furthermore, it returned an optimized value of 0.0 for Gamma—and thus the RMSE is also identical to that in Figure 7.2.

> **NOTE**
>
> The updating formula for the slope in cell E3 of Figure 7.3 is as follows:
>
> =Gamma*(D3-D2)+(1-Gamma)*E2
>
> So when Gamma is 0.0 and the initial slope is also taken to be 0.0 (as it is in one popular initializing scheme) all trend forecasts must also be 0.0. Thus, trend plays no part in the series forecasts.

So including an additive component in the form of trend does not improve the forecast accuracy of simple exponential smoothing when the trend is stationary. In fact, it can *reduce* that level of accuracy when the initial trend estimate, cell E2 in Figure 7.3, is nonzero. Try it yourself: Enter some number other than 0.0 in cell E2, and then use Solver to minimize RMSE by changing Alpha and Gamma. Compare the resulting RMSE to the value now shown in Figure 7.3.

My point is that there's nothing to be gained by applying a model with additive (or, for that matter, multiplicative) trend to a time series that's not trended. Parsimony in constructing models is always a useful goal, and the present example is a useful illustration of that rationale.

Why Use an Additive Model?

A multiplicative model can often provide a more accurate forecast when a time series is trended. This happens when the increase in the seasonal effect, as measured in its original metric, is proportional to the level of the series.

At first glance there appears to be little reason to prefer an additive to a multiplicative model. You can initialize, say, the seasonal effects to values that are proportional to the early level of the time series. Then, as the level of the time series rises (or falls), the amount by which seasonal effects increase (or decrease) the forecasts comes along for the ride.

The problem is that not all time series behave that way. Consider a company that's large enough to be listed on the New York Stock Exchange or on the NASDAQ. Some such companies don't pay dividends at all—among them, in recent years, well-known companies such as Amazon and Berkshire Hathaway. Such firms often invest retained earnings back into product development or asset acquisition rather than distributing them to shareholders in the form of dividends.

Similarly, some companies do pay a minimal dividend, voted annually by their boards and distributed quarterly, which is not necessarily proportional to the current price of a share of their stock, but is a fixed and nominal dollar amount per share. In that sort of case, a multiplicative model might not provide an accurate forecast of the seasonal value of a block of shares. Even if the price per share of a company might be trending steadily upward over a period lasting several years, there's no reason to assume that its seasonal fluctuations will vary in steady proportion to the stock price. Often, of course, it will do exactly that, but not always. That's why you have to apply your own judgment, and knowledge of what drives the time series, to choosing a forecasting model. It's one reason that automated forecasting systems often fail.

Multiplicative and Additive Models Compared

As introduction to multiplicative models, let's take a look at an additive seasonal model shown in Figure 7.4.

> **NOTE** In Figure 7.4, and in the remaining figures in this chapter, I have indicated the end of the initialization period by means of a heavy border. For example, in Figure 7.4, the heavy border is between rows 7 and 8. Row 7 contains the sixth actual observation, the initial values for the level and the seasonal effects and the forecast for the first period of the second year. Row 8 repeats that forecast and has the smoothed values for level and season and the forecast for period 8.

Figure 7.4
In the additive model, seasonal effects are subtracted from the series level.

| G8 | | | × ✓ fx | =Alpha*(Actuals-SameSeasonLastYear)+(1-Alpha)*PriorLevel | | | | | | | |

	A	B	C	D	E	F	G	H	I	J	K	L
1	Year	Season	t	Observ-ations	Forecast for this period	Error	Estimated Level (Smoothing)	Seasonal Index (Smoothing)	Forecast for next period		Alpha	0.1
2	2012	1	1	7950				-220.8			Delta	0.3
3		2	2	7304				-866.8			Year 1 Mean	8170.8
4		3	3	8071				-99.8				
5		4	4	9374				1203.2				
6		5	5	8819				648.2				
7		6	6	7507			8170.8	-663.8	7950.0			
8	2013	1	7	7307	7950.0	-643.0	8106.5	-394.4	7239.7			
9		2	8	7383	7239.7	143.3	8120.9	-828.1	8021.0			
10		3	9	8035	8021.0	14.0	8122.3	-96.1	9325.4			
11		4	10	9084	9325.4	-241.4	8098.1	1138.0	8746.3			
12		5	11	9076	8746.3	329.7	8131.1	737.2	7467.3			
13		6	12	7944	7467.3	476.7	8178.8	-535.1	7784.3			

This is not a Holt-Winters model—it has no trend component. It's an untrended model that has seasonal effects and was discussed in Chapter 5, "Working with Seasonal Time Series" (see, for example, Figure 5.25).

Notice cell G8. Its formula, for the current level of the series, is this:

```
=Alpha*(Actuals-SameSeasonLastYear)+(1-Alpha)*PriorLevel
```

The formula deseasonalizes the level by subtracting the associated seasonal effect, SameSeasonLastYear, from the actual observation. This is analogous to subtracting the dividend dollars paid in a given quarter from the market value of a stock holding, to estimate the value of a holding shorn of the current dividend.

Comparing the Level Estimates

Compare cell G8 in Figure 7.4, both its formula and the result of that formula, with the same cell in Figure 7.5, which shows the multiplicative model for the same data set.

Cell G8 in Figure 7.5 contains this formula:

```
=Alpha*(Actuals/SameSeasonLastYear)+(1-Alpha)*PriorLevel
```

In both formulas, the defined name SameSeasonLastYear refers to the value in cell H2 of both Figures 7.4 and 7.5. It's a mixed range name, discussed in Chapter 6, "Names, Addresses, and Formulas," whose column is fixed at column H but whose row depends on the row of the cell that makes use of the name. The name's reference points six rows up, so its use in cell G8 refers to H2; in G9, to H3; and so on.

The latter two formulas, for the additive and the multiplicative models respectively, are deceptively similar. They differ from one another by only one character: The minus sign in the additive model is replaced by the slash in the multiplicative model. Cell G8 in Figure 7.4 subtracts a seasonal effect of –220.8 (the effect of the first season in the prior year) from the observed, actual value to deseasonalize it and leave only the part of the observation that we can attribute to the current level of the time series.

Figure 7.5
In the multiplicative model, seasonal effects are divided into the series level.

	G8	▾	:	×	✓	f_x	=Alpha*(Actuals/SameSeasonLastYear)+(1-Alpha)*PriorLevel				

◢	A	B	C	D	E	F	G	H	I	J	K	L
					Forecast		Estimated	Seasonal	Forecast			
				Observ-	for this		Level	Index	for next			
1	Year	Season	t	ations	period	Error	(Smoothing	(Smoothing)	period		Alpha	0.1
2	2012	1	1	7950				0.97			Delta	0.3
3		2	2	7304				0.89			Year 1 Mean	8170.8
4		3	3	8071				0.99				
5		4	4	9374				1.15				
6		5	5	8819				1.08				
7		6	6	7507			8170.8	0.92	7950.0			
8	2013	1	7	7307	7950.0	-643.0	8104.7	0.95	7244.9			
9		2	8	7383	7244.9	138.1	8120.2	0.90	8021.0			
10		3	9	8035	8021.0	14.0	8121.6	0.99	9317.5			
11		4	10	9084	9317.5	-233.5	8101.3	1.14	8743.9			
12		5	11	9076	8743.9	332.1	8132.0	1.09	7471.3			
13		6	12	7944	7471.3	472.7	8183.5	0.93	7787.0			

In contrast, cell G8 in Figure 7.5 divides the current, actual observation by the seasonal effect of 0.97. Again, this deseasonalizes the value of the current observation and results in the best current estimate of the level of the series.

Of course, the seasonal effects are measured differently in the two models. When we subtract the effect in the additive model, we're subtracting a value that's in the original metric. In cell G8 of Figure 7.4, we subtract –220.8 (dollars, perhaps, or website hits) from 7307 (again, dollars or hits) to get a current estimate of 7307 – (–220.8) = 7527.8, to be multiplied by Alpha.

But cell G8 in Figure 7.5 divides the current observation by the seasonal effect to deseasonalize it and return a different estimate of the current level of the series. And the seasonal effect is no longer in the original metric but instead represents a fraction, or equivalently a percentage, of the original metric. Dividing the actual observation by .97, or 97%, nudges the level up; so does subtracting the negative value –220.8.

Let's look a little more closely at those seasonal effects. Doing so often helps clarify what's going on in a multiplicative model to distinguish it from an additive model.

Consider first the value of –220.8 in cell H2 of Figure 7.4. It's the initial value of the seasonal effect for season 1. It means that during the year 2013, we expect an observation made during season 1 to fall below the level of the time series by 220.8 dollars or hits or whatever observation is being recorded in column D. By subtracting the negative 220.8 from the current actual observation in cell G8,

```
Actuals - SameSeasonLastYear
```

we're adding that 220.8 back in along with the measured observation to remove the effect of being in season 1, leaving cell G8 with our best estimate of the current level, which is then multiplied by Alpha.

> N O T E
>
> The focus here is on the conceptual differences between additive and multiplicative seasonal models and how those differences play out in Excel formulas. But the way I derived the initial values for the seasonal effects might provide additional context. To keep things straightforward here, I used what's sometimes termed the method of simple averages. For the additive model, the six initial seasonal values are just the first year's grand mean *subtracted from* each bimonthly observation. The effect is the observation less the mean, so a negative seasonal effect means the season pushes the observation below the current level. For the multiplicative model, the seasonal effect is the bimonthly value *divided by* the first year's mean, so a seasonal effect below 1.0 again means that the season pushes the observation down below what the level of the series would lead us to expect.
>
> During the forecasting process, we use those results when we deseasonalize an observation to smooth the level and the trend. Subtracting a negative seasonal effect boosts the estimate of level, and dividing by a seasonal effect less than 100% does the same. Subtracting a positive seasonal effect lowers the estimated level, just as dividing by a seasonal effect greater than 100%.
>
> Just because I used an oversimplified method of getting initial values in this example (to keep the focus on additive versus multiplicative models), don't get the idea that you need to use that initialization method with any seasonal model. You can use any of the methods for seasonal time series that are described in Chapter 4, "Initializing Forecasts."

Now consider the value of 0.97 in cell H2 of Figure 7.5. The formula in cell G8 divides it into the value of the current observation:

```
Actuals / SameSeasonLastYear
```

In this case we divide the actual observation by a seasonal effect that's less than 1.0. So doing necessarily results in a value that's larger than the actual value. That deseasonalized result provides our best estimate of the current level of the time series—in this case, a value that's a little larger than the actual observation, due to the effect of the season when the observation was made. If the observation is the amount of cold-weather clothing sold during the fall months, the normal effect of the season is to raise the observation above the annual average. If the observation occurred during the summer months, the normal effect of the season is to pull the observation down vis-à-vis the annual average.

Again, in the multiplicative model, the seasonal effect is measured as a percentage of the series level during a given season, not—as in the additive model—as a value in the original metric that can be added or subtracted to or from the current level. If the effect of being in season 1 is to depress the actual observation, we should nudge the estimate of the level back up, to remove the influence of the season. To do so in the multiplicative model, we divide by the seasonal effect.

What if the effect for season 1 were positive in the additive model or larger than 1.0 in the multiplicative model? Here are the formula fragments once again:

```
Actuals - SameSeasonLastYear
```

where subtracting a positive value reduces our estimate of the current level, and

```
Actuals / SameSeasonLastYear
```

where dividing by a value greater than 1.0 also reduces our estimate of the current series level.

Comparing the Estimates of Seasonal Effects

The preceding section discussed how the additive and multiplicative models differ in the way that they use seasonal effects to estimate the level. Similar, but hardly identical, considerations apply to the estimation of the seasonal effects themselves. In Figure 7.4, cell H8 uses this formula to estimate the seasonal effect as of season 1 in 2013:

```
=Delta * (Actuals - Levels) + (1-Delta) * SameSeasonLastYear
```

Here, we subtract the current estimate of the series level (Levels) from the actual observation (Actuals). The result of that subtraction is our best current estimate of the effect of season 1 on the time series.

> **NOTE**
> I'm using the smoothing, rather than the error correction, versions of the formulas in this discussion, so I might as well point out that they conform to the basic pattern of the smoothing versions: a smoothing constant (here, Delta) times an actual observation, plus 1 minus the same constant times the previous forecast. Here, we're getting as close as possible to directly observing the seasonal effect by subtracting the level estimate from the actual observation; and the use of the range name SameSeasonLastYear points to the most recent forecast of the seasonal effect.

Contrast the estimation of the seasonal effect by way of subtraction (the additive model in Figure 7.4) with its estimation by way of division (the multiplicative model in Figure 7.5). Here's the formula in cell H8 of Figure 7.5:

```
=Delta * (Actuals / Levels) + (1 - Delta) * SameSeasonLastYear
```

Dividing the current actual observation, 7307 in cell D8, by the current level estimate of 8104.7 in cell G8 returns 0.90, our best estimate of the current seasonal effect based on the current observation. The complete formula in cell H8 combines that estimate with the prior forecast and the smoothing constant Delta to produce the smoothed forecast for the effect of being in season 1 during 2013—that is, 0.95. Again, the forecast value of 0.95 is a weighted average of the current observation, the actual divided by the level, and the prior forecast, SameSeasonLastYear or 0.97.

Producing the Next Forecast

Before I start to describe how the multiplicative model generates the forecasts of the time series itself, I want to discuss how some choices regarding worksheet design can make it easier for you to interpret your forecasts and simultaneously complicate your calculations. These choices have implications for how your worksheet calculates the next forecast.

Where possible, I like to have the worksheets that I design mimic actual workflow. That makes it easier for the people who populate the worksheets to avoid errors, because they understand better how the worksheet goes about its business. It also makes things easier for people who interpret the worksheet's results and who use those results to inform their decisions.

When you're forecasting, particularly when you're making daily forecasts, you generally want to make your forecast as soon as the necessary information is in hand. If your forecasts are based on monthly data, you want to forecast March as soon as February's final results are available, and often that's before March 1.

It helps me to mimic that schedule on my forecasting worksheets. So I show the final calculation of a forecast for the next period as part of the prior period. But I also use that forecast as part of the data belonging to the period that has been forecast.

These notions are expressed better visually than verbally. Have a look back at Figure 7.5, for example. The forecast for season 1 in 2013 first appears in cell I7: At the end of season 6 2012 we forecast 7950 as the value for season 1 2013. The forecast first appears one season earlier, and one row above, the season to which it actually applies.

The same forecast appears in cell E8. That forecast of 7950 actually belongs to season 1 2013 so it should be placed on that season's row. For example, if you want to show the forecast error for season 1 2013 on row 8, it helps to have both the actual observed value *and* the forecast value in the same row.

If for some reason your goal in designing the worksheet is to be as sparing as possible, you won't want these frills around. If you're using the smoothing versions of the formulas, for example, you don't absolutely need the column that contains the forecast errors (in Figure 7.5, that's column F). None of the calculations in the smoothing versions of the formulas makes use of the forecast error. But if you're using the error correction versions of the formulas, it's useful to have the forecast on the row it pertains to so that it's easier to calculate the forecast errors in column F, and use them in conjunction with the level smoothing constant to help create the next forecast.

> **NOTE**
>
> Of course, even when using the error correction versions, it's not necessary to put the forecast error directly on the worksheet. You can leave the calculation inside the formula, with a construct along the lines of
>
> ```
> Alpha * (Actual - Forecast)
> ```
>
> instead of
>
> ```
> Alpha * F8
> ```
>
> But I've always found that, at least in worksheet design, it's best to be explicit.

So if I want to put the forecast for season 1 2013 in cell I7 of either Figure 7.4 or Figure 7.5, I need to make reference to the seasonal effect in cell H2. Here's the formula used by the additive model in Figure 7.4, cell I7:

```
=Levels+NextSeasonLastYear
```

Or, in Figure 7.5's multiplicative model:

```
=Levels*NextSeasonLastYear
```

In an additive model, the forecast of the time series for the next period is the sum of the current level forecast plus the seasonal effect for the next period; in a multiplicative model it's their product. At the time the forecast in cell I7 is made, at the end of season 6 2012, the current level forecast of 8170.8 is added to the most recent forecast of the effect of season 1 in Figure 7.4 and multiplied by the most recent season 1 forecast in Figure 7.5.

We pick up the current forecast of the series level by means of the implicit intersection of row 7 with the range named Levels, defined as G7:G13. The value in that intersecting cell is 8170.8. We also need the most recent forecast of the effect of season 1, and that's in cell H2, with a value of –220.8.

We can't get that seasonal effect by using the SameSeasonLastYear range name in cell I7. That name uses a mixed reference, always pointing to column H, and six rows above the cell where the name is used. So, used in cell G8, SameSeasonLastYear works fine. It points to cell H2, the cell in column H that's six rows above cell G8, where the name is used.

But SameSeasonLastYear isn't helpful in cell I7, where it would point one row too high, at the label in cell H1. We need a new name, a mixed reference, for use in column I where it will point five rows up, not six. The name might as well be something such as NextSeasonLastYear instead of SameSeasonLastYear. Using NextSeasonLastYear instead of SameSeasonLastYear helps keep things straight when you're making the forecast one season in advance of the season you're forecasting.

The following steps will define that name for you:

1. Select cell I7 (or any cell in row 7).
2. Click the Ribbon's Formulas tab.
3. Choose Define Name in the Defined Names group.
4. Type the name NextSeasonLastYear in the box for the Name.
5. I suggest that you set the name's scope to the worksheet you're using, but setting the scope to the workbook might work out for you.
6. Clear any address in the Refers To box, and then click in cell H2.
7. Delete the dollar sign immediately before the 2 in $H$2.
8. Click OK to dismiss the dialog box.

7

Now your formula in cell I7 can be

```
=Levels + NextSeasonLastYear
```

for the additive model, and

```
=Levels * NextSeasonLastYear
```

for the multiplicative model. You can autofill the formula, or copy and paste it, down as far as you have actual observations.

Don't neglect the substantive effect of the formula—with all the business in this section about setting up the range name and arranging for it to have a mixed reference, it's easy to miss the point. The idea is to combine the effect of the season with the level of the time series. In the additive model, we add the current level forecast to the most recent seasonal effect forecast. When that effect is positive, the result is to adjust the forecast up from the current level, so as to recognize the impact of the associated seasonal effect on the time series. When the seasonal effect is negative, it pulls the forecast down below the forecast level of the time series.

Contrast that effect with the multiplicative model in Figure 7.5. There, the forecast for season 1 of 2013 in cell I7 is

```
=Levels*NextSeasonLastYear
```

In the multiplicative model shown in Figure 7.5, the seasonal effects are measured not as dollars or site hits, but rather as fractions of dollars or site hits. You can also think of the seasonal effects as percentages—just select column H and change the number formats from Number to Percent.

Multiplying the current level by a seasonal effect greater than 1.0 has an effect similar to adding a positive seasonal effect in an additive model: It lifts the forecast above the forecast level of the series. Multiplying by an effect less than 1.0 is analogous to adding a negative seasonal effect in the additive model.

Using the Error Correction Formulas

Using error correction formulas instead of smoothing formulas yields the same results. There's no major advantage to using one version instead of another, apart from your own preference—some people prefer to think in terms of weighted averages and others prefer to think in terms of error correction. But as I noted earlier, if you're going to use the error correction forms of the equations, it's helpful to have the difference between the forecasts and the associated actuals right there on the worksheet. See Figure 7.6, which show the additive model with error correction formulas. Notice that the results are identical to those shown in Figure 7.4, which uses smoothing formulas and the additive model.

The error correction formula in Figure 7.6 for the forecast level in the additive model is as follows:

```
=PriorLevel+Alpha*Errors
```

7

Figure 7.6
The results are the same as in Figure 7.4, but here the forecast errors are used in the Level and the Seasonal formulas for the additive model.

G8	▼	:	×	✓	f_x	=PriorLevel+Alpha*Errors					

◢	A	B	C	D	E	F	G	H	I	J	K	L
1	Year	Season	t	Observ-ations	Forecast for this period	Error	Estimated Level (Error Correction)	Seasonal Index (Error Correction)	Forecast for next period		Alpha	0.1
2	2012	1	1	7950				-220.8			Delta	0.3
3		2	2	7304				-866.8			Year 1 Mean	8170.8
4		3	3	8071				-99.8				
5		4	4	9374				1203.2				
6		5	5	8819				648.2				
7		6	6	7507			8170.8	-663.8	7950.0			
8	2013	1	7	7307	7950.0	-643.0	8106.5	-394.4	7239.7			
9		2	8	7383	7239.7	143.3	8120.9	-828.1	8021.0			
10		3	9	8035	8021.0	14.0	8122.3	-96.1	9325.4			
11		4	10	9084	9325.4	-241.4	8098.1	1138.0	8746.3			
12		5	11	9076	8746.3	329.7	8131.1	737.2	7467.3			
13		6	12	7944	7467.3	476.7	8178.8	-535.1	7784.3			

By using the mixed reference in `PriorLevel` and the implicit intersection with the range `Errors`, you can copy and paste that formula from cell G8 through G13. Notice that, consistent with other error correction forms, the formula for this level forecast adds to the prior forecast level to the product of the associated smoothing constant and the current forecast error. Contrast this formula with the error correction formula for the forecast level in the multiplicative model shown in Figure 7.7.

Figure 7.7
Error correction formulas in the multiplicative model also return the same results as do the smoothing formulas in Figure 7.5.

G8	▼	:	×	✓	f_x	=PriorLevel+Alpha*Errors/SameSeasonLastYear					

◢	A	B	C	D	E	F	G	H	I	J	K	L
1	Year	Season	t	Observ-ations	Forecast for this period	Error	Estimated Level (Error Correction)	Seasonal Index (Error Correction)	Forecast for next period		Alpha	0.1
2	2012	1	1	7950				0.97			Delta	0.3
3		2	2	7304				0.89			Year 1 Mean	8170.8
4		3	3	8071				0.99				
5		4	4	9374				1.15				
6		5	5	8819				1.08				
7		6	6	7507			8170.8	0.92	7950.0			
8	2013	1	7	7307	7950.0	-643.0	8104.7	0.95	7244.9			
9		2	8	7383	7244.9	138.1	8120.2	0.90	8021.0			
10		3	9	8035	8021.0	14.0	8121.6	0.99	9317.5			
11		4	10	9084	9317.5	-233.5	8101.3	1.14	8743.9			
12		5	11	9076	8743.9	332.1	8132.0	1.09	7471.3			
13		6	12	7944	7471.3	472.7	8183.5	0.93	7787.0			

The error correction formula for the forecast level in the multiplicative model, Figure 7.7, is this:

```
=PriorLevel+Alpha*Errors/SameSeasonLastYear
```

That formula is entered in cell G8 and copied down through cell G13. It's illuminating to compare this formula for the forecast level in the multiplicative model with the forecast level for the additive model (discussed in conjunction with Figure 7.6):

```
=PriorLevel+Alpha*Errors
```

You might wonder why the seasonal effect shows up in the formula for the multiplicative model but not in the formula for the additive model. The reason is that the errors need to be deseasonalized before they can be used in the error correction formulas for the next season, but that occurs earlier in the additive model than in the multiplicative model. For example, in the additive model, here's how we calculate the forecast errors:

$$e_t = y_t - \hat{y}_t$$

$$e_t = y_t - \left(L_t + S_t \right)$$

$$e_t = y_t - S_t - L_t$$

So in the calculation of the forecast error for period t, the seasonal effect is subtracted from the actual observation in the process of calculating the forecast for period t. But in the multiplicative model,

$$e_t = y_t - \hat{y}_t$$

$$e_t = y_t - \left(L_t * S_t \right)$$

$$e_t / S_t = y_t / S_t - L_t$$

where, in the final expression, y_t is overtly deseasonalized and L_t has no seasonal component.

The same consideration applies to the difference between the error correction formula for the seasonal effect forecast in the additive model

```
=SameSeasonLastYear+Delta*(1-Alpha)*Errors
```

and the seasonal forecast formula in the multiplicative model

```
=SameSeasonLastYear+Delta*(1-Alpha)*Errors/Levels
```

where the effect of level must be explicitly removed from the forecast errors by means of division in the multiplicative model.

The difference between the additive and the multiplicative models is not normally pronounced in a series without trend, despite even dramatic seasonal effects. Things get more active in a trended and seasonal series—in other words, a Holt-Winters model.

Additive and Multiplicative Seasonal Models in Holt-Winters Analysis

Recall from Chapter 5 that Holt-Winters models are designed to forecast time series that combine trend and seasonal variation. In Chapter 5 we looked at additive Holt-Winters models. In this section we'll apply the concepts discussed earlier in this chapter to Holt-Winters models and change them from additive to multiplicative.

Things are in fact a trifle less complicated than the preceding sentence might lead you to believe. Holt-Winters models have a trend component as well as a seasonal component. *Additive* Holt-Winters models are a combination of an additive trend forecast and an additive seasonal forecast. *Multiplicative* Holt-Winters models combine an additive trend component with a multiplicative seasonal component. Although it's certainly possible to combine a multiplicative trend component with a multiplicative seasonal component, as far as I know such models have never been used widely enough to warrant being named after anyone.

Let's return to Box and Jenkins' Series G, which we last saw at the end of Chapter 5 beginning at Figure 5.26. Figure 7.8 repeats a chart from Chapter 5 to remind you what the series looks like when charted.

Figure 7.8
Series G is an ideal candidate for forecasting using a Holt-Winters multiplicative model.

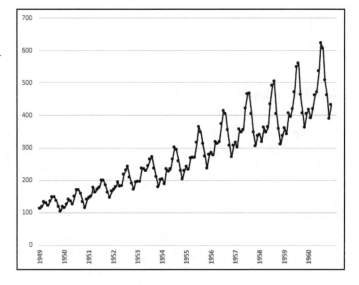

The forecasts, based on the additive model, appear along with the original observations in Figure 7.9.

You can see in Figure 7.9 that the additive model is simply not up to the task of forecasting the swings' peaks and valleys as the level of the series increases as a function of the general upward trend. The next section reviews how the additive model works in the Holt-Winters framework, and then we'll work through the formulas for the multiplicative model.

7

Figure 7.9
The additive forecasts do not swing as far up and down as do the actual observations in the second half of the time series.

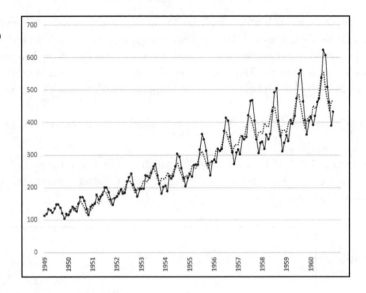

Holt-Winters Additive Models Revisited

When we looked at the additive Holt-Winters model in Chapter 5, we used cell references in the formulas. In this section we'll convert those references to named ranges and intersections. For each component (level, trend, and seasonal effect), I show the smoothing version of the Holt-Winters formula, the season-only no-trend formula given earlier in this chapter, and the error correction version of the Holt-Winters formula.

The Level Equation

Here's the formula used to forecast the series level in the additive Holt-Winters model. It starts in cell G14 of Figure 7.9 and continues down to the 145th row of column G.

    =Alpha*(Actuals-SameSeasonLastYear)+(1-Alpha)*(PriorLevel+PriorTrend)

As you can see from the use of both Alpha and (1 – Alpha), it's the smoothing form of the equation. Notice that the current level is taken to be the deseasonalized value of the actual observation, the current actual observation less the associated seasonal effect. That seasonal effect was most recently calculated the *last* time the season came around.

Here's the equation as used earlier in this chapter, in "Comparing Multiplicative and Additive Models," to forecast the level of the untrended but seasonal series:

    =Alpha*(Actuals-SameSeasonLastYear)+(1-Alpha)*PriorLevel

The only difference between the two formulas is that the first, the Holt-Winters version, adds the estimate of the immediately prior *trend* in the series, PriorTrend, to the immediately prior *level* of the series, PriorLevel. (The second of the two formulas does not include PriorTrend because there we're analyzing a time series that has no trend.) The pattern in these two formulas is consistent with the basic pattern of the smoothing formulas. In the present case, the smoothing of the series level, the Holt-Winters formula is the sum of these two terms:

- Alpha times the current estimate of the level, which we get by deseasonalizing the actual observation
- (1 – Alpha) times the prior forecast, which we get by adding the prior level to the prior trend

The error correction version of the Holt-Winters level equation is this:

```
=(PriorLevel+PriorTrend)+Alpha*Errors
```

That is, it's the forecast of the current period plus Alpha times the error in that forecast.

The Trend Equation

Here's the smoothing form of the equation for the current trend in the additive Holt-Winters model, which follows the same pattern as the levels formula:

```
=Gamma*(Levels-PriorLevel)+(1-Gamma)*PriorTrend
```

We can estimate the current trend, the slope that helps carry the observed value of the time series from the prior period to the current period, as the difference between the current level and the prior level (*not* the difference between the current actual and the prior actual, because that difference also involves the difference in the seasonal effects). That difference is multiplied by Gamma, the trend smoothing constant. The prior forecast of the trend is multiplied by (1 – Gamma), and the two terms are summed to return the current smoothed forecast of the series' trend.

The untrended model discussed earlier in this chapter of course has no trend smoothing equation.

The error correction version of the additive Holt-Winters trend smoothing equation is as follows:

```
=PriorTrend+Alpha*Gamma*Errors
```

The Seasonal Effect Equation

For the seasonal effect in an additive Holt-Winters model, this is the smoothing form of the equation:

```
=Delta*(Actuals-Levels)+(1-Delta)*SameSeasonLastYear
```

Our best estimate of the current seasonal effect is the difference between the current actual observation and the current estimate of the series level. The most recently calculated seasonal forecast available—always one complete turn of seasons back—is the seasonal effect SameSeasonLastYear, which is multiplied by 1 minus the seasonal smoothing constant Delta.

The seasonal equation for the no-trend, seasonal model looks the same at first as the Holt-Winters seasonal equation, but that's misleading. The Holt-Winters model builds the trend component into its estimate of the level. On the other hand, trend plays no part in the horizontal model in general or its level component in particular. (See the earlier section

"The Level Equation" for the details of the two formulas.) Therefore, although the equation for the seasonal effect appears to be the same in the horizontal seasonal model and in the Holt-Winters model, it's not: In Holt-Winters, the level component has the effect of the trend built into it.

The error correction form of the equation for the seasonal effect is

```
=SameSeasonLastYear+Delta*(1-Alpha)*Errors
```

The Forecast Equation

The forecast equation for the additive Holt-Winters model, found in column J of Figure 7.9, is

```
=Levels+Trends+NextSeasonLastYear
```

In the horizontal, seasonal model discussed earlier, it is

```
=Levels+NextSeasonLastYear
```

Multiplicative Holt-Winters Models

Before examining the the formulas used in multiplicative Holt-Winters models, have a look at the forecasts made by those formulas, in Figure 7.10.

Figure 7.10
The forecasts made with the multiplicative model are much closer to the actual observations than with the additive model.

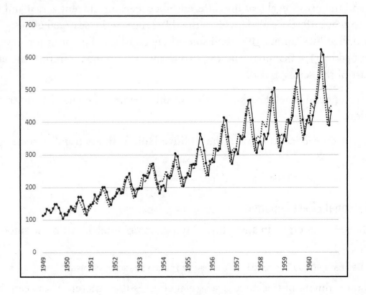

Compare the forecasts shown in Figure 7.10 with those in Figure 7.9. The additive model in Figure 7.9 does not reflect the increasing size of the intra-year swings as fully as does the multiplicative model in Figure 7.10. This is particularly the case with the more recent observations and forecasts charted for the final half of the time series, say from 1954 on.

As I discussed earlier in this chapter, that's largely the result of the fact that the additive model adds values to the series level and trend, values that you usually—not always, but usually—want to react to the current level of the series. In other words, the higher the level, the larger the seasonal swings.

Two general tasks can convert an additive Holt-Winters model to its multiplicative form:

- Changing how the initial estimates of the seasonal effects are made
- Modifying the level and the seasonal smoothing formulas

Both are necessary.

Changing the Initial Seasonal Estimates

In the additive model, the seasonal effects are initialized using some procedure that involves adding or subtracting an observed seasonal value from an annual mean value. (More generally, to extend the discussion to other sorts of seasons such as weekdays or work shifts, we add or subtract an observed seasonal value from the mean of the encompassing period.) Any of various methods covered in Chapter 4 might be appropriate.

For example, you might adopt a regression approach and establish effect or dummy coded vectors to represent a time period's membership in a given season. This approach was mentioned in Chapters 4 and 5. The resulting regression equation, returned in Excel by the LINEST() function, provides regression coefficients. The coefficients, some positive and some negative, are added in the smoothing equations as seasonal effects. Besides seasonal mean differences and the regression approach, backcasting is another possibility.

To keep the focus here on the smoothing process, I've used the simple-averages method to get the initial estimates. As I described earlier in this chapter, the initial seasonal effects in Figures 7.4 and 7.5 were derived by subtracting the first year's mean value from each seasonal observation in the first year (Figure 7.4, additive model) and by dividing each seasonal value in the first year by the first year's mean (Figure 7.5, multiplicative model).

The same procedures are used in Figures 7.9 and 7.10. In Figures 7.4 and 7.9, the seasonal effects are added to the levels and, if present, to the trends, to return the forecast of the next period's observation. In Figures 7.5 and 7.10, the seasonal effects can be thought of as percentages, multiplied times the combined levels and trends, to forecast the next period's observation.

Modifying the Level and Seasonal Smoothing Formulas

With the initial seasonal values changed from simple additive amounts to percentage adjustments, it remains to change the smoothing formulas so that instead of adding the seasonal effects, the formulas use them as multipliers.

There's a lot less to that than it might seem. Here's the smoothing form of the level equation in the additive model:

```
=Alpha*(Actuals-SameSeasonLastYear)+(1-Alpha)*(PriorLevel+PriorTrend)
```

7

Here's the same formula modified for the multiplicative model

```
=Alpha*(Actuals/SameSeasonLastYear)+(1-Alpha)*(PriorLevel+PriorTrend)
```

Notice that the *only* difference between the two formulas is that in the additive model, the seasonal effect is subtracted from the actual observation. In the multiplicative model, the actual observation is divided by the seasonal effect.

An example is shown in Figure 7.11. Suppose that the current season is Quarter 1 2017. The mean quarterly value for the first year is $100, and the first quarter's value during the initialization period of 2016 was $110. In that case, using simple averages, the seasonal effect for the first quarter of 2016 in the additive model was $10 ($110 – $100), and, in the multiplicative model, 1.10 or 110% ($110 / $100). These seasonal effects are in cells G3 and G12, respectively, in Figure 7.11.

Figure 7.11
The same basic worksheet layout works well for either the additive or the multiplicative model.

	A	B	C	D	E	F	G	H	I	J	K
G16					f_x	=Delta*(Actuals/Levels)+(1-Delta)*SameSeasonLastYear					
2	Year	Quarter	Observation	Forecast for this period	Error	Estimated Level (Smoothing)	Seasonal Index (Smoothing)	Forecast for next period		Alpha	0.1
3	2016	1	110				10.0			Delta	0.3
4		2	96				-4.0			Year 1 Mean	100.0
5		3	85				-15.0				
6		4	109			100.0	9.0	110.0			
7	2017	1	115	110.0	5.0	100.50	11.35	110.50			
8											
9											
10					*Multiplicative Model*						
11	Year	Quarter	Observation	Forecast for this period	Error	Estimated Level (Smoothing)	Seasonal Index (Smoothing)	Forecast for next period			
12	2016	1	110				1.1				
13		2	96				1.0				
14		3	85				0.9				
15		4	109			100.0	1.1	110.0			
16	2017	1	115	110.0	5.0	100.45	1.11	110.50			

> **NOTE**
> Figure 7.11 does not show a trend component and therefore does not represent a true Holt-Winters model. It shows a simple seasonal smoothing model instead. But the formulas for level and season are the same for both a simple seasonal model and a Holt-Winters model. To keep the focus on levels and seasons, I have omitted the trend calculations from Figure 7.11. You'll find the full Holt-Winters model shown in Figure 7.12.

In both of the smoothing equations just shown, the first term multiplies Alpha times a deseasonalized measure of the actual observation. To get the deseasonalized measure, the additive model subtracts the seasonal effect of $10 from the actual observation. The multiplicative model divides the actual observation by the seasonal effect of 1.10, again leaving an estimate of the current level, unadulterated by the seasonal effect.

Each method reduces the estimate when the additive seasonal effect is positive or the multiplicative seasonal effect is larger than 1.0; each method increases the estimate when the additive seasonal effect is negative or the multiplicative seasonal effect is less than 1.0.

Now it's April 1, 2017, and the results for Quarter 1 2017 just came in at $115. In the additive model's level smoothing equation, we subtract the seasonal effect, SameSeasonLastYear, or $10, from the actual of $115. The first term in the equation is Alpha * ($115 – $10) or Alpha * $105. After adding (1-Alpha) * PriorLevel, the full equation returns 100.50 (see cell F7).

In the multiplicative model, cell F16 divides the actual result of $115 by the seasonal effect of 1.1 in cell G12. The full equation in cell F16 returns 100.45.

To forecast the next observation using the smoothing equations, the additive model adds the current smoothed level to the most recently updated smoothed seasonal effect. So in Figure 7.11, cell H7 adds cells F7 and G3 to return 110.50. Using defined names, the formula is this:

```
=Levels+SameSeasonLastYear
```

The multiplicative model multiplies the level by the seasonal effect instead of summing them. Still in Figure 7.11, cell H16 also returns 100.50, using this formula:

```
=Levels*SameSeasonLastYear
```

Notice, by the way, that the forecast for the first period in both the additive and the multiplicative cases is identical to the first observation in the time series. This happens when, as here, a simple averages method for calculating the initial values is used with just one year of an untrended series. In the additive case, for example, we initialize the level with the year's mean and the trend with the first observation minus the mean. Then we create the first forecast by means of Level + Trend, or (Mean) + (Observation – Mean), which results, tautologically, in the first observation. This won't happen outside of simple averages, nor in any situation in which the first forecast doesn't simply reverse the effect of calculating the first level and trend estimates.

> **NOTE** It's not hard at first to confuse the use of the seasonal effects in the smoothing formulas with their use in the forecast equations. In the multiplicative model, for example, you *divide* an actual observation by a seasonal effect as you're calculating the smoothed level. You *divide* an actual observation by a level estimate as you're calculating a new seasonal effect. But you *multiply* a level by a seasonal effect to calculate a forecast.

To extend the forecasts past the first quarter of 2017 in Figure 7.11, there are just three steps:

1. Add new observations as they arrive, using columns A, B, and C to record the data.

2. Make sure that the defined names *Actuals* and *Levels* extend far enough down the worksheet to capture the new observations. The Defined Names group on the Formulas tab

has a Name Manager that's handy for this task. Set up properly, an Excel table can be another useful method for extending the reach of a defined range name.

3. Copy and paste the formulas in columns D through H as far down as the new observations are entered.

Modifying the Trend Smoothing Formula

I'm covering the modification of the additive model's formula for smoothing the trend component separately from its level and seasonal effects formulas because it requires a bit more explanation.

At first thought you might expect that the Holt-Winters multiplicative model treats the levels and seasonal effects as multiplicative (as shown in the immediately preceding section) and the trend as multiplicative as well. But a Holt-Winters multiplicative model is generally taken to refer to an *additive* trend and multiplicative level and season.

There's no special reason that a multiplicative trend (more often termed an *exponential* trend) cannot be combined with smoothing equations for levels and seasonal effects. But in smoothing jargon, a Holt-Winters multiplicative model has an additive trend component and multiplicative level and seasonal effect components.

It is a good bit more difficult to disaggregate multiplicative seasonal effects from an exponential trend than to disaggregate them from an additive trend, and I don't cover the details here. (The typical procedure is to convert the actual observations to logs, carry out the smoothing and forecasting on those logs, and then convert the results back to the original scale via antilogs.)

Figure 7.12 shows the trend calculated with the smoothing formula, in the context of a full Holt-Winters model. The data set is once again the Box-Jenkins Series G time series, but Figure 7.12 shows only a subset of the data, through the 13th period. That much data is sufficient to demonstrate the smoothing formulas and how they come together to create the forecasts. To forecast through the end of the full data series, just supply the remaining observations and copy and paste the formulas in columns E through J down through the end of the series.

In Figure 7.12, I have hidden several periods in order to save room for both the additive and the multiplicative model: Rows 5 through 12 and 22 through 29 are hidden. Including the trend component in column H changes the analysis from simple seasonal exponential smoothing shown in Figure 7.11 to a true Holt-Winters model. Using simple averages, the trend is initialized in cell M17, which is named `Year_1_Trend`.

The formula used here to initialize the trend is as follows:

```
=(D14-D3)/11
```

The very simple assumption is that the difference between the starting and ending observations for the first year represents the annual trend. (Note that there are 11 season-to-season—that is, monthly—trends in each year.) Both cells H14 and H31 are linked to cell M17 by means of this simple linking formula:

```
=Year_1_Trend
```

Figure 7.12
Compare the results of the smoothing formulas, particularly the seasonal indexes, in rows 15 and 32.

| I32 | | | × ✓ _fx_ | =Delta*(Actuals/Levels)+(1-Delta)*SameSeasonLastYear |

	A	B	C	D	E	F	G	H	I	J	K	L	M
1							_Additive Model_						
2	Year	Season	t	Observ-ations	Forecast for this period	Error	Estimated Level	Estimated Trend	Estimated Seasonal Index	Forecast for next period			
3	1949	1	1	112					-14.7				
4		2	2	118					-8.7				
13		11	11	104					-22.7			Alpha	0.1
14		12	12	118			126.7	0.5	-8.7	112.5		Gamma	0.1
15	1950	1	13	115	112.5455	2.5	127.5	0.6	-14.2	119.4		Delta	0.2
16												Year 1 Mean	126.67
17												Year 1 Trend	0.55
18							_Multiplicative Model_						
19	Year	Season	t	Observ-ations	Forecast for this period	Error	Estimated Level	Estimated Trend	Estimated Seasonal Index	Forecast for next period			
20	1949	1	1	112					0.9				
21		2	2	118					0.9				
30		11	11	104					0.8				
31		12	12	118			126.7	0.5	0.9	112.5			
32	1950	1	13	115	112.4823	2.5	127.5	0.6	0.9	119.3			

Level Estimates

In Figure 7.12, the smoothing process for the additive model starts in row 15 with the following formulas. The level estimate in column G is calculated with this:

```
=Alpha*(Actuals-SameSeasonLastYear)+(1-Alpha)*(PriorLevel+PriorTrend)
```

Notice that the actual observation is deseasonalized by subtracting the associated seasonal effect from it. Also notice that the presence of trend means that the prior forecast of the level is augmented by adding PriorTrend to PriorLevel. (Compare the formula in cell G15 with cell F7 in Figure 7.11.)

Still in Figure 7.12, the smoothed level estimate for cell G32 (multiplicative model) is virtually identical to that in cell G15:

```
=Alpha*(Actuals/SameSeasonLastYear)+(1-Alpha)*(PriorLevel+PriorTrend)
```

The only difference between the formula in G15 and that in G32 is that in the multiplicative model you divide the actual observation by the associated season, rather than subtracting the season from the observation. This is of course consistent with the differences between the additive and the multiplicative models that we looked at in the immediately preceding section.

As noted earlier in this chapter, in "Holt-Winters Additive Models Revisited," the error correction form of the additive model's level equation is

```
=(PriorLevel+PriorTrend)+Alpha*Errors
```

For the multiplicative model, the error correction form is

```
=(PriorLevel+PriorTrend)+Alpha*Errors/SameSeasonLastYear
```

Trend Estimates

The additive model's smoothing form of the equation for trend is

```
=Gamma*(Levels-PriorLevel)+(1-Gamma)*PriorTrend
```

The multiplicative model's formula for trend, in its smoothing form, is identical to the one used in the additive model.

The additive model's error correction form for trend is

```
=PriorTrend+Alpha*Gamma*Errors
```

The error correction form of the equation for the multiplicative model is

```
=PriorTrend+Alpha*Gamma*Errors/SameSeasonLastYear
```

Seasonal Effects

The additive model's smoothing form of the equation for the seasonal effects is

```
=Delta*(Actuals-Levels)+(1-Delta)*SameSeasonLastYear
```

The multiplicative smoothing form is

```
=Delta*(Actuals/Levels)+(1-Delta)*SameSeasonLastYear
```

The additive error correction form is

```
=SameSeasonLastYear+Delta*(1-Alpha)*Errors
```

In the multiplicative model, the error correction form for seasons is

```
=Delta*(Actuals/Levels)+(1-Delta)*SameSeasonLastYear
```

Forecasts

As you've seen in prior chapters, there is no distinction between a smoothing form and an error correction form of the forecast equations themselves. There is a simple difference between the forecast equations in the additive and the multiplicative models.

In the additive model, the equation in cell J14 of Figure 7.12 is

```
=Levels+Trends+NextSeasonLastYear
```

and in the multiplicative model the equation in cell J31 of Figure 7.12 is

```
=(Levels+Trends)*NextSeasonLastYear
```

The Multiplicative Model with Error Correction Formulas

Over the past few years, from time to time I've found myself seriously frustrated by sources of information regarding exponential smoothing, particularly those that write about the mild complications that accompany the addition of trend to a stationary series and the addition of a seasonal pattern to either a stationary or a trended series.

One of the reasons I've written this book is to try to spare others that sort of frustration. Apart from the problems created by using different symbols for the same factors, there's the fact that many sources use only the smoothing form of the equations and others use only the error correction form. When those sources report different outcomes with the same time series, even given identical smoothing constants and methods of initialization, it becomes very difficult to track down the source of the discrepancies.

Making things even worse is the unaccountable frequency of (apparently) typographical errors, which tend to show up mainly in the formulas' symbols. A hardbound textbook, published by one of the most familiar names in academic publishing, contains no fewer than eight errors in a six-page span that calls out the formulas for Holt-Winters additive and multiplicative models. Some fail to specify in their examples the values of the smoothing constants used to reach their forecasts.

My hope and intention is that two aspects of this book will prevent that sort of problem from plaguing this book:

■ A superior technical edit

■ The availability of the actual worksheets used in this book's figures via download from the publisher's website

Those worksheets, which always contain the actual formulas used to build their forecasts, should remove the sources of ambiguity that typify the sources I've just complained about.

In furtherance of that goal and at the risk of repeating myself, Figure 7.13 illustrates how level, trend, and seasonal effect are calculated in a Holt-Winters multiplicative model, using the smoothing and the error correction versions of the formulas on Box-Jenkins Series G.

Figure 7.13
The trends calculated with the smoothing formula are equal to those calculated with the error correction formula.

| L14 | | | × | ✓ | *fx* | =(PriorLevel+PriorTrend)+Alpha*Errors/SameSeasonLastYear |

	E	F	G	H	I	J	K	L	M	N
1	Forecast for this period	Error	Estimated Level (*Smoothing*)	Estimated Trend (*Smoothing*)	Estimated Seasonal Index	Forecast for next period				
2					0.9					
3					0.9					
4		Alpha	0.1		1.0					
5		Gamma	0.1		1.0					
6		Delta	0.2		1.0					
7		Year 1 Mean	126.67		1.1					
8		Year 1 Trend	0.55		1.2					
9		RMSE	15.82		1.2					
10					1.1					
11					0.9				Error Correction	
12					0.8			Level	Trend	Season
13			126.7	0.5	0.9	112.5				
14	112.5	2.5	127.5	0.6	0.9	119.3		127.5	0.6	0.9
15	119.3	6.7	128.8	0.6	0.9	134.9		128.8	0.6	0.9
16	134.9	6.1	130.0	0.7	1.1	133.1		130.0	0.7	1.1
17	133.1	1.9	130.9	0.7	1.0	125.7		130.9	0.7	1.0
18	125.7	-0.7	131.6	0.7	1.0	141.0		131.6	0.7	1.0
19	141.0	8.0	133.0	0.8	1.1	156.3		133.0	0.8	1.1
20	156.3	13.7	135.0	0.9	1.2	158.8		135.0	0.9	1.2
21	158.8	11.2	136.8	1.0	1.2	148.0		136.8	1.0	1.2

7

Notice in Figure 7.13 that the error correction form figures in columns L through N appear identical to the smoothing form figures in columns G through I. Of course, displaying only one or two decimal places can obscure an actual difference between the results in two different cells, and you can test for genuine equality of two cells (within the roomy limits imposed by the architecture of today's PC processors) using a formula like

    =G14=L14

which returns TRUE if the results of the formulas in the two cells are equal and FALSE otherwise. Some cells that you would expect to equal one another will cause this comparison to return FALSE, and that's almost certainly due to a vanishingly small difference caused by overflow in one of the formulas. You can look more deeply into the discrepancy using something such as

    =G14-L14

and set the number of decimals to something such as 10. I think you'll find the difference between the two values not to be worth any concern.

Damped Trend Forecasts

At the end of Chapter 3, in the section titled "Going Beyond the Next-Step-Ahead Forecast," I noted that you have available some methods to extend the forecast horizon beyond the next period, or the *next-step-ahead forecast*. Figure 3.13 is repeated here as Figure 7.14 to provide the basis for some further discussion.

Figure 7.14
Note that the formulas used in C35:C39 are shown in D35:D39.

	A	B	C	D	E	F	G	H	I
									=SQRT(SUMXMY2(B3:B34,C3:C34)/32)
	Period	Observed, Trended Series	Forecast of Current Period	Forecast Level	Forecast Trend	Forecast of Next Period			
1								Alpha:	0.94769
2	1	9,174		9,174.0	0	9,174.0		Gamma:	0.284488
3	2	9,408	9,174.0	9,395.8	63.1	9,458.8		RMSE:	383.661
4	3	8,540	9,458.8	8,588.1	-184.6	8,403.4			
5	4	8,314	8,403.4	8,318.7	-208.7	8,109.9			
6	5	7,998	8,109.9	8,003.9	-238.9	7,764.9			
7	6	8,202	7,764.9	8,179.1	-121.1	8,058.0			
8	7	7,601	8,058.0	7,624.9	-244.3	7,380.6			
9	8	7,731	7,380.6	7,712.7	-149.8	7,562.8			
10	9	7,468	7,562.8	7,473.0	-175.4	7,297.6			
11	10	7,643	7,297.6	7,624.9	-82.3	7,542.7			
32	31	890	739.7	882.1	-35.6	846.6			
33	32	968	846.6	961.6	-2.8	958.8			
34	33	791	958.8	799.8	-48.1	751.7			
35	34		751.7	=F34					
36	35		703.6	=C35+$E$34					
37	36		655.6	=C36+$E$34					
38	37		607.5	=C37+$E$34					
39	38		559.4	=C38+$E$34					

In Figure 7.14, you can see that after you run out of new actual observations at Period 33, you no longer have a way to estimate the level of the time series in Periods 34, 35, 36, and so on. One generally accepted way to forecast a trended series beyond the next period is to assume that neither the level nor the trend will change. Granted that assumption, you can (as shown in cells C35:C39 of Figure 7.14) repeatedly add the most recent trend estimate to the most recent level estimate. The worksheet formulas to accomplish this are shown in cells D35:D39.

The result of this procedure is a straight line, in which the difference between any two consecutive points is equal to the most recently calculated trend estimate. Figure 7.15 charts the actual observations and associated forecasts for the first 33 periods, as well as the final five forecasts, calculated as just described.

Figure 7.15
The forecasts following Period 33 describe a straight line.

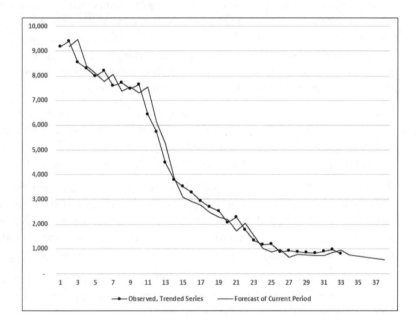

There's good news and bad news about those five forecasts. Let's start with the good news:

- The forecasts continue the downward trend established by the first 33 observations.
- The forecasts continue downward, but at the much less precipitous rate established by the 26th through the 33rd observations.

On the other hand, to have enough faith in the forecasts that you would use them as the basis of an important decision, you can't let these points worry you:

- The final five forecasts assume that the level of the series remains unchanged from the calculation of 799.8 at Period 33.
- The final five forecasts assume that the period-to-period trend remains unchanged from the calculation of –48.1 at Period 33.

Now it's true that those assumptions are the same as the ones made throughout the smoothing process. The forecast made for Period 24, for example, assumes that the level and trend estimates made at the end of Period 23 will hold for Period 24.

But in the case of the final five forecasts, there are five opportunities, not just one, for reality to invalidate the level and trend estimates made at Period 33.

One way to deal with this sort of uncertainty is to stick with one-step-ahead forecasts. The uncertainty is still there, of course, but it does not compound itself the way it does when you pile forecast on top of forecast with no empiric observation to provide correction.

That approach implies that you make your observation periods coincide with the frequency of your important decisions. Suppose that you need to make a product-mix decision at the end of fiscal year 2017 that will materially affect revenues for fiscal year 2018. In that case there's a good argument for treating each fiscal year from, say, 1987 to 2017 as a different period. Then you could smooth through 2018 to estimate results if you make no change to the product mix, and your 2018 forecast would be only one step ahead.

There's a very different approach to dealing with this sort of uncertainty. It ignores the absence of corrective observations when you push trended forecasts well into the future, and instead focuses on the fact that many sorts of trends, from Pet Rocks to PalmPilots, die out as time passes. This approach results in what are termed *damped trend* forecasts.

The classic Malthusian model of population growth creates, on paper anyway, untrammeled periodic increases in population size until we're all, well, hip deep in alligators. In reality, other factors interfere with that growth and force it to level out—harsh realities such as a static food supply impose limits to growth. The problem is to come up with a method of limiting the calculations so that the growth on paper slows to match the growth in reality.

In smoothing, that method is another smoothing constant to go along with Alpha, Gamma, and Delta. The additional constant, which exerts a damping effect on forecast trends, is termed *Phi*, symbolized as the Greek letter ϕ.

Formulas for the Damped Trend

The formulas for the damped trend are similar to those for Holt's linear trend. The only difference is the use of the Phi constant to modify each trend estimate. This section provides the smoothing form of the equations for the additive model.

The level equation for the damped trend is this:

$$l_t = \alpha y_t + (1 - \alpha)(l_{t-1} + \varphi b_{t-1})$$

Notice that the only difference between the level equation for the damped trend and that for Holt's linear smoothing is the use of Phi to multiply the trend coefficient. For comparison, here's the level equation from Holt's method once again:

$$l_t = \alpha y_t + (1 - \alpha)(l_{t-1} + b_{t-1})$$

Because Phi is restricted to the range between 0 and 1, as are the other smoothing coefficients, it reduces—or *damps*—the effect of the trend coefficient.

Couldn't you simply reduce the value of the trend constant, instead of introducing a new one? Yes, for the periods that have actual observations, that's certainly possible. But when you get beyond the end of the observed time series and want to push the forecast horizon forward, it's helpful to have a separate Phi constant that can be raised to increasing powers, separate from the trend constant.

Here is the smoothing form of the additive model's equation for damped trend:

$$b_{t+1} = \gamma\left(l_t - l_{t-1}\right) + \left(1-\gamma\right)\varphi b_t$$

Again for comparison, here's the smoothing form of the additive model's standard, undamped trend equation:

$$b_{t+1} = \gamma\left(l_t - l_{t-1}\right) + \left(1-\gamma\right)b_t$$

Recall that to get the forecast of the next value in the time series, the additive model of Holt's method simply totals the level forecast and the trend forecast:

$$\hat{y}_t = l_t + b_t$$

But with the additive model, a damped trend forecast uses the Phi constant. Suppose you have *n* actual observations. For each period through the *n+1*st, the forecast for each period uses this formula:

$$\hat{y}_{t+1} = l_t + \varphi b_t$$

Further suppose that *t* now equals *n*, the final period for which you have an actual observation, and you want to forecast 5 periods into the future. The one-step-ahead formula is still this:

$$\hat{y}_{t+1} = l_t + \varphi b_t$$

And for the second and subsequent periods following the end of the actual observations, the formula is as follows:

$$\hat{y}_{t+b} = l_t + \sum_{b=1}^{5}\varphi^b b_t$$

where *b* is the number of such subsequent periods. Or, equivalently, it's

$$\hat{y}_{t+2} = l_t + \left(\varphi + \varphi^2\right)b_t$$

for the second step ahead, and

$$\hat{y}_{t+3} = l_t + \left(\varphi + \varphi^2 + \varphi^3\right)b_t$$

7

for the third step ahead, through

$$\hat{y}_{t+5} = l_t + \left(\varphi + \varphi^2 + \varphi^3 + \varphi^4 + \varphi^5\right)b_t$$

for the fifth step ahead.

Notice that if you set Phi to 1.0, you wind up with results identical to Holt's method: No damping of the trend takes place. And if you set Phi to 0.0, you wind up with simple exponential smoothing: All trend estimates are 0.0 and each forecast is equal to the current estimate of the time series' level.

Implementing the Damped Trend on the Worksheet

Figure 7.16 gives an example of how all this works in the context of a worksheet. The discussion and the figures that follow are based on standard Excel column-and-row addressing rather than on defined names, except for the smoothing constants. The reason is that the addresses of the precedent cells become static after you get beyond the end of the observed time series.

Figure 7.16
Forecasts for five periods
following the end of the
time series.

	H	I	J	K	L	M	N	O
								O42 ▾ ⋮ ✕ ✓ ƒx =H41-H42

	H	I	J	K	L	M	N	O
1			Alpha:	0.95				
2			Gamma:	0.28				
3			Phi:	0.65				
4								
5		*Additive Damped Trend*						
6	Forecast of Current Period	Forecast Level	Forecast Damped Trend	Forecast of Next Period				
7		9,174.0	234.0	9,408.0				
8	9,408.0	9,182.0	111.1	9,254.2				
9	9,254.2	9,400.0	113.7	9,473.8				
10	9,473.8	8,588.8	-177.9	8,473.2				
11	8,473.2	8,322.3	-158.5	8,219.3				
12	8,219.3	8,009.6	-162.7	7,903.8				
13	7,903.8	8,186.4	-25.4	8,169.9				
39	892.1	964.0	26.8	981.5				
40	981.5	801.0	-33.9	778.9				
41	778.9	=$I$40+Phi*$J$40						
42	764.6	=$I$40+(Phi+Phi^2)*$J$40						14.3
43	755.3	=$I$40+(Phi+Phi^2+Phi^3)*$J$40						9.3
44	749.2	=$I$40+(Phi+Phi^2+Phi^3+Phi^4)*$J$40						6.1
45	745.3	=$I$40+(Phi+Phi^2+Phi^3+Phi^4+Phi^5)*$J$40						3.9

Figure 7.16 shows, in the range H41:H45, the damped trend forecasts for the periods following the end of the time series (shown in Figure 7.14). The formulas for the forecasts in H41:H45 appear in the range I41:I45. They follow the approach outlined at the end of the

preceding section, and add another term that raises Phi to another power for each subsequent forecast.

Compare the damped trend forecasts in H41:H45 of Figure 7.16 with those shown in C35:C39 of Figure 7.14. In Figure 7.14, the forecasts describe a straight line following Period 34, because they're each calculated by adding the constant –48.1 to the prior forecast.

But in Figure 7.16, the forecasts describe a curved line. The downward trend is damped by the addition of another instance of Phi, raised to the next power. I have shown the forecast-to-forecast differences in the range O42:O45. You can see that the forecast-to-forecast difference gets smaller, from 14.3 to 3.9, as the forecast progress.

It's a little difficult to see in the chart of the damped trend forecasts, but you can make out how the trend flattens for the final five forecasts in Figure 7.17.

Figure 7.17
For greater clarity, this chart shows only the final 27 periods.

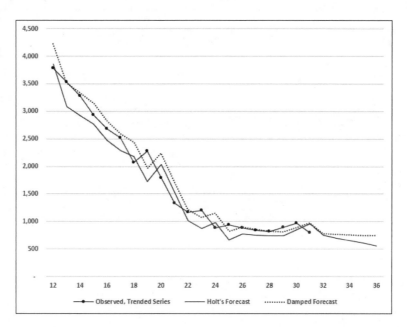

If the straight-line Holt forecasts were allowed to continue, they would eventually drop below zero. That would make no sense if the measure being studied were something such as the incidence of new cases of an antibiotic-resistant virus. The damped trend forecasts, much like the logistic function, take account of logical limits such as true zero points.

7

T I P

Formulas for damped trend forecasts such as

```
=$L$35+(Phi+Phi^2+Phi^3+Phi^4+Phi^5)*$M$35
```

are tedious to enter and prone to typos. Instead of entering them as shown in Figure 7.16, you could array-enter (with Ctrl+Shift+Enter) this formula in cell H41:

```
{=$I$40+SUM(Phi^ROW(A$1:A1))*$J$40}
```

Remember, Excel supplies the curly braces. Then copy and paste or autofill that formula down as far as you want.

7

Index

J - K - L

M

R

S

REGISTER THIS PRODUCT
SAVE 35%*
ON YOUR NEXT PURCHASE!

☐ How to Register Your Product

- Go to quepublishing.com/register
- Sign in or create an account
- Enter ISBN: 10- or 13-digit ISBN that appears on the back cover of your product

🔓 Benefits of Registering

- Ability to download product updates
- Access to bonus chapters and workshop files
- A 35% coupon to be used on your next purchase – valid for 30 days
  > To obtain your coupon, click on "Manage Codes" in the right column of your Account page
- Receive special offers on new editions and related Que products

Please note that the benefits for registering may vary by product. Benefits will be listed on your Account page under Registered Products.

We value and respect your privacy. Your email address will not be sold to any third party company.

* 35% discount code presented after product registration is valid on most print books, eBooks, and full-course videos sold on QuePublishing.com. Discount may not be combined with any other offer and is not redeemable for cash. Discount code expires after 30 days from the time of product registration. Offer subject to change.

quepublishing.com